Slavery on the Spanish Frontier

University of Oklahoma Press
Norman

Slavery on the Spanish Frontier

The
Colombian Chocó
1680 - 1810

by William Frederick Sharp

Library of Congress Cataloging in Publication Data

Sharp, William Frederick, 1941–
  Slavery on the Spanish frontier.

  Bibliography: p. 235
  1. Slavery in Chocó, Colombia.   2. Gold mines and mining—
Colombia—Chocó.   3. Chocó, Colombia—Economic conditions.
4. Chocó, Colombia—Social conditions.   I. Title.
  HT1134.C5S5   301.44'93'098612   76-18767

This book is for my wife,
Elizabeth Allcott Sharp,
and for three Chocoano friends,
Sixto Mayoma,
Esilda Parra,
and
Lucho Parra

Preface

On an October morning in 1963 I arrived in Quibdó, Chocó, with seven other Peace Corps volunteers. The rugged old DC-3 circled for half an hour before breaking through the solid cloud cover to land on the gravel runway that served as Quibdó's airstrip. Within a few minutes we stepped out into one of nature's sauna baths and experienced for the first time the weather of the central Chocó— heat, humidity, and an almost constant cloud cover. Late in the afternoon rain descended and continued throughout the night. Rain, heat, and humidity were my constant companions while I lived and worked with the people of the Chocó town Tadó during the next twenty-one months.

Today's inhabitants of central Chocó are the descendants of slaves, Indians, and Spanish mine owners who peopled the area during the colonial and republican periods. More than 90 per cent of the population is of pure or mixed African ancestry. Despite the Chocó's fame as one of the richest gold and platinum-mining regions of Colombia, the area is underdeveloped, and most of the inhabitants live in varying degrees of poverty. In terms of material progress, there is little to indicate the Chocó's historical and present importance as a source of mineral wealth.

River travel connects Tadó with the other Chocó towns along the San Juan River, but the Chocó's fourth-largest city is physically isolated from the capital, Quibdó, and from the population centers of interior Colombia. A rough road exists to Quibdó, but no bridges span the San Juan or the Atrato rivers. Hence surface transportation

Slavery on the Spanish Frontier

to Tadó via an all-land route is impossible. During my twenty-one months in Tadó I frequently traveled in dugout canoes (*champas*) and walked many miles on roads and jungle trails (*trochas*) that dated back to colonial times. I developed a respect and love for the people of the Chocó and some understanding of the problems they face.

During my visits to the interior cities of Colombia I related my experiences in the Chocó to many interested Colombians. We often discussed the mineral wealth of the Chocó, the racial composition of the region's inhabitants, the area's lack of development, and its high temperatures and copious rainfall. The Chocó was viewed as a frontier on the fringe of modern Colombia. The church officially designated the region as a mission district, and many Colombian officials who worked in the area received special "hardship" benefits. The Chocó, my Colombian hosts emphasized, was entirely unlike other "more civilized" regions of their country.

Perplexed by conditions in the Chocó, I often asked, "Why, if the Chocó is so rich in mineral wealth, has it remained impoverished?" Some Colombians replied that its isolation and forbidding climate provided the answers, and others explained that the black inhabitants of the Chocó were lazy, shiftless individuals incapable of progress. The first two reasons, while correct, do not really explain why the region has not developed. They are simply contributory factors that have been overcome in other areas that contain desired treasures. The third conjecture is obviously prejudiced and ignores the many industrious inhabitants of the Chocó.

The desire to answer the question I had posed led to the formation of this book. What soon became apparent was that the present miseries of the Chocó are closely connected with events of the past. The patterns of exploitation, the doctrine of individualism, and the region's lack of meaningful social organization evolved during the colonial period. This book is a description and analysis of the economic and administrative system which the Spanish used during the colonial period. The first five chapters examine the problems of climate, conquest, supply, mining, and contraband

viii

trade. Subsequent chapters treat with slavery, race relations, manumission, freedmen, and economic productivity.

Any study of the colonial period in the Chocó must be based principally on primary sources. Few secondary works on the history of the Chocó exist. The several books on the area are interesting, sometimes helpful, but usually inaccurate. The one book of genuine value is Robert Cooper West's *The Pacific Lowlands of Colombia: A Negroid Area of the American Tropics* (1957). West surveyed archival material in his brief presentation of the history of the region, but it was not his purpose to describe the system of slavery or to present an economic history of the area. His book is extremely useful in terms of geographical data and a survey of life in the Chocó in the 1950's.

Colombian and North American scholars have developed themes concerning the black in Colombia which are of considerable value. Particularly noteworthy are Jaime Jaramillo Uribe's "Esclavos y señores en la sociedad Colombiana del siglo XVIII;"[1] Alan Kuethe's "The Status of the Free Pardo in the Disciplined Militia of New Granada;"[2] James Ferguson King's "Negro Slavery in the Viceroyalty of New Granada;"[3] Norman Meiklejohn's "The Observance of Negro Slave Legislation in Colonial Nueva Granada;"[4] and, David L. Chandler's "Health and Slavery: A Study of Health Conditions among Negro Slaves in the Viceroyalty of New Granada and its Associated Slave Trade, 1600–1810."[5] Several other studies, including those by David Paul Pavy and Norman E. Whitten, make important contributions concerning the black in coastal regions to the south of the Chocó, but they treat mostly with an analysis of modern problems.[6]

Fortunately the Archivo Histórico Nacional de Colombia in Bogotá, the Archivo Central del Cauca in Popayán, and the Archivo General de Indias in Seville, Spain, are replete with manuscripts relating to the Chocó during the colonial period. In the two Colombian archives the documents are bound, and each manuscript is numbered. Because of this numeration I have not titled each document. A document may be readily found by referring to the volume and folio number (in the Archivo Histórico Nacional de Colombia), or to the *signatura* number (in the Archivo Central del Cauca). Only the year in which each document was written is provided. Citations to material from the Archivo General de Indias follow the usual form of series, *legajo*, and date—with a brief description of each document.

The most important colonial archives in the Chocó (in Nóvita and Quibdó) were destroyed by fires in the nineteenth century. Copies of most of the documents in those provincial archives, however, are in Bogotá, Popayán, or Seville. There are no *cabildo* (town council) records for the Chocó since no town during the colonial period was large enough to merit a *cabildo*. Unhappily, the often-rich notarial records also burned early in the nineteenth century. I have used private collections of family papers and discovered some land titles from the colonial period in the archives of a North American mining company in Andagoya, Chocó (Archivo de la Compañía Minería Chocó Pacifico).

One of the most vexing problems of an economic study treating with the Spanish colonial period concerns weights and measures. Several terms adopted in the Chocó, for example, were not common to other parts of the Spanish Empire, or even in other parts of New Granada; or, if the same expressions applied, they may well have had different values. I have consistently used the values established in the Chocó for various weights and measures. Those most commonly employed in this study include *tercio* (one hundred pounds), *quintal* (one hundred pounds), *arroba* (twenty-five pounds), *bulto* (ten arrobas or 250 pounds), *marco* (eight ounces of gold), *fanegas* (1.6 bushels), *almud* (ten kilos of shelled corn), and *ración* (sixty-four "fingers" of *plátanos*—plantains). The dollar sign, unless specifically noted, signifies the Spanish silver peso of eight *reales* (bits). The North American dollar was based on this famous Spainish coin, and so the value of the silver peso, or piece of eight, was the equivalent of the North American dollar in 1800. Unless specifically designated, no references are made to the gold peso (worth slightly more than two silver pesos); gold dust served as the medium of exchange in the Chocó. The term *castellano* is used on occasion. In the Chocó it was both a weight measure for gold (one hundred *castellanos* in a pound of gold) and a synonym (incorrectly employed) for the gold peso.

I am grateful to the following publications for permission to reprint material that originally appeared in part in article form: Duke University Press, "The Profitability of Slavery in the Colombian Chocó, 1680–1810," *Hispanic American Historical Review*, 468–95 (August, 1975); and Pages 89–110. Taken from *Slavery and Race Relations in Latin America*, edited by Robert B. Toplin, reprinted by permission of the publisher, Greenwood Press, a division of William House-Regency Inc.

I gratefully acknowledge that research for this book was supported by a Waddell Fellowship from the University of North Carolina at Chapel Hill and by Faculty Research and Travel grants from Temple University. I am indebted to many people who have given valuable time and assistance. I am particularly grateful to Professors Harold Alfred Bierck, Margarita Gonzáles, Jorge Orlando Melo, German Colmenares, James Hilty, and Herbert Bass for helpful suggestions and criticisms. I am also grateful to the people of Tadó, Chocó, who befriended and influenced me from 1963 to 1965 while I served as a Peace Corps volunteer; to Elisa Arboleda, Carlos Gil, and Carlos Restrepo Canal, of the Archivo Histórico Nacional de Colombia; to the late José María Arboleda Llorente, of the Archivo Central del Cauca; to the helpful staff of the Archivo General de Indias; to officials of the Compañía Minería Chocó Pacifico, in Andagoya, Chocó; and to Paul Trevor Sharp and Vincent B. Dunlap. Most of all I am indebted to my wife, Elizabeth, and to my mother and father. Their critical knowledge of history and Latin America provided many helpful insights.

WILLIAM FREDERICK SHARP

Temple University

Contents

Illustrations

Maps

Tables

Slavery on the Spanish Frontier

Introduction

Success in the Chocó placer mines during the colonial period depended upon the forced labor of thousands of native Indians and imported African slaves. The Chocó was one of the few tropical mining regions of the New World where the Spaniards subjected both the Indians and the blacks to compulsory service. Neither Indians nor blacks were satisfied with the forced-labor system, and both resisted in a variety of ways. Slaves could and did seek manumission, but the Indians had little recourse other than to flee.

Spanish experience with conquest and settlement elsewhere in the Americas guided actions during the initial frontier stage in the Chocó. Following mission activity the Indians were pacified and forced to reside within specific districts (*corregimientos*). The first local officials were appointed from among those Spaniards who had helped conquer the region. Land was claimed, and mining began in earnest. Authorities soon established lines of communication with older settlements in New Granada (Colombia), and the crown attempted to implement a system of administrative control. Significantly, the Chocó never developed much beyond this rough frontier stage.

The classic waves of frontier development described by Frederick Jackson Turner did not occur in the Chocó. The region remained a mining frontier on the fringe of developing centers of commerce, education, and authority in colonial New Granada. As a mining rather than agricultural frontier, the white inhabitants of the Chocó relied upon the forced labor of slaves and Indians to

3

produce wealth. Topography, isolation, and climate made the region unattractive to white colonists. Guarded by towering mountains and dense, tropical rain forests, the Chocó presented formidable barriers to entry. Unlike other mining regions of the Americas, businessmen, farmers, educators, and pioneer families did not arrive within a few decades to lend stability and further its social development.

Although the Spaniards rarely attempted to settle there, the few who came to the Chocó succeeded in extracting millions of pesos worth of gold. Spanish officials and mine owners constituted the ruling elite and exhibited little interest in anything except the accumulation of wealth. They were not concerned with what Wilbur J. Cash called the "essential frontier process . . . the wresting [of] a stable foothold from a hostile environment."[1] Gold brought the Spanish to an area they otherwise would have ignored; they neither intended nor sought to establish permanent residence.

Clerics and certain royal officials resided in the central Chocó before the final conquest of the region. Thus elements of law, order, and spiritual guidance preceded the rush of miners with their slave gangs. Law, order, and religion played important roles on the Chocó frontier since the whites needed to subjugate and control the colored majority. Spaniards stressed religious instruction and strictly punished Indians, slaves, and freedmen who committed crimes or resisted authority. The enforced regulations were not always those prescribed by Spanish law. At the same time Spanish occupants paid little attention to regulations that restricted their own actions or profits.

Rugged individualism, common on most frontiers, developed in the Chocó. It became so pervasive that virtually no unity existed among whites, Indians, or blacks. There were no significant changes in the methods of exploitation or control for almost a century and a half. Nor did the desires of the inhabitants change. Whites sought wealth, Indians wanted to be left alone, and blacks struggled for freedom.

Slavery constituted the key to Spanish survival and economic productivity in the Chocó. One might well expect the primitive frontier environment and the vigorous exploitation of the placer mines to influence markedly Spanish behavior regarding their slaves. Any study of the Chocó, therefore, must treat with Spanish attitudes and policies regarding slavery and determine what, if anything, was unique about the institution in the Chocó.

A quarter of a century ago Frank Tannenbaum brought new interest and insight into the problems of slavery in the Americas.[2] Tannenbaum concluded that slavery, as it existed in Latin America, was generally a milder institution than the systems practiced by other European colonial powers in the New World. Iberian slavery, he believed, recognized the "moral personality" of the slave, thereby facilitating his acceptance and assimilation into society. Perhaps the most important proof presented to sustain this thesis involved the accessibility of slaves to manumission. In essence Tannenbaum contended that a slave system that offered freedom as a real possibility was ultimately more humane than a system that did not. Manumission, he noted, existed to a much higher degree, both in theory and practice, in the Spanish and Portuguese empires than elsewhere in the Americas.

Tannenbaum's conclusions opened the floodgates of investigation and criticism as scholars examined his thesis.[3] Subsequent studies revealed that he had developed his analysis on the basis of incomplete evidence. Lacking archival data, he relied heavily on a legalistic approach buttressed with evidence that the Roman Catholic church and a centuries-old tradition of slavery in the Iberian Peninsula regulated Spanish and Portuguese actions. He did not know the frequency with which slave laws were applied, although he noted that there was considerable inconsistency;[4] nor, as one critic pointed out, did Tannenbaum fully recognize the different economic conditions in the various European slave systems.[5]

Recent scholarship has done much to present needed data and to define the wide range of issues involved in comparative studies.[6] Despite this research, however, there is still no real consensus regarding slavery in Latin America. David Brion Davis, Eugene D.

Genovese, A. J. R. Russell-Wood, C. R. Boxer, and many others have shown that the life of a slave anywhere in the Americas could be nasty, brutish, and short.[7] Most modern observers would agree with Eric Williams, Eugene Genovese, and David Brion Davis that, regardless which European nation employed the slave system, its basic intent was the economic exploitation of human and physical resources.[8]

During the past two decades, most of the research on slavery in the Americas has focused on the United States, Brazil, and Cuba. Slavery in these regions was extensive and economically more important than elsewhere. Research has shown that in Brazil, for example, slaveholders often lived in close proximity to their slaves, thus creating the variety of relationships described by Gilberto Freyre and Donald Pierson.[9] And, as Carl Degler recently argued, the presence of a "mulatto escape hatch" in Brazil precluded certain patterns of segregation.[10]

In Cuba, as Herbert Klein noted, urban centers provided more opportunities for slaves and free blacks.[11] In both Cuba and Brazil many occupations were open to slaves as plantation laborers, miners, personal servants, dock workers, and urban artisans. Manumission was possible and actual, and free blacks had a greater degree of mobility than those in the United States. Thus social relationships developed among masters, slaves, and free blacks; societal mores became more complex; and free blacks and mulattoes sought elevation within the system.

Many scholars have discussed the merits of the Tannenbaum thesis and the impact of the Roman Catholic church, law, and tradition on slavery in the more heavily populated regions of Latin America. It is also important to study these same forces in the less-well-developed areas. The Colombian Chocó is one region of Spanish America ideally suited for such a study. During the eighteenth century the Chocó constituted a mining frontier physically separated from the centers of Spanish population, law, and refinement in colonial New Granada. It is important, therefore, to examine both the nature of the frontier and the system the Span-

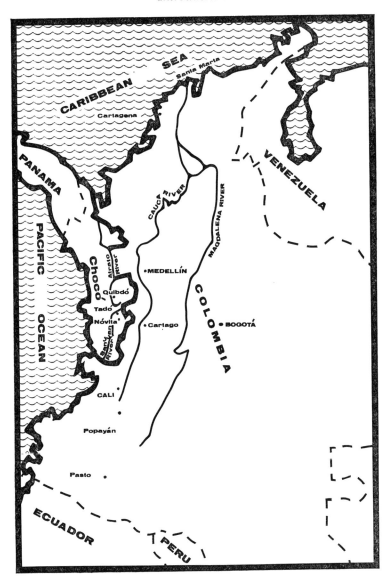

Colombia

iards adopted to exploit this isolated but wealthy region. If traditional religious and cultural attitudes were truly important in shaping Spanish behavior, they should be observable on this frontier.

1

The Land and Its People

The *departamento* (state) of the Chocó lies in the northwest corner of Colombia between the eastern spur of the Andes Mountains and the Pacific Ocean.* Bordered on the north by Panama and the Gulf of Darién and on the south by the Departmento del Valle, the Chocó is an area of heat, humidity, rain forests, jungle, rivers, and heavy rainfall. Jungles, swamps, and meandering streams guard the northern and southern entrances to the Chocó, and on the west and east two mountain ranges, the Serranía de Baudó and the massive, snow-capped Cordillera Occidental, separate the area from the seas and interior Colombia. The isolation thus imposed by these geographical barriers on life in the Chocó has always been one of its most notable realities.

Two great rivers, the Atrato and the San Juan, cut through the center of the Chocó, providing avenues to the Caribbean and the Pacific. The Atrato River flows northward through the central valley of the Chocó, emptying into the Gulf of Darién. Although only some two hundred miles long, the Atrato discharges an enormous volume of water because of the heavy rainfall in the Atrato--San Juan Valley.[1] The Atrato River provides a natural highway into

---

* To present a picture of the Chocó compatible with the views of those who lived in, or traveled through, the region in the colonial period and early nineteenth century, I have used descriptions of the area from that time whenever possible. For modern sources treating geography, land, and peoples of the Chocó, see Robert Cooper West, *The Pacific Lowlands of Colombia: A Negroid Area in the American Tropics*; and, *Geografía económica de Colombia, VI, Contraloría general de la República.*

9

the Chocó, but for most of the eighteenth century the Spanish crown prohibited maritime commerce along this route in the vain hope of controlling contraband trade.* Thus there was no easy access to the Caribbean or ports of the Spanish Main. Internal commerce did take place along the Atrato as canoes carried products to and from Murrí, Quibdó (Citará), and Lloró; both mining and agriculture extended inland from the river banks.[2]

The San Juan River presents a southern entrance into the Chocó as it flows in a southwesterly direction for 120 miles to the Pacific Ocean. The headwaters of the San Juan and Atrato rivers are in the same general region, and the San Juan also drains an area of heavy rainfall.[3] Most of the tributaries of the San Juan and Atrato rivers, particularly those originating in the Cordillera Occidental, are swift-flowing streams, dangerous to navigate. During the eighteenth century, with the Atrato closed to commerce, Spanish merchants and mine owners used the San Juan to introduce products from Panama, Guayaquil, Lima, and Spain. Even this trade, however, was severely restricted by *reales cédulas* (royal orders).† Canoes traversed the San Juan from the Pacific port of Chirambirá as far upriver as Playa del Oro, stopping at Noanamá, San Pablo (now Istmina), and Tadó, or they branched off on the Tamaná and Iró rivers to go to Nóvita and Iró.

The weather of the Chocó conforms to that of a typical tropical area. Temperatures are high but not unbearable, the air is moist and humid, and rainfall is copious. The temperature is remarkably

* The *Real Audiencia* (Royal Tribunal) of Santa Fe de Bogotá first declared the Atrato River closed to maritime commerce in 1698, in order to prevent contraband trade and the *entradas* (entries) of foreigners. The *Real Audiencia* passed similar decrees in 1705, 1717, and 1718. Royal *cédulas* (orders) of 1730, 1733, 1734, and 1736 gave royal sanction to these decrees. The number of decrees issued on this matter show both the importance of the prohibition and the probable lack of enforcement. For a summary of the orders restricting trade on the Atrato River see Archivo Histórico Nacional de Colombia (hereafter cited as AHNC), Bogotá, Colombia, Caciques e Indios 38, fols. 725–31 (1784).
† The crown permitted only basic foodstuffs to be imported by way of the San Juan River, and only two or three ships were allowed to arrive each year. Guayaquil was the only legal port of debarkation for ships destined to the Chocó for several decades.

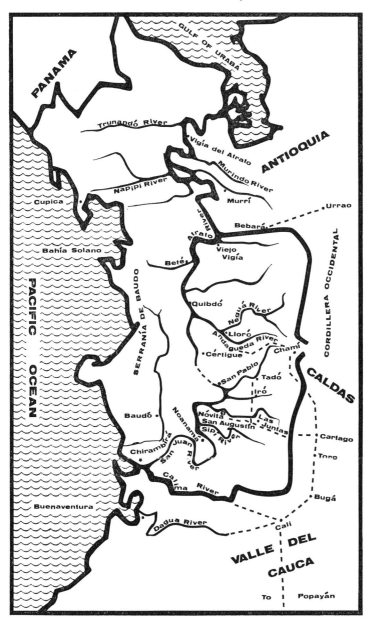

The Chocó

constant with seldom more than a two or three degrees' Fahrenheit change from month to month. The central lowlands of the Chocó, in the Atrato–San Juan depression, is the hottest region. The most important towns of the Chocó—Quibdó, Istmina, Andagoya, Condotó, Cértegui, and Tadó—lie in this area. Quibdó and Istmina have an average mean temperature of 82°, and Nóvita and Tadó 80°.[4]

Heavy and continual rainfall covers the upper San Juan–Atrato region. Andagoya averages 272 inches of rain a year; Quibdó, 347 inches. Rainfall rarely exceeds 8 inches in twenty-four hours, and most of the precipitation comes during the night. The heaviest recorded daytime rainfall measured slightly over 3 inches.[5] The constant precipitation precludes a dry or wet season in the central Chocó, but four months—February, March, July, and August—usually average less rainfall. A week without rain is rare, and because of the area's rapid drainage,[6] can cause a severe water shortage when it occurs.

The heavy rainfall contributes to the growth of the lush tropical vegetation that covers the Chocó. This forest cover falls into two main categories: true tropical rain forest and the swamp forest. The former blankets the central region, the slopes of the Serranía de Baudó, and extends to the Cordillera Occidental to elevations of five thousand feet. The latter flourishes in areas of poor drainage and is more likely to occur in the flatlands of the coastal regions, particularly near the mouths of the San Juan and Atrato rivers.[7] Along the river banks, where erosion, flooding, and cultivation tend to destroy the upper tree layers, a tangled undergrowth presides. What appears to be an impenetrable forest vegetation disappears a few hundred yards inland from the rivers.

Heavy rainfall on the western or windward side of the Cordillera Occidental has caused considerable erosion, cutting deep canyons from east to west in the mountain range. Several of these canyons have been used since pre-Columbian times as corridors of travel from the Chocó to the interior of Colombia. The streams flowing from the Western Cordillera into the Atrato and San Juan rivers become raging torrents during heavy rains, carrying huge boulders and gravel to the flatlands below. Because of the fluctuating water level and the presence of large rocks and rapids in the streambeds, boat travel on most of the tributaries of the San Juan and the Atrato is impossible for more than a few miles.

Quebradas (ravines) flowing with water from the Western Cordillera are the major ore-bearing streams of the Chocó. Almost every stream orginating in the Cordillera Occidental and emptying into the Atrato or San Juan is gold-bearing. Along the base of the Cordillera stretches a belt of gravel, five to ten miles wide, heavy with gold and platinum. Robert Cooper West concluded that the present-day streams do not carry much gold from the Cordillera itself (no mother lode has ever been discovered there) but wash it down from the beds of former rivers whose buried patterns have "no relation to that of modern drainage." The bottoms of these ancient *quebradas* contain the richest gravel deposits. Recent uplift has exposed layers of gold where modern streams cut through the channels of the old rivers.[8]

The Spaniards encountered an area of auriferous streams and alluvial gold deposits with richer gravels on the eastern sides of the Atrato and the San Juan and generally nearer their headwaters. But travel was difficult and dangerous, and the region was hot, humid, and rainy. Only the precious metal awaiting collection enticed them to enter the Chocó. They came bringing their slave gangs to an area described by one early Spaniard as an "abyss and horror of mountains, rivers, and marshes."[9]

Spanish occupation in the Chocó followed the course of least resistance, and communities took on a typical riverine pattern. Population followed the rivers, the gold, and in some instances the supply routes. The land along the rivers was easily accessible, presenting agricultural advantages, and even nonfarmers were attracted to the food sources in and along the streams. Fish, mollusks, and amphibious mammals (manatees) lived in the rivers, and deer, tapirs, and wild pigs used the streams as sources of fresh water. Rivers served as natural, although sometimes treacherous, highways and the mines usually were located along the streams where water was easily available to wash the gravels. The gold-rush mania of disorganized settlements was reflected in the Chocó as it was in many other mining areas. As a result some of the towns (Nóvita for example) were neither well planned nor ideally located. Some of the other villages (Tadó, Citará, Cértegui, and Viró Viró de Iró), though small, followed the usual Spanish pattern of construction; having a central square as the distinguishing feature. On one or both sides of the square the houses spread along the river banks. Towns were seldom more than a few blocks wide. Most of the houses were square or rectangular with thatched roofs. Constructed on piles, those houses nearest the river often stood on stilts ten to fifteen feet high. The rectangular house was undoubtedly a Spanish or African innovation; the Indians' houses (*tambos*), while made of the same materials, were round. The *tambos* generally did not have walls, but the rectangular dwellings had sides made of split bamboo plastered with mud and sometimes whitewashed.[10] These houses, easy and economical to build, had one serious defect—they were extremely susceptible to fire. Even with the heavy rainfall, a number of fires swept through the Chocoano towns, causing major damage on several occasions.[11]

As a series of mining camps or commercial warehouses, the towns of the Chocó contained neither large centers of population nor places that could be designated as cities during the colonial period. Not a single Spanish town was large enough to merit a *cabildo* (town council) or an *alcalde* (mayor). Villages like Nóvita and Tadó in the San Juan River region, and Quibdó and Lloró on the Atrato River, did not compare with the smaller towns of interior New Granada.[12]

During most of the colonial period the Chocó was divided into two provinces: Nóvita, on the San Juan; and Quibdó (Citará) on the Atrato. Since Nóvita was considered the more important of the two, it was designated the capital of the Chocó, and the governor was ordered to reside there.[13] Situated in the heart of the San Juan mining district, Nóvita also served as a commercial clearing house.

14

The town operated as a warehouse for goods carried up the San Juan, and, being close by land to the Cauca Valley, it afforded a natural stopover for travelers and products destined in or out of the Chocó. Although destroyed and abandoned several times in the seventeenth century (because of Indian attacks), Nóvita was always re-established because of its strategic location. Not until the last decade of the eighteenth century did Quibdó become significant as the commercial center of the two provinces.*

In spite of its commercial importance and designation as provincial capital, Nóvita offered scant evidence of the usual Spanish preoccupation with town planning. Situated on a small hill, the village lacked a central square, and streets and houses were strewn together to form a chaotic maze of mud and thatch.[14] In 1817, Lieutenant Governor José María Mallarino y Vargas and a number of Nóvita's leading citizens submitted an especially negative description of their own town and petitioned for relocation. Pleading the need for complete renovation, the advocates for relocation rejected Nóvita's phoenixlike past and asked the crown for permission to initiate new construction at a site some five miles distant on the Tamaná River.[15] Nóvita doubtless was in a state of ruin, and its inhabitants were losing out commercially to those in Quibdó (the Atrato River was by that time receiving considerable traffic from Cartagena), and they sought a location on the Tamaná River that would give them increased transportation advantages.

By the nineteenth century most persons judged Quibdó far superior to Nóvita. The citizens of Quibdó were thought to be more industrious, providing the city with larger, cleaner streets and generally better organization.[16] A French visitor to Quibdó in 1819, Julian Mellet, reported that the city was well known for its wealth and gold mines and also carried on a considerable amount of trade with the interior regions of New Granada and with Cartagena. Mellet remarked that, although prices were high in Quibdó, the

---

* Once the Atrato River was reopened to maritime commerce in 1784, the river quickly became the preferred route for travelers and products destined in or out of the Chocó. Quibdó then replaced Nóvita as the commercial center of the region.

inhabitants were very rich and proud, wearing only the finest clothes and jewels.[17]

Mellet seems to have been overly appreciative of Quibdó for other visitors to the city were more critical. In 1820, Joaquín Acosta, then a young officer in the patriot army, wrote that Quibdó had four hundred houses, all made of wood and straw, and that the women, although "ladies," usually walked about barefoot.[18] Two years later an Englishman, Charles Stuart Cochrane, expressed relief in leaving Quibdó. Cochrane was upset not by the oppressive climate but by the fact that Quibdó was "a place with but little society or amusement—in fact, almost destitute of the positive requisites of life."[19]

During the nineteenth century Quibdó replaced Nóvita in both economic and political importance. Lieutenant Colonel José Cancino, commander of the republican forces in the Chocó, designated Quibdó as the capital of the Chocó during the Wars of Independence.[20] It retained this position until 1842, when Nóvita was temporarily renamed the seat of government for political reasons. The citizens of Nóvita had remained loyal to the conservative central government through the revolution of 1841, but the liberal inhabitants of Quibdó had taken the side of the insurgents. In 1851, with the liberals in control of the national government, Quibdó was again named the capital,[21] and Nóvita quickly faded into insignificance.

The prosperity of Nóvita had depended in great part upon the wealth of the gold mines in the surrounding area, but the abolition of slavery in Colombia in 1851 precipitated Nóvita's demise. In 1853, Agustín Codazzi, a famed geographer of Colombia, related that most of the important people of the town, being unable to exploit the region's minerals without slaves, had left not only Nóvita but the Chocó as well.[22] Quibdó, on the other hand, with its emphasis on trade, remained relatively prosperous.[23]

*Corregimientos** and mining camps (*real de minas*) formed the

---

* The *corregimientos* in the Chocó were all originally *corregimientos de indios* (a district of Indians governed by a crown official called a *corregidor*). The Indians

other centers of population in the Chocó. In the province of Nóvita
the six *corregimientos* Tadó, Noanamá, Los Brazos, Las Juntas,
Sipí, and Baudó served as political and commercial headquarters
for the Indians, slaves, and miners. The number of *corregimientos*
in the province of Quibdó fluctuated. Six *corregimientos* existed
for over a century, but two others, Pabarandó and Cupica, enjoyed
a shorter tenure. Pabarandó, the northernmost *corregimiento*, was
destroyed by Cuna Indians of the Darién region in 1806 and was
not rebuilt. It lasted for almost twenty-five years.[24] Cupica, opened
as a port on the Pacific Ocean in the 1770's, faded out of existence a
decade later, when navigation was permitted on the Atrato.[25] The
other six *corregimientos* were Quibdó, Lloró, Chamí, Beté, Bebará,
and Murrí.

Both provinces had a number of mining camps, although the
province of Nóvita clearly was of greater importance as a mining
district. Mining centers in that province included Ibordó (near
Tadó); San Joaquín, Santa Barbara, Santa Rita, and Viró Viró on
the Iró River; Opogodó on the Opogodó River; Yalí, Salto, El
Playon, El Tigre, San Felipe, and San Lorenzo on the Tamaná
River; San José, El Cajón, Santa Rita, and Torrá on the Cajón River;
and Santa Ana on the River Sipí. Most of the largest *cuadrillas*
(slave gangs) in the Chocó worked in these mining camps. The
province of Citará (Quibdó) contained some mining centers—
including Cértegui on the Cértegui River halfway between Quibdó
and Nóvita; Bagadó and Santa Barbara on the Andagueda River;
Neguá on the Neguá River; and a number of small mines near
Bebará. But the total number of slaves and mines owned in the
province of Citará did not compare with those of the province of
Nóvita.

Peoples from three racial groupings—Indian, black, and white—
combined unevenly to form the population of the Chocó. Whites,
though only a small percentage of the total population, held vir-

residing within these areas had their own chiefs (*caciques*), governors, and mayors
(*alcaldes*), but were primarily responsible to and under the control of the *corregidor*.

tually all the important or controlling positions. Whites reaped the wealth, while Indians labored under corregidors to produce food and serve as cargo carriers (*cargueros*) and black and mulatto slaves toiled in the mines. Miscegenation was common, but, as will be seen later, social relationships among the various groups remained distant or nonexistent.

Whites living in the Chocó were generally owners or overseers of small mines, crown officials, priests, or merchants. The wealthier mine owners and the *dueños* (owners) of the large slave gangs almost invariably lived outside the Chocó in the interior towns of New Granada—especially Buga, Cartago, Cali, Anserma, Popayán, and even Santa Fe de Bogotá.[26] The hot, humid climate of the Chocó was not considered healthy for whites, and few remained if they could hire overseers to handle their affairs. Whites arrived as exploiters, not as settlers. Ideally, one made a fortune in as brief a time as possible and retired to a life of comfort in more agreeable areas. The major mines of the Chocó were almost always owned by absentee proprietors.[27]

Whites contracted smallpox in the Chocó and were particularly susceptible to many tropical fevers. Because seventeenth- and eighteenth-century accounts describe the Chocó simply as fever-ridden, one can only surmise that a major illnesss was malaria.* Royal officials assigned to positions in the Chocó bitterly complained about the climate, and many resigned their positions for reasons of health.[28] In fact, climate and disease presented such problems that the crown offered better pay to officials, from governors to scribes in the Chocó as an inducement to remain in the "unhealthy and costly" district.[29]

Neither high salaries nor gold attracted many white settlers.

---

* See, for example, AHNC, Caciques e Indios 10, fol. 532 (1693); AHNC, Aguardientes del Cauca 5, fol. 75 (n.d.). In a report in 1914 United States Consul Louis G. Dreyfus wrote that it was almost impossible for a white man to remain in his district for more than three or four months without contracting malaria. See "Health and General Conditions at Quibdó," Dreyfus to Secretary of State, Quibdó, March 21, 1914. The National Archives of the United States, Washington, D.C. Post Records, Republic of Colombia (Record Group # 84).

During the five-year period from 1778 to 1782, an average of only 340 whites resided in the Chocó. They constituted about 2 per cent of the region's total population (see Table 1*). In 1782, when the central Chocó contained 17,898 inhabitants, only 359 were whites. The remaining poulation included 7,088 slaves, 6,552 Indians, and 3,899 free people of color (*libres de color*).[30] The percentage of whites in the Chocó increased slightly during the nineteenth century, but it remained low.[†]

Most of the whites who lived in the Chocó were single, and males outnumbered females 204 to 131 in 1779 (see Table 2). Since the number of married males (67) was greater than that of married females (49) a few whites may have wed Indians or blacks. It is more likely, however, that they left their wives and families in the interior provinces of New Granada while they worked in the Chocó. Census data for the neighboring province of Popayán support this assumption. In the year 1779 there were 4,280 married males and 4,333 married females in that province.[31]

The history of the Indian in the Chocó is one of demographic decline and physical disaster. The Indians of the central Chocó[‡] were initially hostile to the Spaniards, withstanding conquest for almost two centuries. After 1686, when the Chocoes were finally pacified, many Spanish miners began to enter the Chocó. Originally, Indians were used for labor in the placer mines, but their hostility, high death rate, and conflicting Spanish ideologies concerning their treatment and religious conversion soon forced the Spaniards to

* All tables not appearing in the text are presented in the Appendix.

† By 1918, the total Chocó population was enumerated at 68,335 and only 7,030 were whites. However, 2,805 of these resided in the all-white and mestizo (Indian-white offspring) *municipio* of El Carmen. High on the Western Cordillera near Antioquia, El Carmen was not a part of the Chocó until 1883. Only 4,225 whites lived in the central provinces of the Chocó, or less than 6 per cent of the total population. See Manuel Roca Castellanos, *10 luces sobre el futuro*, 60.

‡ Four major Indian groups ruled in the Chocó at the time of the Spanish Conquest: the Cunacunas (Cunas), in the northern Darién region; the Zitares, along the upper Atrato River; the Noanames, along the San Juan River; and the Chocoes, along the Baudó River. The Zitares, Noanames, and Chocoes have often been grouped together under the common name Chocó. See Henry Wassen, *Estudios Chocoes*.

use blacks to fill the labor shortage. After the Spanish crown prohibited the use of Indians in the mines of New Granada early in the eighteenth century,[32] the indigenous inhabitants were shifted to other necessary occupations. Herded into *corregimientos,* they were forced to pay tribute, grow corn and plantains (*plátanos*) for the slave gangs, build houses for the miners and slaves, construct canoes, and serve as the primary transportation force.

It is impossible to determine how many Indians lived in the Chocó when the Spaniards first entered the region, but in 1660, Jesuit missionaries estimated the number of Indians in the central Chocó to be over 60,000. Undoubtedly the Indian population had already declined by 1660, for smallpox epidemics in 1566, 1588, and 1589 to 1591 had decimated the Indian population. In 1591, Melchor Velásquez, son of the governor of the Chocó, reported that the recent smallpox epidemic had been particularly severe. Many had died, and others had fled from settlements and towns hoping to escape the disease.[33] Smallpox was not the only disease that ravaged the Indian inhabitants of the Chocó. In 1749 a priest from Bebará informed the viceroy that an epidemic of measles had killed many Indians in the Bebará-Murrí area of the Atrato.[34]

By 1778, when the first major census was completed in the Chocó, only 5,414 Indians remained in the central region. The census included the Indians of the upper Atrato, the San Juan, and Baudó but did not include the still hostile and unconquered Cunas.[35] Listed both by corregidors and the local priests, the 1778 census provided a fairly accurate enumeration of the Indians.* During the next five years the Indian population grew, reaching a high of 6,552 in 1782 (see Table 3). This constitutes an astounding increase of 20 per cent (1,138) in just five years. While it is likely that the enumeration techniques improved, accounting for part of this gain, 918 of the newly counted were children.[36] Hence the Indian birthrate for these years must have been high. The 1808 census, however, revealed that the number of Indians had decreased by more

---

* Since the corregidor paid tribute on the basis of male Indians counted, he was not trusted to make the enumeration by himself.

than 2,000 to 4,450. Disease was a factor as smallpox contributed to the decline.[37] Between 1782 and 1808 a number of Indians also fled north from the Atrato River basin, joining the still independent Cuna Indians.[38]

The largest centers of Indian concentration were the *corregimientos* Quibdó, Lloró, and Chamí in the province of the Atrato, and Tadó and Noanamá in the province of the San Juan.* The data also demonstrate the ratio of the male and female Indians in the Chocó was almost equal and that many Indians were married. Agricultural production was one of the major occupations of the Indians, and the distribution of the indigenous inhabitants demonstrated the importance of the province of the Atrato as a food-producing region. In the 1780's the province of the Atrato contained at least twice as many Indians as the province of the San Juan. This constitutes a reversal of the 1660 estimates given by the Jesuit missionaries, but, as will be seen, it was in the province of the San Juan that the Spanish concentrated their mining ventures.

Blacks composed the third major racial group inhabiting the Chocó, and by the last half of the eighteenth century the African peoples had replaced the Indians as the largest segment of the population. By 1782 the various black peoples represented almost two-thirds of the population.†

The early use and need for black slaves in the Chocó resulted in part from the rebellious nature of the Indians. Late-sixteenth-century attempts to establish mining centers in the Chocó failed because of the hostility of the Indians, but by the year 1704 the Spaniards had imported over six hundred slaves into the Chocó.[39]

As the mining ventures prospered during the first decades of the eighteenth century, the number of slaves residing in the region

---

* Table 4 shows the Indian population recorded in each of the *corregimientos* of the two provinces in 1782.

† Doubtless many of the people listed as black were in fact mulattos or *pardos* (black-white offspring), or *zambos* (black-Indian offspring). The census records simply employed the terms *blancos* (whites), *indios* (Indians), *esclavos de various colores* (slaves of various colors), and *libres de varios colores* (freedmen of various colors). Hence the word *negro*, or black, as used in the Chocó, did not apply only to those of pure African descent.

increased rapidly. By 1724 an estimated 2,000 slaves worked in the Chocó. The slave population continued to increase and the 1782 census recorded the largest number of slaves, listing 7,088. However, the slave population declined during the next two decades, even though the Spanish crown permitted the special importation of *bozales* (blacks from Africa) in an attempt to increase mineral production in the Chocó mines. By 1808 the number of slaves in the Chocó had dropped to slightly under 5,000. Manumission accounted for much of this decrease, and of course disease and various epidemics also affected the black population.*40

During the eighteenth century the number of freedmen living in the Chocó also increased steadily. Owners voluntarily freed slaves, often in their wills, and slaves fortunate enough to save money could purchase their own freedom. Manumission in the Chocó was not only possible but actual. Census reports began listing *libres* (freedmen) in the 1770's, and by 1782 3,899 *libres* were counted in the Chocó. Quite possibly there were many more; many of them lived in inaccessible places and were difficult to find. Large numbers of the *libres*, joined by runaway slaves (*cimarrones*) both from the Chocó and outside regions such as the Cauca Valley and Antioquia, retired to isolated sites near the headwaters of the various streams in the Chocó. In 1808, Governor Carlos de Ciaurriz asserted that an accurate count for the two provinces of the Chocó was impossible owing to the wide dispersal of the population.[41]

In the nineteenth century the Wars of Independence and manumission laws greatly reduced the number of slaves. At the time of their final emancipation in 1851 only 1,725 slaves remained in the Chocó to be freed (see Table 5).

From at least 1755 to 1851 most of the blacks, slave or free, lived in the province of the San Juan. Extensive mining along the San

---

* Despite these factors, unless one accounts for the profitability of slavery in the Chocó, the decline in the slave population at the end of the eighteenth century is difficult to explain. Slave prices dropped, the crown facilitated the sale of slaves, and slaves were easily purchased directly from the nearby slave port of Cartagena. The profitability of slavery and its effect upon the slave trade will be discussed in a later chapter.

Juan and its tributaries created a greater need for slaves in this province.* The 1782 census figures show that the highest percentage of blacks resided near Nóvita, Tadó, Los Brazos, and Sipí. In the province of Citará most slaves and *libres* lived near Quibdó, Lloró, and Bebará. Very few slaves were listed in the predominantly Indian towns Noanamá, Las Juntas, or Baudó in the province of Nóvita; or Chamí, Beté, or Cupica in the province of Citará. The Spaniards attempted to keep blacks and Indians separated,† and—except during the early years of conquest in the Chocó—there is no indication that blacks or Indians respected each other or had many interrelationships.[42]

During the 150 years of Spanish rule in the Chocó there was a significant decrease in total population. But it was an uneven demographic decline noticeably along racial lines. As the mining districts prospered in the late seventeenth and eighteenth centuries, the racial composition of the region changed from one almost exclusively Indian to one predominantly black. Even if the 1660 Jesuit estimate of the number of Indians is taken as only a rough approximatation, the decimation of the indigenous inhabitants—because of conquest, disease, and doubtless misuse as well—was staggering: from 60,000 in 1660 to 4,450 in 1808. But, although the once numerous Indian population stabilized at between 4,000 and 6,000 in the latter part of the eighteenth century, the total number of inhabitants in the Chocó almost doubled several times—first from 1763 to 1808 and then again between 1808 and 1856 (see Table 7). Thus, from 1763 onward, the population of the Chocó grew by about 1.5 per cent a year. This percentage of increase is similar to that in the viceroyalty of New Granada as a whole, where the population was increasing by 1 to 1.5 per cent a year from 1778 to 1788.[43]

---

* Table 6 shows in detail the distribution of slaves and *libres* within the various *corregimientos* of the Chocó in 1782.

† The crown repeatedly prohibited blacks from living among or around the Indians, but the proscription could not be completely enforced. See Konetzke, ed., *Colección de documentos para la historia de la formación social de hispanoamerica*, I, 213, 321, 513, 554, 572, 627ff.

The patterns of settlement and the occupations of the inhabitants focused on mining as the primary purpose. Whites governed, slaves labored in the placer mines, and Indians undertook the necessary (if, in the eyes of many miners, secondary) tasks of producing food and transporting products. Many officials, white miners, merchants, and overseers viewed their tenure in the Chocó as a temporary hardship—endured only because of the wealth it produced. Few white families settled in the area, and, because most of the wealthy *dueños* were absentee owners, they did not establish elaborate residences in the region nor aid in the refinement or development of the Chocó's population centers. Mining camps and villages remained scattered, small, and unimpressive. The growing group of *libres de color*, instead of congregating in or near the Spanish settlements, often preferred secluded homes in the jungle. Slaves made up most of the population in the *real de minas*, and Indians peopled the agricultural and transportation districts. Of course, neither the slaves nor the Indians had much choice in their occupations or places of residence. Blacks followed the desires of their masters, and Indians were forced to remain in centralized communities governed by corregidors.

Thus the Chocó contained an expanding series of widely dispersed frontier mining camps, Indian *corregimientos*, and seclusion-seeking *libres*. As a result, neither urban centers nor the "Big House" existed to add structure, complexity, or social development. The population was dispersed, absentee ownership was common, urban centers did not develop, slave gangs were isolated, officials were few in number, and a profitable slave-dependent monoculture evolved.

2

The Struggle for Conquest: The First Two Hundred Years

The legendary Chocó Indian goddess Dabaibe (Dabaiba)* proved a reluctant mistress, yielding her treasures to adventurous Spanish suitors only after a a two-hundred-year courtship. By gradually revealing her secrets and the promise of much more to come, Dabaibe became the Lorelei for countless Spanish dreamers. She promised gold, but, aided by climate, geography, and hostile Indian tribes, she often inflicted death. Mosquitoes infected the blood with burning fevers; thick jungle growth on the riverbanks prohibited exploration in a set direction, forcing gold seekers to follow the treacherous winding streams; poison darts skillfully aimed by hidden avengers meted out swift destruction, mercifully ending the intense pain they produced; and the grim specter of famine continually accompanied those lured into the Chocó searching for Dabaibe's treasure. Conquest of the brooding jungle area the Spanish called the Chocó was a long and arduous task, but the precious yellow metal within its borders provided a powerful incentive.

The northern coastline of the Chocó was among the first parts of terra firma discovered and explored by the Spaniards. Vasco

* According to Indian legend, Dabaibe was a beautiful woman who had come down from heaven to aid and instruct the Indians. Having accomplished her mission, Dabaibe retired to the mountains, building a beautiful golden city before she ascended to heaven. See *Geografía económica de Colombia*, VI, *Chocó*, 94; as an example of early sixteenth-century Spanish accounts about Dabaibe see Friede, ed., "Carta del Cabildo de Cartagena sobre varios asuntos de la gobernación (November 26, 1535)," *Documentos inéditos para la historia de Colombia*, IV, 11–15.

Núñez de Balboa, Pascual de Andagoya, Francisco Pizarro, Diego Almagro, and their followers explored and mapped the Chocó's Pacific coast over a decade before other conquistadors penetrated interior New Granada.[1] For almost two centuries, however, the central part of the Chocó remained virtually unsettled by the Spaniards and to a large extent unknown.

As early as 1511 the Spaniards knew that there was gold in the Chocó,[2] but topography, climate, and irascible natives rebuffed attempts to enter this potential El Dorado.[3] By 1570 several *entradas* (expeditions of entry) into the Atrato–San Juan basins had reported rich gold deposits, but the Spaniards were unable to establish a firm foothold. *Entradas* and temporary settlements became more common in the seventeenth century. From the north Spaniards used the Atrato River or journeyed overland through the Urrao Valley from the population centers of Antioquia. Expeditions beginning in the south were either fitted out in Popayán, Cali, Anserma, Toro, or Cartago and entered through passes in the Cordillera Occidental, or came up the San Juan River from Buenaventura. *

Spanish steel and armor initially proved ineffective in the Chocó. Conquest was delegated to brown- and black-robed friars carrying wooden (and thus rust-proof) crucifixes as their only protection against the Indians' poison darts. In 1624, Governor Valenzuela Fajardo of Popayán dispatched a team of Jesuits to establish missions in the upper San Juan area among the Noanamaes. The first two Jesuit fathers to attempt the spiritual conquest of the Chocó, Pedro de Caceres and Francisco de Orta, worked in the region for more than ten years before more Jesuits arrived to share in the mission.[4] The Jesuits successfully formed several *reducciones* (settlements) and pacified a number of the Noanamá Indians. In the years 1659, 1660, and 1661 groups of these former savages swore allegiance to the Spanish king and agreed to pay tributes and *diezmos* (tithes).[5]

---

* Several excellent primary sources exist for this period of Chocó history including Friede, ed., *Documentos*; Juan de Castellanos, *Elegías de varones ilustres de Indias*, and Ricaurte, ed., *Historia documental del Chocó*.

Jesuits held no exclusive right to work in the Chocó; in fact, their missions did not have official crown approval. Other Spaniards (mostly miners) entered the Chocó from Antioquia and the Cauca Valley, sometimes with the crown's permission.[6] Other religious orders also became interested in the Chocó and the Franciscans first sent a missionary to the region in 1648. In that year, Fray Matías Abad, a brother working in Cartagena, received authorization from his superior to enter the Chocó and undertake a personal mission among the Zitarares. After traveling through Antioquia to the Atrato River basin, he founded a church on the banks of the Atrato.

Both the mission and Fray Matías were short-lived; Chocó Indians killed the ill-fated friar a year after his arrival. While in the Chocó, Fray Matías wrote three letters to his provincial superior in Cartagena describing the region as the richest in the world and asking that more missionaries be sent. Three Franciscans did arrive shortly after Fray Matías' death, but they were unable to do anything more than return with the martyred priest's body to Cartagena.[7]

The Franciscans continued their interest in the region, and in 1669 Fray Miguel de Castro Rivadeneira journeyed to Spain to solicit a license and crown support for a mission in the Chocó. The Spanish monarch sanctioned the request and instructed the governor of Antioquia to aid the Franciscans in their venture. Twelve Franciscans embarked on the apostleship, and within two years they had formed a number of *reducciones* along the Atrato River. The Indians, although peaceful at first, did not relish being herded into the newly established towns. They soon rebelled, killing four of the Franciscans. The rest of the missionaries escaped death by fleeing the area.[8]

The massacre took place in the Atrato region, but the Jesuits along the San Juan remained unharmed—probably because an armed expedition had been sent earlier from Popayán to aid them in the pacification of the Indians.[9] The governor of Popayán, Gabriel Díaz de la Cuesta, who had objected when the Franciscans received the license for proselytizing in the Chocó, requested that the Jesuits be awarded the mission on the basis of superior results.[10] The issue of which religious order, and where it would originate, formed part of the early rivalry between the provinces of Antioquia and Popayán, for both areas wished to gain political control over the potentially rich Chocó.

In the 1670's, Spanish civilians trickled into the Chocó, some of them bringing small *cuadrillas* (slave gangs). With few Spanish officials in the region to enforce the king's rules, the Chocó remained a lawless frontier. One Spaniard, Santiago de Arce, entered the Chocó in 1677 hoping to carve a personal empire out of the Atrato region. Making his own rules, he forced Indians to work for him without any official authorization, and he severely punished any Indian or Spaniard who opposed him. One fellow white, Diego Díaz, who disagreed with Arce's strict policies and monopolistic control of the Indians, was taken prisoner by Arce's men, and, on his orders, hanged.

The Indians, seeking escape from Arce's intolerant measures, fled from their towns to the mountains and began raiding the Spanish mines in the region. The newly appointed governor of the Chocó, Juan Bueso de Valdés, requested help in subduing the Indians and in restoring peace and order to the district. Supplies and munitions were sent from Anserma, and soldiers under Captain Felipe Rodríquez arrived from Antioquia.[11] The Spanish forces quickly ended the rebellion. Arce was taken prisoner and sent to the capital of New Granada, Santa Fe de Bogotá. The Indians were returned to their villages where, under the guidance of priests, they began to rebuild the churches and houses they had so recently destroyed.[12]

Arce's self-appointed fiefdom collapsed with his arrest, but the increased number of Spaniards in the Quibdó area caused further problems with the Indians. A report written several years later by Sergeant Major Antonio Joaquín de Veroís intimated that difficulties arose when some *hombres de mal vivir* (men of disreputable character) flaunted the authority and respect of a Spanish official in

Quibdó. On one occasion these men gathered around the official, ridiculing him in public. One of the pranksters grabbed the startled official's walking cane (which served as a symbol of authority), broke it in half, and threw the pieces to the ground in a gesture of contempt. The offended official, apparently an indecisive, weak-willed man, either could not or would not punish the culprits. Sergeant Major Veroís contended that a number of Indians witnessed this particular incident, and, seeing it possible to defy royal authority, chose to do likewise. A major Indian uprising resulted shortly thereafter in 1684.[13] Official titles meant little on the frontier if the men holding them did not command respect. A timid official was worse than no official because the crown's authority was made to look weak. Respect had to be earned; it was not afforded automatically by an official title.*

During the 1684 rebellion Indians from Quibdó, Tadó, and Las Juntas joined in a common effort to dislodge the Spanish. The Indians slaughtered several Spanish miners and officials in the Quibdó area and completely drove the rest of the disorganized Spaniards from the region. Near Tadó some runaway black slaves joined with the Indians, dug trenches, and set up fortifications. On November 10, 1685, the king commanded the complete pacification of the province of Citará.[14] By the time this order arrived in New Granada, however, under the leadership of Governor Juan Bueso de Valdés, the Spanish had already regrouped near Nóvita and with aid from the Cauca Valley reconquered the recalcitrant tribes and slaves. The blacks were executed, and the governor rewarded his soldiers by granting them Indian prisoners for use as slaves.[15]

Although the rebellion ended in 1686, the Spanish authorities experienced extreme difficulties in persuading the remaining Indians to return to their homes and towns along the Atrato River.

* Wilbur J. Cash described several of the most important characteristics of the frontier when he wrote: "For it is characteristic of the frontier tradition everywhere that it places no such values on wealth and rank as they command in an old and stable society. Great personal courage, unusual physical powers, the ability to drink a quart of whisky or to lose the whole of one's capital on the turn of a card without the quiver of a muscle—these are at least as important as possessions and infinitely more important than heraldic crests" (*The Mind of the South*, 38).

Before the revolt there had been over 1,300 warriors and 100 chiefs in the area,[16] but when Antonio Ruiz Calcedo arrived in Quibdó in 1689 as the new lieutenant governor, he found virtually no Indians. Some had died during the uprising or been made prisoner by Governor Bueso de Valdés, but most had fled to the Western Cordillera, congregating in the Urrao Valley in Antioquia. The lieutenant governor feared future assaults from this group of run-away Indians, but when 30 Spanish troops and 160 now friendly Noanamá Indians arrived to protect the province, the expected attacks did not materialize.[17]

By 1690 the Chocó was generally considered pacified. For the first time sizable numbers of Spaniards began to enter the area with their *cuadrillas*. The Jesuits had withdrawn in 1687, but this did not mean that they believed the region sufficiently Christian-ized to leave. They had been having increasing difficulties with their missions in the Chocó. On the one hand, an ever-growing number of miners wanted to use the Indians of the Jesuit mission as a labor force; and on the other hand, secular priests were eager to take over the clerical duties (which could be quite lucrative) in the Chocó. Thus the Jesuits retired from the Chocó after thirty-two years of service, and in 1689 they began to establish missions in the Amazon region, where they were not as likely to be hindered in their apostolate.[18]

With the Indians of the central Chocó pacified, if not Christian-ized, the Spaniards faced the new threat of foreign invasion before finally securing the Chocó. Pirates had first appeared in 1679, when, led by the famous English captains Coxen and Cooke, they entered the Chocó via the Atrato River. Lured by reports of gold, the marauders made a quick foray up the Atrato as far as Quibdó. The pirates were overly optimistic: each took with him a large trunk to carry back the loot he expected to steal. Financially the raid was a dismal failure, since little gold had been accumulated in the new Spanish settlement of Quibdó. But the buccaneers did barter with the Indians for some gold, and they received a false impression of the ease with which they could enter and leave the region.[19]

In 1689 and again in 1691 authorities in the Chocó requested supplies from Popayán claiming that English freebooters, aided by Cuna Indians from the Darién, were preparing to invade.[20] Raids did not occur at this time, but foreign adventurers lurking near the mouth of the Atrato River continued to threaten the internal security of the province. Late in 1701 the Spaniards again received notice of an impending English and Cuna attack. On this occasion information from various sources and locations led the captain general of New Granada to send warnings on June 22, 1702, to Popayán and the Chocó to expect an invasion. The lieutenant governor of Citará, Manuel de Herrera, was instructed to enlist all available fighting men, regardless of color (mulattoes, blacks, *zambos*, mestizos, Indians and whites), provided they were free men, and assemble them in Quibdó, where they could move at a moment's notice. The governor of Popayán was commanded to send all men, munitions, and supplies on hand.[21]

Lieutenant Governor Herrera, upon receiving the captain general's orders, began recruiting in his province and sent several letters to Lieutenant Governor Gómez de la Asprilla of the province of Nóvita asking him to send troops and Indians from the San Juan region. Gómez de la Asprilla complied, enlisting 26 soldiers (Spaniards, freedmen, and mestizos) and 112 Indians from Tadó; 56 soldiers from Nóvita; 40 soldiers from Las Juntas; and 135 Indians from Noanamá. Only whites possessed guns, but mulattoes carried pikes and knives, and the Indians were armed with bows, arrows, and blowguns.[22]

The first major battle with the English and Cuna Indian forces took place before many of the recruits sent from the San Juan reached Herrera. With news that the enemy had entered the Atrato River, Herrera took his troops downriver from Quibdó, encountering the English near the mouth of the Bebará River on November 26, 1702. Herrera's forces completely routed the invaders, killing 105 Englishmen, sinking seven of the enemy boats, and capturing three large canoes. Herrera also took several English prisoners, who informed him that 150 more Englishmen had gone

Slavery on the Spanish Frontier

up the Río Bebará attempting to invade Antioquia through the Urrao Valley. Herrera knew that the marauders would have to return to their ships by way of the Chocó, and he decided to greet them in force. He asked that more powder (although guns had been captured in the battle of November 26, the powder Herrera's troops had taken was wet and thus useless) and men be sent.[23]

The trails into the Urrao Valley from the Chocó existed only in the memories of the Indian guides who traversed them. For all other travelers an almost impassable wall of thick jungle growth blocked the way. The English had managed to employ several Indian guides (and some Cunas apparently accompanied them) to lead them through the obscure green forest, but from the start they experienced difficulties with the natives. Discouraged by the lack of food and the slow pace of the raiders, the guides deserted, leaving the buccaneers to wander aimlessly through the jungle.

Without Indians to lead them, the English could not go forward to their objective, but, once they found a stream, they could at least return. Separated, sick, and hungry, the disheveled invaders tried to get back to supplies and safety at the mouth of the Atrato River. Herrera's troops ambushed one bedraggled group that straggled out of the Río Bebará, killing 35 Englishmen and capturing a Frenchman.[24]

Herrera's forces soon took 113 more prisoners (Englishmen), and plans were made to send them to Cartagena or Santa Fe de Bogotá for trial. The Spaniards' Indian allies, however, did not understand or agree with this apparent benevolence, and they massacred all the captives by slitting their throats. A subsequent investigation of the incident showed that Herrera had been absent during the bloodbath and that those Spaniards left in charge had been "unable" to prevent the slaughter.[25]

Herrera feared another invasion,[26] but it never materialized, doubtless owing in part to the reports of disaster carried to the enemy forces waiting in the Gulf of Urabá by the survivors of the first two expeditions lucky enough to defeat the jungle and slip past the waiting Spaniards.

Foreigners and the Cuna Indians presented problems to the Spanish authorities in the Chocó for the next 115 years. But never again was there a full-scale foreign invasion. By 1703 more and more Spaniards were occupying the Chocó, and neither the Indians nor the foreigners could dislodge them. For the Indians there was no recourse. Those in the central region were soon, if they had not already been, placed in *corregimientos*. For the foreigners, however, there was a profitable alternative to war. They simply traded with the Cuna Indians and set up settlements to send merchandise into the Chocó and receive contraband gold in return. The conquest of the Chocó had ended, but the story of slavery, mining, food supply, and contraband trade had just begun.

3

From Chaos to Colony: The Establishment of Government in the Chocó

From the early 1540's onward the Chocó had been considered a jurisdictional part of the province of Popayán. This had come about naturally, without direct instructions from the king. Following the failure of Pascual de Andagoya to implant a colony within the present confines of the Chocó in the late 1530's (Andagoya received the title governor of the San Juan in 1538),[1] Sebastián de Belalcázar, the original conquistador of the Cauca Valley, assumed governmental powers over the area, granting licenses for *entradas* and titles to several Spaniards. The title governor of the Chocó granted in the sixteenth and seventeenth centuries was doubtless given more to increase the prestige of the individual who received it than to describe the position he held. The correct Spanish title for such an adventurer would have been *adelantado* (conqueror, pacifier, pathfinder), but the terms were often interchangeable in that early period. Certainly the early governors could not administer a region that had not yet been conquered.

Officials in Popayán had no monopoly on the Chocó, however, and for almost 180 years appointments were made from various seats of Spanish authority. Spaniards such as Captain Gómez Fernández and Lucas de Avila, who tried to conquer the Chocó in the second half of the sixteenth century, received commissions and titles from the *Real Audiencia* in Santa Fe de Bogotá. The Spanish monarch even exercised his royal prerogative on occasion to grant permits for missions and *entradas* to the Franciscans and to individuals as well.

Spanish officials were fastidious in their attempts to create an orderly chain of command. When the Indians were finally pacified late in the seventeenth century, a more systematic method of government had to be implemented. In 1687 the Chocó underwent a political restructuring when the four existing provinces, Payá, Tatamá, Citará, and Noanamá were eliminated and three *tenencias* (lieutenantcies—governed by a lieutenant governor), Nóvita, Citará, and Baudó*, were created.[2] At the same time Governor Carlos de Sotomayor selected the first corregidors in the Chocó. Although the Jesuits and Franciscans formed some *reducciones, corregimientos de indios* had not been established. The creation of the new *corregimientos* was not so much for the benefit of the Indians as it was a method of controlling them and rewarding Spaniards who had helped in their conquest.

Sotomayor's appointments did not have crown sanction, but it proved an easy matter to have them approved by the *Real Audiencia* in Santa Fe de Bogotá. One such post went to Sergeant Major Antonio Joaquín de Veroís, whom Sotomayor described as an active and loyal participant in the pacification of the province of Citará. Judging him to be a man of strong character, contemporaries stated that Veroís was capable of handling the rough, adventuresome Spanish miners, as well as the Indians, of the area. He was named corregidor of Citará on the provision that he instruct the Indians in the Christian doctrine and collect tributes. The sergeant major readily accepted this standard pledge and suggested that he levy a yearly tribute of twelve pesos on each Indian male of working age; retaining as corregidor two pesos and sending four pesos to the crown. The remaining six pesos would be used as stipends for the clergy. One of the consuls (*fiscals*) of the *Real Audiencia* reviewed the appointment and the recommendation of the appointee and approved both.[3]

Some of the early corregidors set a pattern of opportunism which

---

* Little gold was discovered near Baudó, and it was soon changed from a *tenencia* to a *corregimiento*. Thus only two *tenencias*, Nóvita and Citará, were in existence during the eighteenth century.

their successors followed until the abolition of the *corregimiento* system at the beginning of the republican era. In the middle of the 1690's, for example, reports reached the crown that the corregidor of Noanamá had been mistreating his charges. The *Real Audiencia* appointed one of its members, *Oidor* (Judge) Merlo de la Fuente, as *Visitador* (Inspector) to the province of Nóvita. While investigating the accusations, De la Fuente discovered that a corregidor, named by the governor of the Chocó had forced some of the Noanamaes to travel to Nóvita to build houses for the miners and slaves of that growing settlement without giving them proper food or paying them sufficient wages (he paid them only four pesos a month, often in goods they did not want). The corregidor had sent other Noanamá Indians to transport goods along the San Juan River to Nóvita, awarding them only four pesos a canoe load, though the correct wage was determined at double that amount.[4] It usually took the Indians twenty to twenty-four days to make the trip down the San Juan River to the port of Chirambirá, load, and then return to Nóvita. The Indians were required to make several such trips each year.[5]

Visitador de la Fuente also noted that the corregidor had violated Spanish law when he permitted his friends to use the Indians for personal service. The Indians had not been paid in cash but given only *aguardiente* (liquor) and wine. Spaniards had been allowed to reside in the Indian village of Noanamá, and many treated the Indians as personal slaves. The treatment of the Noanamá Indians, the *oidor* concluded, had been unjust, particularly so since the loyalty of this tribe had been demonstrated recently by their help in quelling the Citará Indian rebellion and repelling the pirate invasions. The corregidor was admonished and told to obey the laws, but he was neither removed from office nor fined.[6]

Crown officials in the seventeenth century seemed unwilling to enforce the king's edicts concerning mismanagement of the Indians —perhaps because the officials were themselves some of the major violators. The same was true in the implementation of other official regulations, most notably those concerning contraband trade. Once the immediate problems of discovery and conquest ended, the hundreds of new arrivals—slave and white—became consumers rather than producers of basic necessities. Virtually every item important to support or enhance life, excluding corn, plantains, and some meat and fish, had to be imported. Salt, wine, oil, wax, fresh and salted meat, iron and steel for tools, clothes, and most luxury items like chocolate had to be purchased and brought in. The surreptitious extraction of gold dust and the introduction of various illegally imported articles presented Spanish officials with perhaps their most vexing problem.

Mines in the Chocó yielded the product desired by Spaniards and foreigners alike, for gold provided an immediately acceptable medium of exchange. Spanish merchants in Panama, Cartagena, Guayaquil, and Lima took Chocó bullion in return for credit and provisions.[7] English, Scots, French, and Dutch marauders and merchants living among the Cuna Indians near the mouth of the Atrato River eagerly exchanged supplies for gold,[8] and non-Spanish European possessions in the Caribbean became well-known centers for contraband trade with the Spanish Main. By the late seventeenth century Jamaica had gained notoriety as a hotbed of illicit commerce.[9] Individuals from Cartagena, Panama, and the Chocó doubtless traded directly with British merchants in Jamaica in the seventeenth and eighteenth centuries.

The Spanish crown tried repeatedly to prevent colonial contact with foreigners, but officials ordered to restrict intercourse often engaged in it themselves. In 1691, for example, a company of Spanish regulars sent from Cartagena to guard the mouth of the Atrato River from pirates deserted their post, and officers and soldiers alike traded with foreigners in the Darién region. They sent contraband clothes, liquor, tools, and slaves into the Chocó via the Atrato River. Crown officials in the Chocó were also implicated since they permitted the fraudulent introduction of these products.[10] Four years later a Spanish merchant, Juan de Andalueza, complained that he faced unfair competition in the Chocó as other merchants and officials undersold him with contraband products on which no duties had been paid. He estimated that in a few months more than 6,000 pesos worth of merchandise had illegally entered the Chocó by way of the Atrato River. He also denounced the lieutenant governor of Noanamá not only for permitting contraband along the San Juan River but also for being a partner in the company most heavily engaged in the business. Maintaining a legitimate business in the Chocó, Andalueza stated, was extremely difficult.[11]

Concerned with reports of contraband trade in the Chocó, the *Real Audiencia* took immediate measures designed to curtail the illegal traffic. On October 20, 1698, the Atrato River was declared closed to maritime commerce on pain of death.[12] The order arrived at an inopportune time, for the Chocó had just begun to develop an organized mining industry. In the period from 1695 to 1710 Spanish immigration increased and there was a five-fold growth in the number of slaves. The proscription concerning trade along the Atrato did not deal a crippling blow to the expanding economy, since the San Juan River remained open to maritime commerce and products could still be imported legally from Panama, Lima, and Guayaquil. Transportation costs were higher, for the Atrato River afforded a more natural entrance into the Chocó for many products, but at least necessities could be purchased without extreme difficulty.

Vessels from Panama, Peru, or Guayaquil either unloaded at Port Chirambirá at the mouth of the San Juan River, or, if boats of low draft, they proceeded up the San Juan to a site known as Boca Calima where the Calima River joins the San Juan. From Chirambirá or Calima, Noanamá Indians poled canoes loaded with merchandise to Noanamá, Nóvita, or San Pablo. During the last decade of the seventeenth century commerce flourished along this route, and in a three-year period Indians freighted more than 200,000 pounds of salt, wine, and *aguardiente* from Chirambirá to Nóvita.[13]

Evidence also exists that trade along the Atrato continued because officials lacked the means of preventing it even had they so desired. As a result, in 1712 the crown ordered Vicente de Aramburo, *oidor* of the *Real Audiencia* de Nueva Granada, to travel to the Chocó, create a *junta de guerra* (council of defense) and select a site for a fortress on the Atrato. The crown gave three specific reasons for the construction of this fortress: first, to quell the repeated and dangerous attacks of the English upon the region which threatened the security of the Chocó and posed a strategic challenge to the wealthy Spanish territories southward (it was feared that foreigners might gain direct access to Peru via the Atrato and San Juan rivers); second, to prevent the frequent and illegal entry of contraband merchandise and the fraudulent exportation of gold dust; and third, to control the Indians and prevent them from running away and forming raiding parties which endangered the peace of the Chocó.[14]

After much deliberation the newly formed *junta de guerra* finally selected a site near the mouth of the Beté River as the most desirable location for a *vigía* (fort, lookout post). The land near the proposed *vigía* was fertile; plantains already grew in the region (but no farther downriver), and could be used to feed the men manning the post; and, as the Atrato narrows at this point, both banks of the river could be defended from one side. The junta also decided that a squad of twelve soldiers would be on guard duty at the fortress (there is no evidence that this decision was ever implemented), each receiving a salary of eight pesos a month. The commander of the outpost was to be paid sixteen pesos a month. In order to ensure the soldiers' vigilance in halting contraband trade, they were offered the inducement of one-third of all they captured. Indians helped build the fort and for the first time the Chocó had a fixed military encampment.[15]

A similar outpost was established on the San Juan, although it did not compare in size or importance with the *vigía* of the Atrato. Despite their supposed significance in the prevention of illicit commerce, both *vigías* led a sporadic and chaotic existence. The *vigía* of the Atrato became a favorite target for marauding Cuna Indians—several times they completely destroyed the lookout post.[16] No one seemed very interested in the continued presence of the San Juan *vigía*. It sputtered in and out of existence for almost a century.[17]

There is no evidence that the *vigías* prevented contraband trade. In fact, they presented no barrier to those who wished to bypass them. The *vigías'* locations were well known and could be avoided by traveling overland around them, and the guard posts could be openly passed at night. This was especially true on a night when heavy rainfall muffled sounds and made vision virtually impossible. Despite the junta's stipulation that twelve Spanish soldiers remain at the fortress, only one Spaniard (the captain of the *vigía*), assisted by a half-dozen Indians, manned the *vigía* of the Atrato. The sentry posts were located miles downriver from the lieutenant governors and governors in Nóvita and Quibdó: *vigía* captains were seldom bothered by responsible officials. Finally, the captains were poorly paid, thus creating a situation fraught with the possibilities of bribery and collusion.

The steps taken by the crown to halt or limit contraband trade by creating *vigías* were typical Spanish reactions to problems of the moment. But geography, climate, and temptation nullified any effectiveness of the lookouts. In fact, shortly after the creation of the *vigía* of the Atrato several prominent Spaniards, including a priest, José de Cordoba, and the lieutenant governor of Citará, Antonio de Ordóñez, were indicted for introducing contraband clothes and slaves along the Atrato and for trading with Dutch and English merchants in the Gulf of Darién.[18]

Accusations concerning misdeeds in the Chocó continued to arrive in Santa Fe de Bogotá, and a number of them originated from the regions of the Cauca Valley that were already settled. Merchants in the Cauca Valley sent food supplies grown in the interior provinces and also merchandise from Spain that arrived in the Cauca Valley either from the western port of Buenaventura or from Cartagena on the Magdalena and Cauca rivers. Cauca Valley merchants asked the *audiencia* to enforce proscriptions concerning navigation along the Atrato, and they also asked that maritime commerce entering the San Juan be prohibited. They claimed that much of the traffic on the San Juan constituted contraband trade, and, perhaps more to the point of their own concern, they indicated their financial interest in the matter.[19]

Concerned about the charges of illicit commerce, in 1717 the *audiencia* placed a moratorium on trade entering the San Juan and sent an inspector (*visitador*), Mateo de Zepes, to investigate the allegations of fraud. Reaction from the Chocó was immediate and bitter. Spaniards in the Chocó, accustomed to few restrictions, protested both the complete closing of the region to maritime commerce and the sending of a *visitador*. Mine owners decried their inability to feed their *cuadrillas* even with the San Juan open. They estimated that in the preceding year alone over three hundred slaves had perished from hunger.

Petitions to the lieutenant governor of Nóvita asserted that neither the mine owners nor their slaves could exist without the supplies which entered the San Juan from Guayaquil and Peru. Halting traffic on the river would force them to leave the area or starve. The mine owners proclaimed their innocence with regard to illicit commerce and argued that there was no need for an inspector from Santa Fe de Bogotá to visit the Chocó since officials from Popayán kept a close surveillance over the region. The Chocó petitioners also denounced the merchants and farmers of the Cauca Valley, saying that these providers did not raise enough to feed themselves, let alone the Chocó. Old trails from the interior provinces might have served in 1685 when there were few slaves to support, but, the owners asserted, in 1717 these *trochas* no longer sufficed. Although the lieutenant governor expressed sympathy for the mine owners, he informed them that he was powerless to lift the embargo or halt the *visita*.[20]

Despite these claims of innocence, Zepes' *visita* confirmed the rumors of corruption. Contraband trade not only existed in the region but thrived. This is doubtless the reason petitioners in the Chocó sought to prevent Zepes' arrival. The *visitador* reported that the crown suffered indeterminable losses because foreign merchants openly shipped prohibited products to the Chocó, receiving bullion in return. Zepes also validated accusations of Indian mistreatment in the region. The captain general of New Granada, Antonio de la Pedrosa y Guerrero, reasoned that the widespread contraband trade Zepes reported could only be occurring with the knowledge and involvement of the corregidors and lieutenant governors. As a result he initiated sweeping changes in the administration of the Chocó.

The captain general removed from office all existing lieutenant governors and corregidors and appointed a superintendent to oversee all the crown's business in the Chocó. He also placed the Chocó under the direct control of the *Real Audiencia*. The new superintendent, Luis de Espinosa de los Monteros, received specific instructions to prevent contraband, protect the welfare of the Indians, and nominate new lieutenant governors and corregidors who were men of good faith. All new officials were required to place bonds to ensure their good conduct. Superintendent Espinosa accepted the appointment, personally placing a bond of 5,500 pesos.[21]

Two years later, in 1720, the new viceroy of New Granada, Jorge de Villalonga, confirmed Pedrosa's actions and repeated prohibitions concerning commerce on the Atrato River. But he went much further, placing strict limits on the number and origin of ships that could arrive at the San Juan, and on the products they could transport to the Chocó. The viceroy forbade boats from landing at Port Chirambirá or Boca Calima, which did not have a specific permit to do so from Guayaquil. Only basic provisions (*los efectos y frutos de la tierra*) could be unloaded. Products from Spain (*mercancías y ropa de Castilla*) and slaves could not be imported on the San Juan, and under no circumstances could vessels from Panama put in at either Chirambirá or Boca Calima.

The illegal extraction of gold dust remained a primary consideration, and the viceroy sent specific instructions regarding the management of bullion. Officials in Nóvita and Quibdó were ordered to collect rigorously the *quinto* (the royal "fifth," or tax on mining) on all gold mined in their provinces and to keep detailed records of the levies. The viceroy specifically denounced the custom whereby merchants and mine owners in the region used gold dust as a medium of exchange, and he suggested, but did not order, that a credit system be implemented for merchants and mine owners in the Chocó which would effectively limit the amount of gold changing hands.[22]

The actions of the captain general and the viceroy were designed not only to prevent fraud but also to tighten control over the Chocó by removing it from the political domination of Popayán. Objections from Popayán to this new redistricting were immediate. The governor of Popayán, the Marqués de San Juan de la Rivera, sent several urgent letters to the king arguing that the separation of the Chocó from the province of Popayán would cause great damage to the royal treasury. Ignoring the stated reasons for the appointment of Superintendent Espinosa, the marqués claimed that the Chocó was a frontier region in need of constant supervision from high-ranking officials in Popayán. In 1721, acting on the strength of the governor's letters, the Spanish crown dispatched two royal *cédulas* to the *Real Audiencia* of New Granada, ordering the return of the administration of the Chocó to the jurisdiction of the governor of Popayán.[23]

Three years later, however, the crown rescinded this decision. In 1723, Viceroy Villalonga forwarded several reports to the crown concerning the Chocó which he had received from treasury officials in Santa Fe de Bogotá. Contrary to the pessimistic warnings of the governor of Popayán, the Chocó had experienced a definite increase in gold production and in the profits accrued by the crown during the brief period when the province had been under the control of Superintendent Espinosa.[24]

The viceroy also submitted testimony from important individuals regarding the lack of proper administration by the governors of Popayán. Not only was control inefficient but Popayán governors illegally sold offices in the Chocó. *Tenencias* in Nóvita and Citará had been sold for 4,000 to 6,000 pesos. Individuals purchasing these offices were notoriously corrupt, recouping investments through contraband trade and by accepting bribes from mine owners and

43

corregidors.[25] The evidence proved persuasive, and, upon recommendation of the Royal Council of the Indies, the king abrogated the *cédulas* of 1721.[26]

By the time the 1724 order reached New Granada, the governor of Popayán had reassumed control of the Chocó and Superintendent Espinosa and most of the officials he had appointed had left the region. Further complicating matters was the fact that New Granada itself was undergoing a series of administrative changes. In 1717 the captaincy general of New Granada was raised to the position of a viceroyalty. But six years later, mainly for reasons of economy, the crown returned it to a captaincy generalship. Thus, with the central government of New Granada in a state of flux, one could hardly expect regional changes to be swiftly carried out.

Finally, in a royal *cédula* dated November 28, 1726, King Philip V informed the *Real Audiencia* of New Granada and the governor of Popayán that from that day forward the Chocó would be a separate administrative unit with its own governor. In order to prevent contraband trade, increase the production of the mines and royal *quintos*, and administer justice to the Indians, the crown desired the Chocó to have its own set of officials appointed by, and directly responsible to, the king. The crown deemed the modification necessary because of the distances separating the Chocó, Popayán, and Santa Fe de Bogotá. The Spanish monarch further affirmed the appointment of Francisco de Ibero, who had served loyally for sixteen years in the king's Italian corps, as the new governor of the Chocó.[27] Although many previous Spaniards had held the title governor of the Chocó, Ibero was in all likelihood the first to have been appointed directly by the crown, and certainly he was the first governor of the separate and independent provinces of the Chocó.

With the initiation of the *vigías* and the creation of the Chocó as a separate political entity with one governor, two lieutenant governors and a dozen *corregimientos*, the basic administrative structure was set and did not change for almost a century. Minor shifts were made to ensure peace and prosperity in the province. A few new officials were later added, different plans were attempted to control the contraband trade, and various innovations were made to increase production in the mines. But, in 1726, the chain of command was established, and the system remained essentially intact.

Despite the intentions of the crown, the creation of the separate provinces of the Chocó did not change the basic character of the region. Within the Chocó the frontier expanded during the next century as new mines were opened and more slaves were imported. But the barrier presented by the Cordillera Occidental and restrictions on commerce along the Atrato and San Juan rivers meant that the region remained physically cut off from the rest of New Granada. The crown hoped to create order, but the new administrative structure provided only minimal control. Without strong support and surveillance from centers of Spanish authority Chocó governors and lieutenant governors either could not or would not effectively police the mines, *corregimientos*, and settlements.

4

From Mine to Smeltery: The Problems and Methods of Gold Production in the Chocó

Anyone could mine gold in the Chocó, and any free person— Spaniard, Indian, or black—could own a mine. Registration of a discovery with the nearest crown official constituted the only real regulation.[1] By requiring prospectors to register their mines, the crown hoped to avoid legal difficulties whereby two individuals claimed the same property. Many *mazamorreros* (independent prospectors), realizing the probable temporary nature of their find, did not bother with this procedure, even though there would have been no difficulty receiving title to land that had never been worked or previously claimed.[2]

Following the period of initial discovery and conquest it became increasingly difficult to find unclaimed land in easily accessible locations, and many *mazamorreros* worked territory belonging to others. Many individuals sought ownership of "abandoned" areas. Under the mining code commonly accepted in the Chocó, anyone discovering a mine that had not been worked during the previous year could legally claim it.[3] In most instances this procedure was relatively simple since the property had been vacant for years, or the original owner relinquished his rights to the territory in question.[4] When titles were challenged, however, lawsuits ensued until the exact ownership of the land could be determined.[5]

Claims could also be transferred with little difficulty from one owner to another. The property was often worth a considerable sum, especially if it included agricultural improvements and inventories demonstrated that the land itself was valuable.[6] Territory claimed by mine owners included more than just the sites of the placer mines. Owners usually hoped to produce food for their *cuadrillas* and thus held land for agricultural purposes.[7] Apparently a limit was placed on the amount of land a person could claim, depending in part upon the claimant's ability to use it. This limitation, however, was not clearly defined. In 1690, for example, the Caicedo family appropriated five leagues (about thirteen miles) of land around Las Animas on the San Pablo Isthmus. Since the area contained rich gold deposits, other miners wanted to stake claims in that region. One of the miners, Francisco de Arboleda, requested title to part of the huge Caicedo claim. The *Real Audiencia* ruled that five leagues was more than the Caicedos could possibly use and granted Arboleda title to some land within the Caicedo holdings.[8] However, mine owners continued to retain large acreages in the Chocó.

Agricultural land did not have to be situated near rivers and *quebradas,* although it was preferable, but mine owners always wanted their mines as near running water as possible. When several miners worked separate claims on the same streams, disputes over riparian rights could, and did, occur.[9] Projects noticeably restricting the flow of a stream or changing its course needed a special license from the crown.[10] Potentially rich stream beds led some mine owners to request permission to build dams and dig trenches to change the courses of these *quebradas.* Most of the projects were small, and local officials readily granted approval. On occasion, however, rulings had to be made by a higher authority. Early in the eighteenth century, for example, an ambitious Spaniard suggested changing the course of the Andágueda River above Lloró. Wealthy mines had been discovered in this region, and many believed the bed of the Andágueda River to be heavy with gold. Manuel de Herrera, the lieutenant general of the province of Citará, first conceived of the idea in 1703. He drew a map of the river, including the proposed changes, and sailed for Spain to request the king's approval. However, the lieutenant general was captured by the French and put to death. The idea was revived in 1741, but, because of the size of the project and doubts of its successful completion, a license to initiate the scheme was denied by the viceroy of New Granada.[11]

Although pockets of gold were discovered in the Chocó, because of the alluvial nature of the deposits veins of the yellow metal were rare and few shafts were dug in the region. The most common type of placer mining in the Chocó was ground sluicing. Robert Cooper West described the process as follows:

A sluice channel, or *canelón* is excavated along the base of a gravel bench to the depth of false bedrock (hardpan, *peña*), where the richest pay streaks are usually encountered. With iron bars (*barras*) the miners dig into the face of the bench, dumping paydirt into the sluice. Water is then run through the sluice and the finer materials are washed to the bottom of the sluice; large cobbles are thrown from the *canelón* with pairs of concave wooden plates (*cachos*); next, the bottom of the sluice, containing both the settled gold and the highly auriferous clay layer immediately above the false bedrock, is scraped with *almocafres*, short handled dibbles with hooked metal blades; a second washing ensues; finally the fine residue, rich in gold, is heaped in piles within the sluice and the precious metal panned out with the *bateas* (gold pans). One sluicing operation from the time of the initial terrace excavation to the final clean up requires two weeks of labor by ten or fifteen workers.[12]

The final cleanup with the *bateas* was the most important step in the operation. It was at this time that the overseers and the slave captains maintained an exceedingly vigilant watch over the slaves to prevent theft.[13]

Open-pit placers were also popular during the colonial period,[14] and in these a primitive type of strip mining was employed. Water was always of prime importance to the mine owners because in the ground sluices and pit placers volumes of earth had to be moved and washed to extract the gold. Fortunately for the mining industry in the Chocó, accessibility to water, because of the heavy rainfall, did not usually present a major problem.

Not all the gold discovered in the region was directly adjacent to flowing water. Individuals who found gold on high ground, or where it was impossible to utilize the *quebradas*, sometimes built reservoirs to catch rain water.[15] When droughts occurred, there were serious, if temporary, difficulties. During one such dry period in 1782, Ignacio Mosquera, a mine owner near Tadó, indicated that many of the slaves in the province of Nóvita could not pan gold because of the *mucho verano* (drought—"excessive summer").[16]

Rainfall also washed gold from the soil into the streams and rivers of the Chocó. Many of the *mazamorreros* panned gold directly from the rivers when they did not have the labor force necessary to undertake a ground sluice or a pit placer. Slaves or *mazamorreros* dived into deep holes in the rivers, which served as nature's sluice boxes, trapping the heavy precious metals, to gather gravel from the bottom. When the rivers were low, workers panned from the exposed sand bars or waded into the streams,* collecting *bateas* filled with sand, rocks, and gold from the stream bed itself.[17]

Slave owners did not always keep their bondsmen occupied in their mines because of the kind of mining in the Chocó. It took time to select a suitable site for a ground sluice or a pit placer. Until a section proved valuable, the owner did not want to commit his entire labor force to a venture that might not pay expenses. Slaves were rented out to other owners whenever possible, and this arrangement had advantages for the owners. The owner received income even though his slaves were not engaged in his own mines, and the individual who rented slaves did so only when he specifically needed them. The amount paid for renting slaves averaged one peso a working day. Religious holidays were not included when the total rental fee was computed.[18]

Many owners also permitted certain slaves to work for periods of time independently, paying a set sum (also one peso per working day) to the owner. Self-rental by slaves was common, but the

---

* Because the streams were very swift even when low, workers commonly tied large rocks to the small of their back to gain weight and stability against the current—a feat that requires exceptional balance. A slip in thigh-deep water with a large stone tied to one's back is hazardous. I witnessed this dangerous procedure on many occasions; it is still practiced by independent prospectors in the Chocó.

49

agreement rarely involved more than twenty or thirty days a year.*
Owners allowed their slaves to rent themselves only during slack
periods when little work was being done around the mine. In one
recorded instance, however, a male slave in his twenties worked
entirely on his own for a period of six years.[19]

Despite the frequency of self-rental, no mention was made about
which slaves were eligible or what happened to slaves who failed
to pay the specified fee. In the larger mines overseers were responsible for selecting the slaves who worked independently and for
collecting their payments. Since overseers had to deduct shortages
from their own pockets, they were doubtless persuasive in their
collections.† Nonetheless, incentives to enter such an agreement
were high for healthy slaves since they could keep what they earned
above the stipulated one peso a day.

The term *jornales* was used to record the sums paid to owners
either by slaves working independently or by individuals renting
them. The one-peso-a-day fee for *jornales* was customary, but it
was also officially recommended in 1719, when Superintendent
Espinosa determined one peso to be the average amount a healthy
slave could produce through one day's labor.[20] Accounts from
various mines show that these wages added significant amounts to
an owner's income.[21] When a specific sum had to be sent to an
owner each year, the overseer rented out a certain number of slaves
to ensure the stipulated amount.[22] This might possibly limit over-all
production, but it also guaranteed the owner a minimum fixed
income, even when his mine did not yield as much gold as expected.

Although mine owners rented slaves from one another, they
rarely used free labor in their mines. Slave owners were perhaps

* It is difficult to determine how many slaves were actually involved in self-rental
because few account books from the mines remain. However, many of the extant
ledgers show that individual slaves paid twenty to thirty pesos a year for *jornales*
(rental fees).

† Overseers necessarily were acquainted with the abilities and work habits of all
the members of the *cuadrilla*. Doubtless they only selected slaves who were good risks
to earn at least one peso a day. The revenue from rentals was considered income of
the mine, and overseers normally received, as their salary, 10 per cent of all such
income. Therefore, they also gained revenue from careful rentals.

fearful that free labor could not be depended upon, and throughout New Granada it was considered less profitable than the system of slavery.[23] More to the point, in the Chocó owners found it almost impossible to induce white or freedman labor to work in the mines even at high wages; and they did not entirely trust the latter group. Free labor, when hired, received one peso a day in wages.[24]

Although gold was not the only thing mined in the Chocó, it was the only metal that had any real value for most of the colonial period. Miners also extracted platinum, but it was worth nothing until the 1780's. Several theories developed about platinum. Some thought that gold and platinum "grew" together[25] and that platinum, or white gold (*oro blanco*) as they called it, was a type of gold that simply had not been in the ground long enough to turn yellow or mature.[26] Spaniards in the first part of the eighteenth century had no use for platinum and threw it away in disgust—perhaps in the hope that it would mature. Actually crown officials became quite annoyed by the high percentage of worthless *oro blanco* encountered in the Chocó gold. Stiff penalties were imposed on anyone bringing in a mixture of the two metals. In 1720, Viceroy Jorge Villalonga judged the mixing of platinum with gold as fraud against the royal interests. He established a two-thousand-peso fine for any Spaniard committing the fraud, and any *zambo*, mulatto, black, mestizo, or other person of "inferior caste" (*inferior calidad*) convicted of the offense was to receive two hundred lashes.[27]

The decree created difficulties for the Chocó miners, for it was not easy to separate platinum from gold. The product from the final washing in the mines was a mixture (*jagua*) containing heavy black sand, tiny flakes of iron oxide, gold, and platinum. The precious metals could be isolated from the *jagua* by various methods[28] but not from each other without expense or considerable difficulty. By 1720 the smeltery in Popayán was using quicksilver (*azogue*) to separate the two metals, but it was expensive, and there are few records of mine owners in the Chocó using mercury at that time.[29] The process they developed was laborious and time consuming, and the results depended upon the care taken. Gold and platinum do not have the same atomic weights (gold, 197.2; platinum, 195.23). By placing them in a flat metal dish, tilting the container slightly and tapping the bottom, the heavier gold slid to the downward side of the plate. Too strong a tap or a sudden jerk negated minutes of careful work. Even the most expert individuals left some platinum in the gold.* Several mines in the province of Nóvita (where placer deposits contained a higher percentage of platinum than in the province of Citará) were closed by the viceroy in the early 1720's.[30]

Scientists studied platinum in Europe as early as 1748,[31] and in 1759, Juan Vendlingen, the *cosmógrafo mayor de Indias* (royal cosmographer), ordered the viceroy of New Granada to send four or five thousand pounds (four or five hundred *quintales*) of platinum to Spain for experimentation.[32] The governor of the Chocó, Francisco Martínez, was asked to help fill the request, and he replied that steps had been taken to acquire the metal.[33] Platinum was shipped to Spain at that time, but no mention has yet been found of the actual amount freighted.†

In 1774, Francisco Benito, an official in the *Casa de Moneda* (mint) in Santa Fe de Bogotá, refined platinum, perhaps for the first time.[34] Twelve years later Francisco Chavaneau, professor of physics and chemistry in Vergara, Spain, perfected and refined the technique.[35] The crown suddenly became interested in the metal calling it "a perfect metal, as ductile and malleable as gold." The New Granadan Viceroy Antonio Caballero y Góngora was commanded quickly to collect all the platinum possible while at the same time keeping the new value of *oro blanco* a secret.[36]

The viceroy hastily informed the Marqués of Sonora in Spain that the major area in the Viceroyalty of New Granada that contained platinum was the Chocó. One stream, the viceroy reported,

---

* This is a folk-mining technique that most merchants and miners still use in the Chocó. During the colonial period female slaves, supervised by the overseer, usually separated gold from platinum. Owners believed this task was best performed by women because of their dexterity, care, and patience.

† A few years later, in 1766, Viceroy Pedro Messía de la Zerda reported that platinum was abundant in the Chocó and that some platinum had already been shipped to Spain from that province. See Viceroy Messía to Julian de Arriga, Santa Fe de Bogotá, January 18, 1766, AGI, Seccion 5, Audiencia de Santa Fe, leg. 835.

was so rich in this metal that it had been named *La Platina*. However, Caballero y Góngora cautioned that he would have to proceed carefully in order to maintain secrecy.[37]

The viceroy then transmitted confidential instruction to Chocó Governor Carlos Smith, ordering him to acquire all available platinum without disclosing the metal's new importance. Soon afterwards, Smith confirmed a shipment of 149 pounds of platinum to Cartagena and reported that he had paid mine owners two or three *reales* a pound for their platinum. The governor added that the purchase of any more platinum would probably arouse suspicion and raise the price.[38] Caballero y Góngora then ordered Governor Smith to pay up to four *reales* a pound, publish a ban on the exportation of platinum, and investigate the possibilities of establishing mines to be owned and operated by the crown in the platinum-producing regions and of hiring *libres* to extract the white metal. The viceroy again stressed the need for secrecy.

Governor Smith replied that he had gathered another one hundred pounds of platinum, but he advised against publication of the decree prohibiting the exportation of platinum since it would alert mine owners that platinum suddenly had value. If this happened, he warned, they would smuggle platinum out to foreign sources as contraband. He also reasoned against the initiation of crown-owned mines and the use of freedmen to mine platinum, saying that they would be expensive and that the *libres*, because they were *vagabundos* (shiftless, vagabonds), could not be trusted.[39]

Obviously the crown hoped to acquire platinum quickly and cheaply. A separate laboratory was set up for Chavaneau,[40] and in 1787 the Marqués of Sonora ordered Viceroy Caballero y Góngora to speed up transmission of *oro blanco*; they wanted to make a special table service of platinum for the king and use the metal in the royal chapel. The Márques of Sonora wrote that, in order to facilitate collection, the price could be raised to one peso a pound.[41]

By 1788 the crown was officially paying two pesos a pound for platinum, and the viceroy approved a plan to import tools, iron, steel, and slaves to the Chocó for sale to the mine owners in hopes of increasing productivity.[42] Large-scale attempts to acquire platinum, however, meant that secrecy was no longer possible. In 1788, Visitador Vicente Yáñez decreed that henceforth platinum was to be sold only to the crown (making it a crown monopoly) and established penalties for those caught "hoarding" the *oro blanco*.* Yáñez also encouraged *mazamorreros* to bring platinum into the royal treasuries (*cajas*) in Quibdó and Nóvita by allowing them to pay their yearly taxes (*quintos*) with two pounds of platinum.[43]

Apparently these measures proved temporarily effective, for in 1788 Visitador Yáñez sent more than three thousand pounds (120 *arrobas*) of platinum from the Chocó to Cartagena for consignment to Spain.[44] Production shortly declined, however, perhaps in part because the old hoards of platinum (perhaps piles where it had been maturing) had been expended. In 1802, Lieutenant Governor José María Mallarino y Vargas (of Nóvita) asserted that the price paid by the crown did not induce mine owners to keep slaves working in areas of high platinum rather than gold yields. He also indicated that much of the platinum mined was smuggled to foreign sources that paid more for the metal.[45] The price paid for platinum rose to six or eight pesos a pound in 1804,[46] but miners still preferred to sell their platinum to foreigners. Baron Von Humboldt, writing at the beginning of the nineteenth century, indicated that platinum brought twenty-five or thirty pesos a pound in Paris.[47] Hence, at the end of the colonial period, platinum as well as gold added to the contraband trade, provided profits for Chocó miners, and increased the number of problems for the officials in the region.

It was in the crown's interest to limit the clandestine exportation of bullion. One regulation enacted to this end concerned the establishment of a *casa de fundición* (smeltery) in Nóvita late in the eighteenth century. In a royal *cédula* dated December 20, 1777, the Spanish crown ordered the creation of a smeltery in the Chocó. The royal order stipulated that only gold made into bars could be

---

* Guilty parties were fined sixteen pesos per pound of platinum found in their possession and second offenders, thirty-two pesos a pound. A third conviction was punished by four years' service without pay at Fort Caimán at the mouth of the Atrato River. See, AHNC, Minas del Cauca 5, fols. 845–46 (1788).

exported from the Chocó once the smeltery opened.[48] Since all gold dust legally had to be taken to an official smeltery, the construction of a *casa de fundición* in the Chocó should have simplified the problems of miners and merchants in transmitting *oro en polvo* (gold dust), and, by prohibiting the exportation of gold dust, the crown hoped to curtail contraband trade. But opposition to the new building germinated even before its inauguration, and objections to its existence continued through the remaining years of the colonial period.

In 1779 a group of mine owners, including José Marcelino de Mosquera, Bartola de Arboleda, and Vicente Hurtado (all major slave owners in the Chocó), petitioned for abandonment of the project. They owned mines northwest of Nóvita near Tadó and Iró and preferred to take their gold directly to Popayán along the Tadó–Iró–Las Juntas trail.* The initiation of a *Casa de Fundición* in Nóvita would force them to ship their gold along the Iró, San Juan, and Tamaná rivers, which they characterized as swift and dangerous. They feared the loss of their bullion along this water route.

Arguments were presented depicting Nóvita as an undesirable location for such an important building. The town was said to contain few trustworthy people; slaves, free blacks, and mulattoes comprised almost the entire population. In fact, there was not a single location in the Chocó that would be safe for a smeltery. In addition, the mine owners warned that construction costs would be high because of exorbitant prices in the region, and they predicted difficulty in locating a trustworthy *fundador* (foundryman) willing to live in Nóvita. Testimony supporting the contention that the river routes to Nóvita were perilous and costly was later presented.[49]

An analysis of the petition presented by the Chocó mine owners discloses both racial prejudice and serious omissions and errors. Mine owners protested have to use a water route if they sent their

---

* The trail from Las Juntas to Cartago, on the edge of the Cauca Valley, was for several centuries the major land route into the Chocó. The main trail continued from Las Juntas to Nóvita, but a branch went from Las Juntas to Iró and Tadó.

gold to Nóvita and exhibited a preference for the trails from Tadó and Iró to Popayán. However, they failed to mention that this path crossed Las Juntas only a few miles upriver from Nóvita. Thus travel along the San Juan and Iró rivers could easily have been avoided. Even more important, the mine owners failed to mention that they legally had to send their gold to Nóvita whether or not the *Casa de Fundición* was built there. According to law, the lieutenant governors in Nóvita and Quibdó deducted the *quinto* (crown tax on mining) on all bullion before it could be transported from the Chocó. Obviously, many mine owners had not been complying with this regulation and were accustomed to sending gold dust directly to Popayán or Santa Fe de Bogotá—or what is even more likely, to foreigners.

In 1781 Visitador General to New Granada Juan Francisco Gutíerrez de Pineres studied the petition sent from the Chocó concerning the foundry and denied the mine owners' requests. The *visitador* did not doubt that some might find it more convenient to send gold directly from their mines to Popayán or Santa Fe de Bogotá, but since the purpose behind the construction of a *casa de fundición* in the Chocó was to impede the fraudulent extraction of gold dust, there could be no exception.[50] By December, 1782, a *fundador*, Juan Suárez, had been appointed, and the foundry had been inaugurated in Nóvita.[51]

Those objecting to the establishment of the *Casa de Fundición* discovered new reason for dissatisfaction once the foundry opened. Objections to the high *merma* (loss in gold through the smelting process) and rate of *displatinar* (removal of platinum from gold dust) became common, and many claimed that the *merma* at the foundry in Nóvita was double that of the smelteries in Popayán and Santa Fe de Bogotá. In 1792, Manuel Garín, on behalf of the mine owners in the Chocó (*gremio de mineros*), wrote the viceroy reasoning that if the purpose of the *Casa de Fundición* was to prevent the illegal extraction of gold from the Chocó, inefficiency of the smeltery in Nóvita had created the opposite effect.[52]

The following year Governor Joseph Michaeli, after receiving many complaints from more than thirty members of the miners' guild, conducted a brief investigation of the *Casa de Fundición*. He concluded that the *merma* in Nóvita was indeed double that of the smelteries in Popayán and Santa Fe de Bogotá, and he agreed with the miners' guild that the foundry in Nóvita had stimulated rather than impeded smuggling. Governor Michaeli went on to report that even loyal subjects of the crown illegally shipped gold dust out of the Chocó rather than send it to the foundry in Nóvita. These individuals, the governor explained, were not trying to defraud the crown and avoid the *quinto*. They sent their gold to the Cauca Valley, claimed to have mined it there, paid the *quinto*, and then took the gold to the foundries in Popayán or Santa Fe de Bogotá. Though technically these men were guilty of contraband trade in bullion, Michaeli sympathized with their refusal to suffer an excessive *merma* at the smeltery in Nóvita.[53] Later, in 1795, Governor Michaeli informed the viceroy that nothing could be said in favor of retaining the *Casa de Fundición* in Nóvita.[54]

Several arguments against the foundry kept reappearing. In 1792 members of the miners' guild complained of the dangerous river routes to Nóvita. They explained that in order to prevent loss they had to use their best and most agile slaves in transporting gold, and, in order to keep slaves from stealing the bullion, overseers had to accompany them. Without the overseer at the mine the rest of the *cuadrilla* would not work. The owners lamented the loss of income they correspondingly suffered from washings and *jornales* while prime slaves and the overseer were absent from the mine.[55] In the same year José de Niolta and Manuel de Herrera, merchants from Cali who traded in the Chocó, along with several Chocó mine owners who resided in Cali—Gerónimo de Escobar, Gertrudis Caicedo, and Marcela Caicedo—also complained that the foundry damaged their interests,[56] thus adding negative testimony from individuals residing outside the Chocó.

Despite expressed hatred again the *Casa de Fundición* from mine owners and merchants the *Real Audiencia* reaffirmed continuation of the foundry in 1794. A *fiscal* (consul) did suggest that the efficiency of the smeltery be improved to eliminate several of the most obvious grievances.[57] Weights and measures in the foundry had already been checked,[58] and in 1795 officials in Santa Fe de Bogotá experimentally removed Suárez as *fundador* but quickly reinstated him when the new foundryman, José de Castro, proved even worse.[59] Slaves and freedmen working at the foundry were instructed to maintain a constant temperature in the furnace, and new supplies necessary in the smelting process were brought in.

But despite efforts to improve conditions, ten years later, in 1805, the *merma* still ranged as high as 8 per cent (in Popayán the *merma* averaged 3½ to 4 per cent).[60] Suárez had continued as foundryman, although he had several times been suspected of dishonesty.[61] Now, however, he was charged with incompetence rather than personal dishonesty. A petition from twenty mine owners in the province of Citará sent to the lieutenant governor of Nóvita, José María Mallarino y Vargas, said that Suárez was old and incapable of managing the slaves and freedmen working in the foundry or of overseeing the smelting process. Even though Lieutenant Governor Mallarino had appointed a new assistant to Suárez, Manuel San Clemente, the petitioners claimed that the stubborn *fundador* scarcely permitted his young aide to enter the foundry, let alone assume any responsibility. The petition prompted a closer watch, and San Clemente soon apprehended one of Suárez' slaves stealing gold. The subsequent investigation concluded by Mallarino proved conclusively that slaves and free blacks working in the *Casa de Fundición* had pilfered gold regularly since the smeltery first opened.

Officials estimated that the blacks had stolen thousands of pesos worth of gold. One freedman, Cristóbal, was charged with having taken over four thousand pesos' worth in two years, which he passed off to slaves and freedmen in Nóvita in return for minted silver and favors. He spent freely on several mistresses and bet heavily on cock fights.[62] It seems incredible that such actions could have gone undetected for so long. As early as 1785 several mine owners voiced suspicions of Cristóbal, since the black had purchased his freedom after working in the foundry for less than a year.[63]

The convicted blacks were whipped and thrown in jail. Suárez was not charged with theft, but he was removed from his post and reprimanded for having been exceedingly negligent in his duty.[64] If anyone hoped that these actions would solve the problems of the *Casa de Fundición* or remove the mine owners' resentment, however, they were mistaken. Miners owners, especially those in Citará, continued to express dissatisfaction with the foundry.[65]

Throughout the colonial period gold production in the Chocó relied on forced labor (Indians and slaves), *mazamorreros*, crude tools, and folk-mining techniques (ground sluices, pit placers, the separation of gold and platinum). Although mining codes and custom governed ownership of the mines, Spanish laws designed to regulate the extraction of gold from the region and the deduction of crown taxes were often ignored. Crown officials in the Chocó could not, or would not, control the shipment of gold from isolated mines in the area. A ground sluice could be opened, worked, and closed in a matter of weeks, and only overseers or the owners knew exactly how much had been mined. *Mazamorreros* panning gold along the rivers and streams were even more difficult to police. Hence the crown established a *Casa de Fundición* in Nóvita. But the initiation and retention of the smeltery was doubtless a serious mistake. As the miners' guild and Governor Michaeli suggested, the foundry stimulated rather than curtailed contraband trade in gold.

The inefficiency of the *Casa de Fundición* and the inability of local officials to correct problems clearly showed the difficulties of maintaining crown agencies on the frontier. Distant officials made suggestions but resisted all attempts to abolish the foundry, claiming that it was necessary to the crown's over-all scheme for preventing contraband trade. Unfortunately the Santa Fe officials did not understand local conditions in the Chocó, and Chocó officials, perhaps concerned with their own welfare, were unable to prevent theft or oversee an operation far outside their own experience. The smeltery was always inefficient and expensive, and merchants and miners were convinced that it limited their profits and restricted their freedoms. Mining in the Chocó was successful, but miners preferred to employ their own systems and they resented royal authority that limited their independence.

5

The Chocó and the Cycle
of Contraband

The citizens of the Chocó exported gold and imported many necessities. Good supply lines employing the natural river routes were considered vital by the mine owners. For almost one hundred years, however, Spanish authorities experimented with legislation governing the Chocó's supply routes—not in hopes of stimulating economic growth but in an effort to exert greater and more direct control over the region. The Spanish crown, reacting to suspected and actual contraband, choked off or closed the water highways into the Chocó. All navigation above the *vigía* of the Atrato was prohibited from 1696 to 1782, and maritime commerce entering the San Juan was severely restricted.*

There is no evidence that these measures effectively prevented the furtive shipment of gold, but they did place extreme limitations on the amount of merchandise that could be easily conveyed into the Chocó. The scarcity of food, clothes, tools, and some luxury items created a situation conducive to contraband trade. Two kinds of illicit commerce, therefore, soon developed in the Chocó: gold was smuggled out of the region, and a wide variety of articles were illegally introduced.

Several factors made the fraudulent exportation of gold attractive to Chocó inhabitants. A mine owner or merchant wishing to comply

* From 1720 to 1810 only two or three ships a year were permitted to enter the Chocó by way of the San Juan River. These ships had to be licensed in Guayaquil, where cargoes were listed and duties paid. In order to pass over sandbars at the mouth of the San Juan River, the ships had to be of low draft and therefore of limited capacity.

with crown regulations concerning bullion paid several duties that reduced the net value of his gold dust and made the rewards of smuggling more enticing. First, the crown collected the *quinto real* on all bullion. The *quinto* did not remain constant throughout the colonial period. Originally 20 per cent, the crown reduced the *quinto* to 10 per cent in the sixteenth century for miners who brought gold to the assay offices. Bullion merchants, however, still paid 20 per cent.[1] By the eighteenth century the *quinto* was reduced first to 6½ per cent and then to 6 per cent on gold. And by 1777 the duty had dropped to its final level, of 3 per cent.*

Quintos were not collected directly in the Chocó until 1722. Before that date miners legally had to ship their bullion to interior New Granada for the deduction of crown taxes. In 1721, Viceroy Antonio de la Pedroza y Guerrero concluded that a high percentage of Chocó gold dust was fraudulently being sent to foreign buyers. In an attempt to prevent this trade, he ordered the collection of the *quinto* in Nóvita and Quibdó.[2]

After royal officials in the Chocó collected the *quinto*, mineowners or bullion merchants shipped their gold dust to the royal assay offices and mints in Popayán or Santa Fe de Bogotá.[3] There officials assayed, weighed, and founded the gold and affixed the royal insignia on the newly cast bars. The crown charged a *derecho de fundador, esayador y marcador* (smelter's duty) of between ⅝ and 1½ per cent at the assay office.[4] Following the initiation of the *Casa de Fundición* in Nóvita in 1782, all gold mined in the Chocó had to be taken there, and the same founding process occurred. Owners could expect at least a 4 per cent *merma* (loss in weight) from the smelting process. If conducted incorrectly, or inefficiently, as was the case in Nóvita, the *merma* could be as high as 8 per cent.[5] Also, gold coming from many regions of the Chocó contained a considerable amount of platinum, and owners had to pay the cost of having the platinum removed from their gold (*displatinar*),

---

* From 1722 to 1750 the tax collected on bullion produced in the Chocó (*quintos y cobos*) was six and one-half per cent. This tax was reduced to six per cent in 1751, and then to three per cent in 1777.

and accept the corresponding weight loss in their gold bullion.[6] Finally, mine owners or bullion merchants had to pay the transportation costs for sending gold dust to the assay offices and run the risk of theft or loss. Including freight costs, the total amount deducted for the *quinto, derechos de fundir, displatinar,* and *merma* averaged at least 10 per cent of the gold's value.

Despite the crown taxes many individuals in the Chocó became bullion merchants. The system had advantages for both the sellers and the purchasers. Mine owners did not have to bother with delivering gold to Nóvita or Quibdó or to the foundries in Santa Fe de Bogotá, Popayán, or, after 1782, to the foundry in Nóvita. They thus avoided the risks, labor, and paperwork involved in transporting the precious metal. The bullion merchants, on the other hand, accustomed to the business, were not bothered by the paperwork and cut expenses by conveying large amounts to the smelteries. The gold dust had to be protected against possible theft, and it was certainly more economical to employ several trusted individuals to guard one large shipment.

People dealing in bullion had several profitable possibilities. First, many of them were also store owners who traded in products for gold dust. Second, if they purchased gold directly from the mines, they paid, in return for their services, less than the gold was actually worth. Third, extra profits were accrued because a *castellano* (100 *castellanos* in a pound) of gold brought a higher price at the foundries than it did in the Chocó. And last, there was always the possibility of contraband trade.

In the Chocó, perhaps for the sake of convenience, both a peso of gold and a *castellano* were equal to 16 *reales*, and the terms *castellano* and gold peso were used interchangeably. But officially a *castellano* of gold was worth much more. A pound of 22-carat gold was worth 256.2 silver pieces of eight (256 pesos, 64 *maravedi*). Thus, there was a 56-peso difference between the actual value of the gold and the price paid in the Chocó. The profit made by the bullion merchants, however, was less than 56 pesos a pound since the gold mined in the Chocó was not 22 carat.

Slavery on the Spanish Frontier

Records from the *Casa de Fundición* in Santa Fe de Bogotá for the year 1754 (Table 8) have been used to deduce the number of carats in the Chocó gold and the actual worth a *castellano* of the precious metal. Gold extracted from the province of Nóvita averaged 20½ carats, and that mined in the province of Citará yielded 21½ carats. By the time the cost of cleaning the gold (*displatinar, merma*) and smelting it into bars of 22 carats had been deducted, gold mined in the province of Nóvita produced 2.3 pesos a *castellano*, and that mined in the province of Citará averaged 2.4 pesos a *castellano*. Similar records for the year 1755 demonstrated that the same ratios applied.[7] Thus a bullion merchant legally tendering a pound of gold from Nóvita to the foundry in 1755 would have received at least 30.5 pesos a pound more than he paid for the gold dust in the Chocó. A trader from the province of Citará would have made 44.5 pesos profit a pound.

Normally, however, the profit a pound was not quite that high. Gold was worth 200 pesos a pound on the open market in the Chocó (100 *castellanos* at 2 pesos a *castellano*). Following the deduction of the *quinto* and losses from *merma* and *displatinar* (10 per cent), the actual return for a pound of gold for the Chocó mine owners selling to bullion merchants was only 180 pesos. The bullion merchants received 210 to 220 pesos a pound because of the true value of the gold at the mints.

Although bullion merchants made profits by following legitimate channels, they realized a greater return by sending gold fraudulently to foreigners. They paid no crown duties and suffered no weight loss from the *merma* and *displatinar*. In addition, foreigners, especially the British, paid 280 pesos or more for a pound of gold.[*] Mine owners could sell their gold to foreigners for 100 pesos a pound more than to the mints, and bullion merchants made 60 to

* In 1792 the governor of the Chocó stated that the crown value of a *marco* (eight ounces) was 128.1 pesos. He disclosed that the British paid at least 140 pesos a *marco*; see AHNC, Minas del Cauca 6, fols. 410–13 (1792). In 1824 Charles Stuart Cochrane declared the difference per pound between Chocó gold sold in Colombia and that sold in Jamaica to be 50 pesos; see *Journal of a Residence in Colombia . . .*, II, 423.

64

70 pesos per pound. Profits from contraband thus ranged between 30 to 60 per cent.

The fact that gold merchants made more by selling their bullion to outsiders prompted officials in the assay office in Popayán to suggest in 1791 that the crown raise the price of gold 4 pesos a pound and lower the *quinto* to 2 per cent. The officials intimated that this would nullify several of the obvious advantages of contraband and in the long run increase crown revenues because more people would bring their gold to the assay offices.[8]

Economic motives for engaging in the fraudulent extraction of gold dust were obvious. Since the crown could not contend that the taxes, the smelting process, or the price paid for gold encouraged individuals to remain within the realm of legality, stiff punishments were promulgated as persuasive arguments against contraband trade. The crown hoped that laws requiring the confiscation of smugglers' property, heavy fines, and even the death penalty would keep the illegal shipment of bullion at a minimum.[9]

Actually, the laws restricting commerce or advocating strict punishment for smugglers proved useless in halting the illegal traffic. Conditions in the Chocó and the nature of the contraband trade in gold provided *contrabandistas* (smugglers) with only the remote possibility of detection. Even with *vigías* placed on the Atrato and San Juan rivers, and officials stationed in Quibdó, Nóvita, Las Juntas, San Agustín, and other locations, it was difficult to impede the illegal shipment of gold. *Vigías* could be avoided, or officials could be bribed. Although governors were ordered to name honorable men who had never been connected with illicit commerce to the Chocó's points of entry,[10] it must have been difficult for these appointees to remain honest in view of their isolation and the temptations they faced.

Because of the ease with which gold could be taken from the Chocó, there were many large shipments. In 1730, for example, four Dutch ships anchored off the mouth of the Atrato River and took on an estimated 312 pounds (12½ *arrobas*) of gold over a period of several weeks.[11] Since a pound of gold was worth approximately 280 pesos to the Dutch, the total value of contraband bullion in this one instance was 86,360 pesos.

Many of the leading citizens of the Chocó were engaged in the business of contraband, but in most instances nothing more than suspected duplicity could be documented.* In 1783, for example, a simple complaint of debt quickly evolved into accusations of contraband. One mine owner, Dr. Francisco Renteria, charged that another, Luis José Beserra, owed him more than 3,000 pesos for some slaves. Beserra disputed the claim, but was jailed by the lieutenant governor of Nóvita pending settlement of the suit. Beserra wrote the *audiencia* in Santa Fe de Bogotá explaining his case and, in an obvious attempt to slander his opponent, denounced Renteria for fraudulently exporting forty pounds of gold with the collusion of the lieutenant governor. It was common knowledge in the province, Beserra said, that Renteria had been an active *contrabandista* for many years.

The *audiencia*, interested in the charges of fraud, ordered testimony taken. As the case developed, several other mine owners in the region were singled out as smugglers. One witness, Dr. Jorge Agustín Bermudez, the priest of Lloró, testified that he had suspected Renteria for some time since the mine owner often freighted very heavy boxes from the region. Father Bermudez admitted that he could not prove anything against Renteria, but he did claim to have firsthand knowledge that one of Renteria's friends, Antonio Gutiérrez y Foral, was guilty. Father Bermudez discovered this violation quite by accident. Gutiérrez often sent food supplies, including cakes of *panela* (brown sugar), to another mine owner, Francisco Lloreda, whose mines were located near the *vigía* of the Atrato. The priest disclosed that the *panela* cakes contained a more expensive item, gold dust. Whereas the normal weight of the *panela*

---

* Although few mine owners were actually convicted of contraband trade, many paid minor fines of fifty to one-hundred pesos for irregularities in *quinto* payments. Generally, this meant that bullion produced by a certain mine could not be accounted for, but officials lacked solid evidence of contraband and could not press charges. See Cuentas de la Real Hacienda, Nóvita and Citará, 1760–1802, AGI, Section 5, Audiencia de Santa Fe, legs. 881, 882, 1603, 1604.

66

cakes was about one pound these weighed more than five pounds.[12] If the testimony was correct—and there is no reason to doubt it— the allegation demonstrated the ingenious methods *contrabandistas* developed to escape detection. The golden brown *panela* would have passed most inspections with no difficulty. The litigation dragged on for some time, and authorities in the Chocó gathered no solid evidence. There were no convictions. However, a *fiscal* (judge) of the *audiencia* later stated that the lieutenant governor, and perhaps others as well, had done a half-hearted job in pursuing the case.[13] As will be seen, Manuel Junguito Baquerizo, who served as governor at the time of the Renteria-Gutíerrez-Lloreda accusation, had his own motives for not following complaints of fraud too diligently.

Hoping to curtail illegal shipments of gold dust, crown officials several times suggested auditing the records of all the major mines in the Chocó. One such audit was made in 1743, when Governor Manuel Martínez de Escobar was instructed to check all account books (*libros sobre derechos*) at the major mines. The governor uncovered a number of "bookkeeping" errors, and fines were levied against twelve mine owners (slightly over one-fourth of those audited) who had failed to declare all the bullion their mines produced.* Eleven of the twelve owners paid their fines without protest, but one, Father Felipe Valencia, appealed his case to the *audiencia*. The evidence against Valencia proved to be strong. The priest's *libros sobre derechos* showed that his mine had produced 6,500 pesos worth of gold, but there was no indication that any *quinto* had been paid to royal officials in Quibdó or Nóvita. Following a lengthy investigation, Governor Martínez concluded that Father Valencia had smuggled his bullion. The governor ordered Valencia to pay the missing *quinto* (390 pesos), as well as a fine of 1,070 pesos (three times the value of the attempted fraud).

Despite the evidence against him, Father Valencia presented

---

* Governor Martínez had himself been fined 400 pesos in 1741, for submitting tardy, inaccurate accounts. His desire to prove his own loyalty and efficiency perhaps explains the unusual diligence with which he pursued the 1743 audit.

two separate arguments in his own behalf before the *audiencia*. First, he claimed to have shipped his bullion directly to Popayán, where the proper *quinto* had been paid. However, no record of gold received under Valencia's name could be found, and he could not produce receipts of payment. Second, Valencia argued that he had devoted his time and efforts to the priesthood, assigning the administration of his mine to a manager. The manager, he protested, had been responsible for satisfying the proper duties.

Testimony from Valencia's manager failed to corroborate the priest's position. The manager stated that he had recorded all the gold produced (as required by law), and then sent it directly to Valencia as instructed. The *audiencia* concluded that Valencia was ultimately responsible for the management of his mine, that the *quinto* had not been paid, and that the missing bullion could not satisfactorily be accounted for. Therefore, Governor Martínez' original decision, and fine, were sustained.

The case did not end with this official decision from the highest court in New Granada. Although Valencia paid the missing 390 pesos *quinto* without further argument, he refused to pay the additional 1,070-peso fine, claiming clerical *fueros* (special privileges). He appealed his case to his clerical superior, the bishop of Popayán. The bishop upheld Valencia's position stating that civil officials had no authority to judge and fine a priest. However, the bishop noted that the evidence of fraud was overwhelming, and he ordered Valencia to make a "voluntary" contribution of 1,000 pesos to the crown.[14]

Valencia was apprehended and convicted because Governor Martínez conducted a surprise audit and because the priest's administrator had maintained honest accounts. Other owners were more careful. Official ledgers for each mine were not kept before 1721, for the *quinto* was not collected in the region until 1722. However, it soon became common practice in the Chocó for owners, or administrators, to keep two sets of books: one official and public for the purpose of declaring *quintos,* and the other private and secret which listed actual bullion produced. Late in 1722 administrator Juan Bonifacio Roman revealed that his employer, Domingo Carvajal, had ordered him to maintain two separate accounts. Roman complied with the order, although he knew that it was illegal, because he needed the job. Besides, he explained, all the administrators he knew had been similarly instructed.

Roman disclosed that during the past year and a half, Carvajal officially declared as mined 5,700 pesos while the actual value had been 17,500 pesos. The undeclared 11,800 pesos had been exported from the province as contraband. Roman volunteered this information to Superintendent Espinosa because he had been abruptly fired by Carvajal for mismanagement. The disgruntled administrator, unable to find other employment, admittedly sought revenge against his former employer.

Carvajal denied the allegations against him but was unable to answer Roman's charges. Carvajal presented a weak circumstantial case on his own behalf. In the main he argued that no owner would willingly tolerate a duel-account system since it would openly invite administrators to steal from their employers. Testimony from other mine owners agreed, but officials concluded that it proved nothing. The argument was actually counterproductive when Superintendent Espinosa noted that Carvajal had in fact fired Roman when the latter was discovered skimming off some of the undeclared bullion.

Roman finally produced conclusive evidence by presenting the two ledgers signed by both men and by soliciting testimony from slave captains about the amount mined. Testimony from other mine owners, while sympathetic to Carvajal, reluctantly supported Roman. Witnesses agreed that Carvajal's personal property had accumulated too rapidly to justify his declared earnings. From 1710 to 1722, his slave gang had increased from eight to forty-six, and total production in his mines was estimated at over 54,000 pesos. Officials suspected, but could not prove, that all of the gold produced in Carvajal's mine prior to 1720 had been illegally exported. Carvajal paid the *quinto* on the missing 11,800 pesos (711 pesos), and he was fined 500 pesos for his crime.[15]

A periodic auditing of accounts might have prevented some fraud, but it would not have stopped the contraband trade. The official *libros sobre derechos* were too easily altered. Besides, officials in Popayán later noted that much of the gold illegally exported from the Chocó passed through several hands, and *mazamorreros* (independent prospectors) rarely sent their gold directly to the lieutenant governors or smelteries.[16]

The needs of the small independent prospectors could be supplied in the Chocó by merchants, gold traders, and even the larger mine owners who gathered the metal produced by the *mazamorreros* and gave them merchandise or cash in return.[17] It would have been impossible to keep good records on the transactions among the merchants, the mine owners, and the *mazamorreros*. The bullion merchants buying the gold dust could and did send the bullion out of the area as contraband.[18]

Occasionally a *contrabandista* was apprehended in the act. On October 30, 1719, an informant told José Gonzáles de la Torre, the lieutenant governor of Quibdó, that Miguel de Vielma was attempting to smuggle gold out of the province. Gonzáles, piously communicating that his obligation as a loyal official of the crown compelled him to pursue the culprit, recounted the subsequent events. The men chasing Vielma captured him some distance upriver from Quibdó. When confronted with the allegation, Vielma swore that he carried no gold. A search of his personal belongings, however, revealed a pouch containing 485 pesos worth of gold dust stitched to the lining of his coat. Vielma then argued that the gold did not belong to him but to another individual who had paid all the proper duties. He had denied carrying any gold because he feared the men who had stopped him might be thieves. Further search uncovered three smaller packets of gold worth 25 pesos, 105 pesos, and 9 pesos sewed inside his trousers. Vielma offered no more excuses and was thrown in jail as a *contrabandista*.[19]

In another instance, in 1738, Governor Bartolomé Montes was informed by his brother, Joseph Montes, that mine owner Francisco Maturana intended to smuggle forty pounds of gold past the *vigía* of the Atrato. A canoe belonging to Maturana was apprehended near the *vigía* carrying gold, but Maturana claimed his intent had not been contraband. Maturana and the Montes brothers were bitter enemies, and, although Maturana paid a fine, he protested that he had been framed.[20]

Those engaged in gold smuggling actually ran few risks. The gold was not in their possession for any length of time, and there was little likelihood of officials discovering a few pounds of carefully concealed gold dust. Once bullion had been carried out of the region, it was easily exchanged for cash, products, or letters of credit. Few if any records were kept of these transactions. Gold smuggling, once completed, left scant evidence to convict a *contrabandista*. Behavior might be labeled suspicious, but fraud could not usually be proved. Those caught in the act of smuggling were few indeed, and either had been informed on or framed or were unlucky.

Although no one placed a monetary value on the total amount of gold surreptitiously sent out of the Chocó during the colonial period, royal orders and letters from governors, viceroys, and other officials stressed the huge volume of gold dust illegally exported. One man, Francisco Silvestre, a former governor of the province of Antioquia and secretary to the viceroyalty of New Granada, did estimate in 1789 that more than half of the gold mined in the Chocó was fraudulently transported from the region.[21]

Silvestre's estimate is helpful in determining the total amount of bullion produced when added to the amount of gold legally declared as mined in the Chocó. After 1721 all miners and merchants were required to send their gold dust to either Quibdó or Nóvita for the deduction of the *quinto*. Thus *quinto* accounts can be used to calculate the total bullion presented to royal officials for the deduction of crown taxes. Since the *quinto* did not remain constant, the drop in the *quinto* collected, especially after 1777, did not necessarily signify a decline in the amount of bullion produced.

A tabulation of *quinto* records between the years 1724 and 1803 shows that the yearly average of gold known to have been mined in the Chocó amounted to 320,435 pesos (see Table 9 for complete averages). Average annual production was higher for the province of Nóvita (194,535 pesos) than in the province of Citará (125,900 pesos), and the total declared production was higher during the first half of the eighteenth century. While it is possible that contraband trade was not as well established in the first half of the eighteenth century (there are many indications to the contrary), it is more likely that the easily accessible and richer gold deposits were more commonly exploited during this period.[22]

It is reasonable to conclude that the eighty-year average of 320,435 pesos is a reliable yearly average for the amount of gold legally declared as mined from 1680 to 1810. The total amount mined during the entire period would thus be 41,656,550 pesos.

Table A
Gold Mined in the Chocó on Which the *Quinto* Was Paid*

Years	*Quinto* Collected in *Castellanos*			Total Amount Declared Converted to Silver Pesos†			Yearly Average
	From Nóvita	From Citará	Total	From Nóvita	From Citará	Total	
1724–1750	163	112	275	5,783	4,130	9,913	367
1751–1775	112	78	190	4,296	3,120	7,416	297
1776–1803	75	38	113	5,484	2,822	8,306	297
1724–1803	350	228	578	15,563	10,072	25,635	320

* Figures are rounded off to the nearest ten-thousandth. See Table 9 for complete figures and sources.
† Figures are calculated by multiplying the total number of *castellanos* declared by the assay value per *castellano* (2.3 pesos for Nóvita anl 2.4 pesos for Citará).

Obviously, 41,656,550 pesos is not the total value of gold extracted from the region. *Quinto* records do not include gold smuggled from the Chocó to foreign sources or list bullion sent directly to the foundries in Popayán or Santa Fe de Bogotá. Nor do the *quinto* accounts include gold collected by the church for alms or stipends.[23]

Acceptance of Silvestre's estimation on smuggled gold yields a sum of 83,313,100 pesos for gold mined in the Chocó during the

72

period of Spanish domination. Perhaps Silvestre exaggerated, but even assuming that only one-third of the mined gold ended as contraband, the amount illegally exported would be almost 21,000,000 pesos. Although the sums calculated in Table B for the total value of gold mined in the Chocó (including contraband) can only be approximations, they gain added credibility from data presented by Vicente Restrepo in his nineteenth-century study of mining in Colombia. Restrepo reported that 77,200,000 pesos worth of gold was mined in the Chocó during the colonial period[24]—an evaluation that falls between my two calculations which include contraband.

Table B
Total Gold Mined in the Chocó, 1680–1810*

Amount	17th Century	18th Century	1800–10	Total
Amount derived by averaging *quinto* records	6,409	32,044	3,204	41,657
Total if one-half of the gold mined was fraudulently exported	12,817	64,087	6,409	83,313
Total if one-third of the gold mined was fraudulently exported	9,613	48,065	4,807	62,485
Estimate given by Vicente Restrepo	20,000	52,000	5,200†	77,200

* Figures are rounded off to the nearest ten-thousandth in silver pesos.
† Figure based on estimate that 520,000 a year was mined.

Another kind of contraband trade also occurred in the Chocó. The illegal importation of goods, particularly merchandise from Spain, constituted big business. Crown restrictions on supply routes and trade designed to prevent the extraction of bullion created an environment in which certain products became both greatly desired and expensive. Merchants of legally introduced products paid certain crown taxes, such as the *alcabala* (sales tax) and the *almojarifazgo* (import tax). Of more importance, however, was the fact that most products could not be introduced by way of the most natural routes, the river highways. Merchants had to use overland trails from the interior provinces, and transportation costs, more than crown taxes, dictated high prices. If they were ferried along the Atrato or San Juan, the goods cost much less. Since it was illegal to do so, these who used these routes also avoided crown duties. Under the most profitable arrangements smugglers tried to smuggle out gold and return with merchandise.

Convictions and accusatiosns for contraband trade entering the Chocó greatly outnumber those related to illegal exportations. The actual number of persons engaged in the business may have been smaller but, because, of the products they carried, it was more difficult to escape detection. It might have been simple to slip articles past the *vigías* through the judicious application of bribes or avoidance, but the corregidors in the various towns and officials in Nóvita and Quibdó presented a greater problem. For an item to be sold it had to be displayed openly in stores, or at least individual buyers had to be approached. At any time an official could ask to see the import license (*guía*) and receipts for duties paid. Thus apprehension was much more likely.

The profits from illicit commerce, however, were so great that many chose to engage in the trade despite the danger of detection. Methods were developed that minimized the risks of capture. Contraband goods were introduced by smugglers who also imported similar or other items for which they held legal *guías* and had paid some official duties. If the authority checking the itemized cargo list did not carefully search the cargo itself, merchants could slip in their extra products unnoticed. The fact that officials discovered persons attempting to do this on many occasions is evidence that this method was often employed.[25] Once the shipment passed the official entrance inspection, merchants could show cargo lists and receipts for duties paid and claim that any questioned item had been legally imported. Depleted stocks on which merchants retained legitimate import licenses were doubtless replaced with contraband products.

Although commercial restrictions designed to prevent contraband along the San Juan and Atrato rivers had been issued in 1696, 1717, and 1720, it became apparent in the late 1720's that the illegal activites had continued. In 1730, Joseph Joachín Martínez Malo, a judge of the *audiencia*, traveled to the Chocó to investigate new charges of illicit commerce. Martínez Malo concluded that fraud existed, and on September 5, 1730, he reiterated both the ban on travel below the *vigía* of the Atrato and Viceroy Villalonga's 1720 decree regarding the San Juan.

Ships from Panama, although excluded from the San Juan, could still land products in Buenaventura, and after shipment to Cali some goods were carried back into the Chocó. The favorite Cali-Chocó route did not pass through Cartago but was the Calima River, which flows from east to west, emptying into the San Juan River. Merchants floated supplies down the Calima to Boca del Calima and then ferried them up the San Juan River to Nóvita and Noanamá. Martínez Malo suppressed this route because of the difficulty in distinguishing products coming from Cali from those illegally introduced from Panama. He ordered merchants wishing to freight clothes, slaves, or products from Spain into the Chocó to use overland trails from Cartago.[26]

Merchandise from Spain entered the Chocó after 1730, but the legal supply lines were long and therefore expensive. Products were first shipped from Spain to Cartagena or Panama: those from Cartagena went up the Magdalena River and then overland to Cartago and into the Chocó; the supplies from Panama went through Buenaventura, Cali, and Cartago before arriving in the Chocó. Hence by 1730 commercial routes to the Chocó had been carefully legislated. Only basic necessities could enter through the San Juan. Clothes, all luxuries, manufactured goods, and many staples had to come overland from the interior provinces.

Commerce with Guayaquil supplied many of the Chocó's basic needs. Merchants in the Chocó established companies to handle the trade and retained agents in Lima and Guayaquil. In 1744 one such merchant, Julián de Trespalacios Mier, sent a detailed list of instructions to his agents in Lima. The set of instructions is valuable because of its detail and because of the implied ease with which officials in Guayaquil and Nóvita would grant permission to ship and land merchandise. Nowhere did he warn his agents that certain products were inadmissible.[27] It would appear that, if the technicalities of acquiring and presenting a license were followed correctly, few difficulties arose.

Fortunately for the people in the Chocó, the strict proscriptions concerning shipments along the San Juan seem rarely to have been enforced. Perhaps changes in administartion in the Chocó caused uncertainty about the commercial regulations. The lieutenant governors appointed to the Chocó were almost always new to the region.* Although copies of the old orders were kept in the official archives in Nóvita, there was confusion about the exact laws and about who had the responsibilty of checking incoming vessels. New lieutenant governors and governors several times asked the *audiencia* to clarify trade regulations and specific duties with regard to enforcement of the rules.[28]

Legally the lieutenant governor of Nóvita was responsible for checking the cargoes of ships arriving at Calima. When a vessel docked at Calima, the lieutenant governor was supposed to travel to the *vigía* to inspect the merchandise. Occasionally he delegated someone else to go in his place, but it was his responsibility. If the lieutenant governor was zealous—most were not, since the trip downstream from Nóvita to Calima took four days and ten days to return upstream[29]—and discovered contraband articles, he then confiscated the illicit merchandise in the name of the crown.† It is clear from the instructions sent by Trespalacios Mier to his agent that many lieutenant governors simply accepted cargo lists presented to them in Nóvita and did not bother with the legal formality of inspecting cargo at Calima. Doubtless, with the lieutenant governors residing in Nóvita, it was not difficult to slip prohibited goods into the Chocó along with legitimate products at Calima.

* All the governors and many of the lieutenant governors in the *Chocó* were *peninsulares* (whites born in Spain).
† One confiscation included twelve vicuña hats from Peru, hardly a practical item for the Chocó. See AHNC, Aguardientes del Cauca 4, fol. 273 (1747).

To make matters even more complex and contraband eminently more probable, Martínez Malo's 1730 ban of the Cali-Calima route does not appear to have been enforced for over three decades. In 1761 the viceroy sent Governor Luis Ponce de León strict instructions to permit only two ships a year to land at Calima from Guayaquil and also ordered the Cali-Calima route closed.[30] The reasons for the order and the complaints which swiftly followed were strikingly similar to the controversy in 1717, when the moratorium had been placed on shipping on the San Juan River. Again petitions from merchants and farmers in the Cauca Valley wanting to sell "surplus" products in the Chocó and tales of contraband trade prompted the viceroy's action.[31]

On September 6, 1763, mine owner Joseph López García, sergeant major of the militia and designated representative for the miners' guild, argued against the viceroy's recent orders. López first testified to the loyalty of all members of the miners' guild, saying that to accuse them of contraband insulted their honor and dignity. He then dismissed the petitions from the Cauca Valley as nonsense, saying that the Cauca Valley merchants only sent products to the Chocó because of the large profits involved. Of more importance, however, was the apparent contradiction between the viceroy's orders and the desires of the king. The Spanish monarch had recently requested the miners' guild to seek methods for improving gold production, while the viceroy, perhaps unwittingly, prevented it by curtailing the supply lines. Everyone agreed that merchandise was desperately needed in the "sterile but wealthy" Chocó, but the natural solution to this problem was to turn toward the south or north for supplies, not the east. What was needed, the sergeant major contended, was not a policy of restriction but one permitting the unlimited entry of vessels to Calima.

López was not overly concerned with limitations concerning the Cali-Calima route; his best arguments supported a "free-trade" program. He estimated a total population of 13,963 for the Chocó, and taking only one product necessary to all, salt, he demonstrated that under the new commercial regulations this one item alone could not be supplied. He reasoned that each individual needed a minimum of one ounce of salt daily. The total salt consumed, therefore, was more than 3,185 *quintales* (318,500 pounds) a year. The average freight carried by a ship arriving at Chirambirá or Calima amounted to only 1,500 *quintales* (150,000 pounds). Thus two ships a year could not bring enough salt to maintain the people in the Chocó for one year. This, López stressed, was only one necessary product—there were many more.[32] The analysis made by López, whatever its merit,* had no effect on the issue of free trade; however, the number of ships that could arrive at Calima was raised to three a year.

Despite their predictions of impending disaster, the miners' guild really had no cause to worry. Either they had little faith in the smuggling process or they simply hoped to improve the legitimate channels of commerce. There is no indication that the 1761 orders concerning contraband were any more effective than previous commands. In practice, the threat of punishment did no more to intimidate those illegally importing goods than it prevented the extraction of bullion.

Harsh penalties were rarely imposed. Fines constituted the usual penalty for contraband, and in many instances the levy assessed was simply double the regular duties (*dobles derechos*).[33] On other occasions the contraband items were themselves confiscated and sold for the benefit of the royal treasury.[34] Smugglers might suffer the indignity of being thrown in jail[35] or of having their property impounded,[36] but with the payment of a fine they were free to resume their personal business. There is no evidence that the death penalty was inflicted or even suggested. The stigma of having been convicted of fraud doubtless remained and may have harmed a person in official or even private circles, but the punishments themselves were not a deterrent to others.

Individual merchants could and did engage in contraband trade. But if they attempted to bring in too much merchandise (and

---

* It should be noted that López' argument rested on the unlikely premise that each individual in the Chocó consumed 23 pounds of salt a year.

profits depended in part on volume), the officials in Nóvita and Quibdó should have detected the fraud—unless, that is, the officials in the Chocó were themselves involved in illegal activities. As might be expected, this was exactly the case. Instead of halting illicit commerce, some of the lieutenant governors, governors, and other officials became the major violators.

That the crown's officials were corrupt had been established by 1691, and this pattern continued despite the removal in 1718 of all existing officials (because of their connection with contraband). In 1726, when the Spanish king declared the Chocó a separate province and appointed Francisco de Ibero as the first governor, he specifically instructed Ibero to prevent contraband trade. Four years later Governor Ibero was formally charged with fraud against the king.[37] Not only had the crown's "loyal subject" not paid duties on clothes and other items he had introduced, but he had imported them by way of the strictly prohibited Atrato River route. To make the scandal complete, the governor had openly traded with one of the foremost enemies of Spain, the Dutch. Ibero had maintained a locked warehouse in Quibdó full of clothing and other items. By the time of his arrest he had sold an estimated 30,000 pesos' worth of goods.[38]

Others in the Chocó had been involved with Ibero. The large amount of contraband the governor introduced did not escape the notice of Chocó merchants or the lieutenant governors. The governor purchased their silence by permitting them to bring in contraband products of their own.[39] The judge presiding over the case ordered Ibero's property impounded, reviewed lengthy testimony, found the governor guilty, and fined him 4,000 pesos (2,000 pesos *de oro*).[40] The fine, though large, could scarcely be considered severe punishment, considering the crime and the one who had committed it. Ibero doubtless made much more profit from his illicit dealings than he was fined.

The most famous instance of contraband occurred in 1786, during the administration of Governor Manuel Junguito Baquerizo, although he was not denounced until 1797. Governor Junguito and six leading merchants and mine owners were implicated in a common suit.[41] The governor and his associates were prosecuted for introducing 64,623 pesos' worth of products from Cartagena without a proper license, paying incorrect duties on the goods, importing slaves and merchandise (rifles and gunpowder) from Jamaica, and shipping gold dust out of the Chocó.*[42] The case dragged on for over a decade, and by 1808, Junguito and his cohorts had been found guilty, fined, and those who remained alive (several had died natural deaths), had all taken the *indulto*[43] (a crown pardon excusing guilty parties from future punishment for admitted transgressions).

Other governors, lieutenant governors, corregidors, and priests were accused of fraudulent negotiations during the eighteenth and early nineteenth centuries;[44] and, even though legally governors had to reside in Nóvita, most lived in Quibdó, where it was said they engaged more easily in contraband activities along the Atrato River.[45] Doubtless many of the Chocó's leading officials entered the commerce, and if they did not become excessively greedy or offend someone who might report them to higher authorities, they ran little risk. After all, who was in a better position to practice commerce than the officials who supposedly regulated it?

Ironically, several of the crown's attempts to control fraud in the colonial period actually helped increase it. The normal laws of supply and demand did not apply in the region since trade restrictions, and the inhabitants' obvious need for many products, made demands much greater than the possibilties of supply. Scarcity dictated high prices and provided temptations too powerful to ignore. Individual merchants and mine owners engaged in illicit commerce, as did the officials who were assigned to prevent it. The

---

* By the time Governor Junguito was using the Atrato River to ship his products into the Chocó from Cartagena, it was officially reopened to maritime commerce. However, one of the original reasons for closing the Atrato had been to impede unauthorized trade. Governor Junguito and his associates had swiftly taken advantage of the newly improved trade possibilities. The shipment of gold dust out of the region was strictly prohibited because by then the smeltery in Nóvita was in operation.

The Las Juntas–Iró–Tadó trail crosses the Iró River at this point. The Cordillera Occidental is visible in the background. (All the photographs in the book were taken by the author.)

The Atrato River winds through the rain forest of the central Chocó.

81

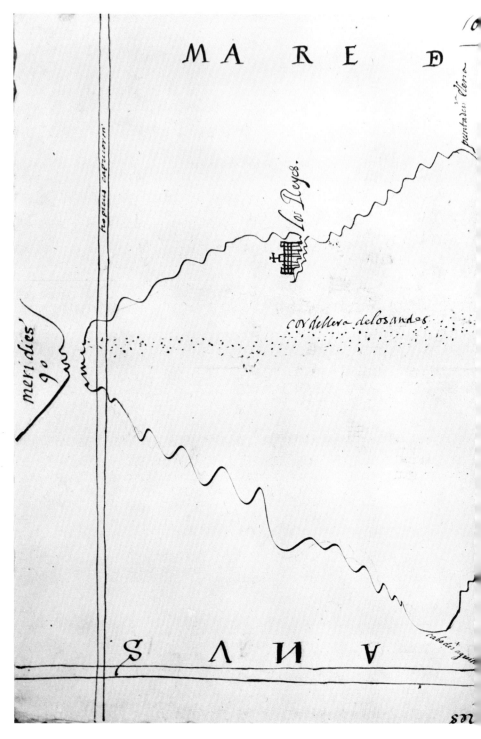

MARE D

puntadeuelena

Los Reyes.

cordellera delosandos

meridies 9°

tropicus capricorni

S A N V A

cabadeuguia

ssn

This 1597 map drawn by Melchor de Salazar predates the final pacification of the Chocó by almost one hundred years. Although very few places located in the Chocó are shown on this map, the San

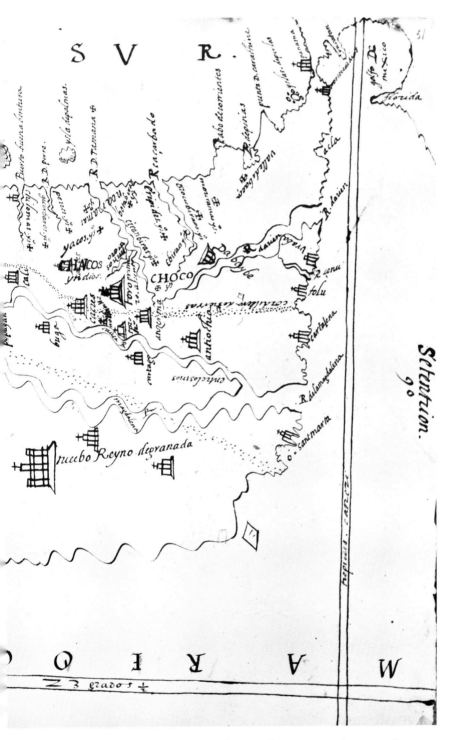

Juan and Atrato rivers are clearly delineated. Importantly, near the site of what later became Nóvita there is the notation minas de oro *(gold mines). AGI, Mapas y Planos, Panama, 329 (1597).*

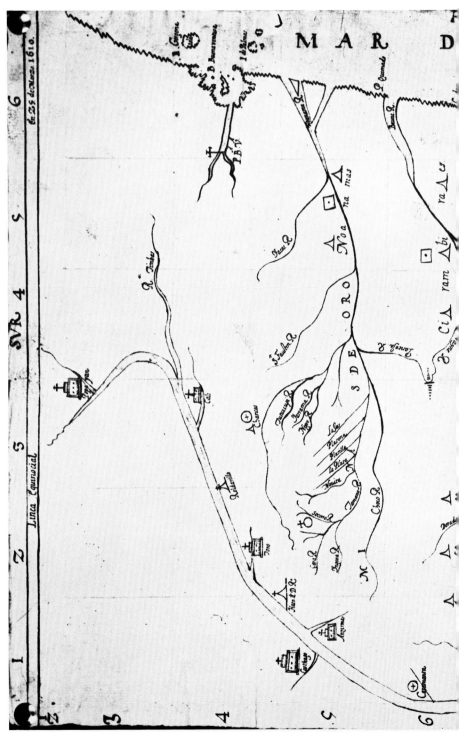

This map shows considerable detail of the San Juan region. Although the San Juan River is called the Chocó River, names such as Nóvita and Tamana are noted. The general location of the Indian

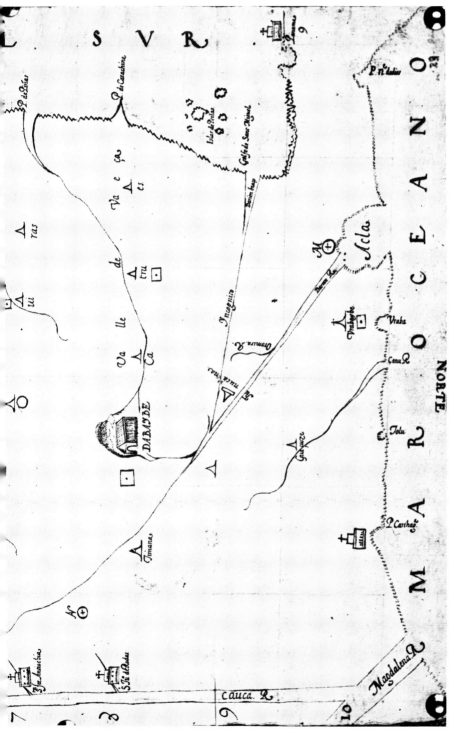

tribes in the region is given in addition to the label minas de oro *along the entire upper San Juan region. AGI, Mapas y Planos, Panama, 29 (1610).*

Plano que demuestra la immediaci

los Indios Barbaros nombrados C

... dos diferentes Vaciones c

... A d

Todas las Poblaciones toman el nombre

This map was drawn to demonstrate the vulnerability of Quibdó. The note on the map reads: "Map that demonstrates the proximity of Quibdó, last major of the Chocó, with savage Cunacuna Indians.

Quibdò ultimo Pueblo de Chocó con
...as entre los que se hallan mescla-
Ingleses, Francesses &.ª

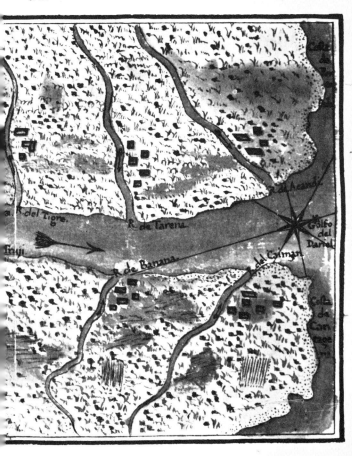

...ia...
o immediato que las baña...

Individuals from two diferent nations, the English and the French,
are found together [mixed] with them [the Cunacunas]." AGI,
Mapas y Planos, Panama, 151 (1753).

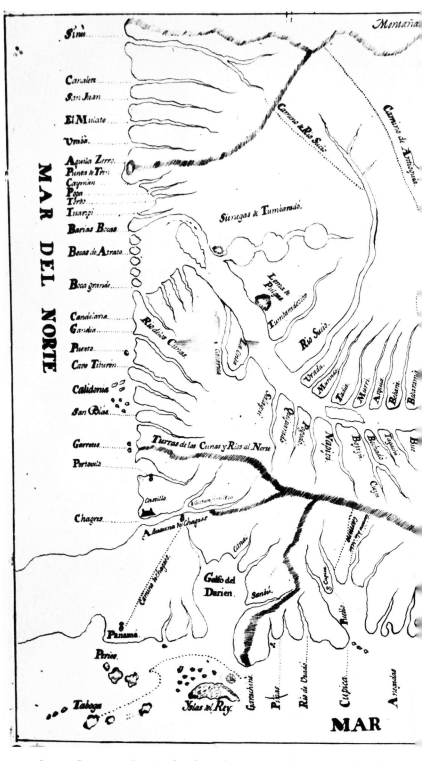

This is the most detailed colonial map ever drawn of the Chocó.
includes the major place names, trails, and rivers of the regio

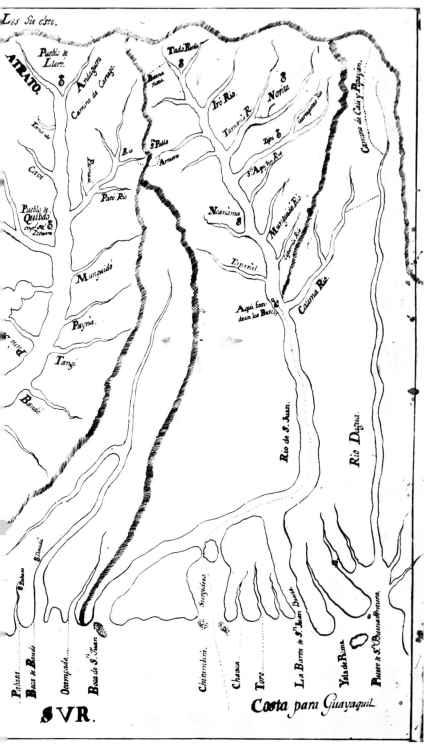

Les Su este.

ATRATO.

Pueblo de Lloro.

Andaguera

Camino de Cariagi.

Buena Vista.

Tado Pueblo.

Iro Rio.

Tamana R.

Nonia

Zipi

Camino de Cali y Popajan.

Taros de

Cava

Parraguera

Rio

S.ta Pablo

Armata

S.to Agu. Rio

Munguido Rio

Cipido Rio

Cuerampana Rio

Pueblo de Quibdo con S.to Zitura

Pato Rio

Noanama

Munguido

Payna

Tarqi

Tiparul

Cajuna Rio

Aqui fondean los Barcos

Payna

Baudo

Rio de S. Juan.

Rio Dagua

Cubasa

Docampado

Boca de S.ta Juan

Surquidero

Chitambira

Chanca

Toro

La Barra de S.ta Juan Igrande

Yela de Pitna

Puerto de S.ta Buena Ventura

Costa para Guayaquil.

SVR.

ecause it includes Cupica, the map was probably drawn about
780. AGI, Mapas y Planos, Panama, 193 (n.d.).

Istmina (formally San Pablo) is typical of the river towns in the Chocó. The houses are elevated on stilts to permit the circulation of fresh air under the house and to protect them from the frequent flooding of the rivers.

Houses in Tadó stretch over half a mile along the San Juan River.

Champas *(dugout canoes)* are tied to the bank along the San Juan River on market day in Tadó.

The dugouts are hand-fashioned with axes, adzes, and small chisels.

This large dugout serves as an open-air playroom for three children on the Atrato River.

Dugouts are poled upriver by skilled bogas *(boatmen) along the swift-flowing San Juan River.*

River travel, though possible, is difficult along the streams leading into the San Juan and Atrato rivers.

Walking along the trochas (trails) of the Chocó is difficult because of the heat, mud, and insects. Poisonous snakes sun themselves along the trails. The shotgun was carried in case of an encounter with them.

Chocó women pan gold and platinum on a playa (beach) on the Platino River.

The typical Chocoano house is rectangular with split bamboo sides and a thatched roof. Note the different stages of construction.

Indian tambos (houses), though made of the same materials as those used in Chocoano dwellings, are round.

This Chocoano house could have been standing two hundred years ago, the isolated residence of a libre *(freedman) or* cimarrón *(runaway slave).*

tricks and devices for sending gold out of the region and bringing merchandise in were highly refined.

Even the opening of the Atrato River to maritime commerce did not end the contraband trade. Transportation costs were reduced, but since smuggling was easier, duties could still be avoided, and cheaper, better, or prohibited products were still desired from outside sources. The entire story of the contraband trade will never be known: that, of course, is the nature of the business. Because of the struggle to exist and the passion to amass huge fortunes contraband trade was as much a part of the life of the Chocó as mining and slavery.

6

Citizen or Slave:
The Indian in the Chocó

Fortunes were made in the Chocó, and many individuals profited from their ventures in the region. There were also those, however, who lost. Blacks suffered while amassing capital for the Spanish overlords. Indians, captives in their own land, lost everything— their land, their dignity, their independence, and, as the census data dramatically reveal, their lives as well.

Ironically, the Indians had many champions. As early as the sixteenth century the Spaniards became concerned about the treatment of the native Americans. Susceptible to the strange diseases carried by the conquering race, the disappearing Indians became a matter of conscience for Spanish clergymen, philosophers, and monarchs. By the time of the pacification of the Chocó at the end of the seventeenth century, a vast body of law had been promulgated regarding the Indians. But, lured by the prospects of quick wealth, few white immigrants to the Chocó complied with humanitarian aspects of the crown's regulations concerning treatment of the Indians.

Spaniards who first entered the San Juan and Atrato river basins seized upon the Indians as a labor force for the placer mines. Many miners, with experience in the interior provinces of New Granada, doubtless believed that blacks were better suited for labor in the tropical region, for both physical and legal reasons. But blacks cost money, while Indians in the Chocó could be freely taken during the late seventeenth century. Indians were utilized because they were present, not because they were preferred.

Theoretically, corregidors protected Indians from physical and psychological abuse by those individuals who might take advantage of the natives' "innocent nature." Indians were required to work, but they had to be fairly compensated for their labor and could not be overworked. The corregidor served as the administrator of the reservation, assigned tasks, collected fees, paid wages, and oversaw the Indians' Christian instruction. In return the corregidor received a portion of the Indian tribute. Of course actual conditions rarely approached the designed model, but even when corregidors administered justly, the Indians lost almost all aspects of self-determination.

The first corregidors swiftly took advantage of their Indian charges. Indians were overworked, poorly paid, and enslaved by Spaniards residing in their villages. In 1695, the *audiencia* reacted by sending a *visitador*, Merlo de la Fuente, to correct abuses. Although he wrote a scathing report condemning the Chocó corregidors, there is no indication that any action was taken to improve conditions. In 1713 more than five hundred Indians ran away from the *corregimientos* of Bebará and Citará because of overbearing corregidors.[1]

Indians, like slaves, sought to escape mistreatment by fleeing. In the following year, 1714, Indians deserted the settlement of Los Brazos because of the actions of the *justicia mayor* (chief judge) of the province. No one accused the *justicia mayor* of harshly handling the Indians. On the contrary, observers condemned him for being too lenient. Besides committing scandals against the church (for some inexplicable reason he stole the church bell from Los Brazos and persisted in disrespectfully entering the church with his sword unsheathed), the official informed the Indians that they were free to act as they pleased. If they wished to leave the *corregimientos*, that was their prerogative; if they no longer wished to grow crops for the Spaniards, attend church, or be taught the Christian doctrine, no one would hinder them.[2] Although the *justicia mayor*'s curious behavior probably stemmed from a quarrel with several of the local officials or priests, his actions were considered not only sacrilegious but also threatening to the existence of the whites in the region, who depended upon the Indians to produce their basic food supplies. The *justicia mayor,* unlike corregidors accused of being too harsh, was removed.[3]

Although a myriad of laws protected the Indians, Spanish justice seldom punished a corregidor who violated these regulations. In 1720 the Indian chiefs of Tadó charged their corregidor, Joseph Torijano, with continually forcing them to build houses, construct canoes, and plant crops, which he then sold to other Spaniards in the region. In return they received *aguardiente* unrealistically valued at six pesos a bottle by the corregidor. The chiefs strenuously protested that the liquor made them drunk and that their real need was food and free time. They could not tend their own crops because Torijano compelled them to hunt and fish on his account when they were not actually doing other work for him. He then confiscated their catch and gave them nothing in return.[4]

Although these charges were seemingly grave enough, there was nothing particularly unusual about them. They would probably have attracted no attention since they merely involved protests of overwork and insufficient pay. But the Indians also denounced Torijano for deflowering Indian maidens and forcing Indian children to serve as personal servants in his house. He did not permit them to leave to visit relatives or even to attend mass. Indians who complained were severely punished by Torijano, and several males were given one hundred lashes a day for three successive days.

These complaints were serious enough to merit immediate attention. But they did not. Indians stated that they had appealed to their priest for help, but since he was a close friend of the corregidor, nothing had been done to correct the abuses. The superintendent of the Chocó likewise had been informed and had not acted. The Tadó chiefs complained that the superintendent, other officials, and mine owners had arrived in the Chocó poor men but had become very rich in gold, jewels, and slaves. The whites, the Indians said, had gained their wealth through a ruthless exploitation of the red men. Having exhausted the legal channels in the Chocó the chiefs petitioned directly to the *audiencia* in Santa Fe de Bogotá.[5]

The *audiencia* and the viceroy (Jorge de Villalonga), already upset by reports that gold from the Tadó area contained a high percentage of platinum, ordered a complete investigation of the matter of fraud and the allegations made by the Indians. In the lengthy testimony that followed, the Indians were concerned with correcting abuses and the whites with clearing themselves of the charges that they deliberately mixed platinum with gold. The questions asked of the white witnesses were arranged so that the specific charges made by the Indians were not answered. Torijano was said to be a firm man but a successful one. White witnesses lauded the corregidor for rounding up *cimarrón* (runaway) Indians and keeping the peace in his region. Torijano had increased the royal tributes in the area, seemed to be instructing the Indians in the Christian doctrine, and had successfully halted the fraudulent mixing of platinum with gold. The answers apparently satisfied the *audiencia*, for Torijano served as corregidor for three more years (until 1723), and was never punished or reprimanded for misusing the Indians.[6]

Although the Indians' complaints did not lead to the removal of Torijano, their problems were reviewed by the Royal Council of the Indies in Spain. The council concluded that clerics in the Chocó had been lax in their religious duties and had not protected the interests and rights of their Indian charges. The council noted that priests maintained virtually no records of vital statistics and that many Indians had not been baptized. In a royal *cédula* dated June 30, 1720, the king ordered priests to learn Indian languages, to remain in their assigned districts, and to request a leave of absence from the bishop of Popayán for any stay outside their district of more than seven days. The king also commanded the bishop to conduct a *visita* to the Chocó.[7]

The bishop of Popayán, prodded by stories of Indian mismanagement and the royal order of 1720, made a *visita* to Nóvita, Noanamá, Quibdó, and Lloró in 1722. Religious instruction, he found, had been very poor, although he felt the blame lay with the corregidors rather than with the clerics. The corregidors, in his opinion, did not allow the Indians enough time for adequate religious indoctrination. The bishop also reported that the distribution of products like *aguardiente* and clothes had been badly mismanaged by the corregidors, who charged outrageous prices for the goods they disbursed to the Indians in return for labor.[8] The bishop did admit that several priests had taken advantage of their favored positions to enrich themselves. He was forced to remove two priests from Lloró and another from Quibdó who had been actively engaged in commerce, owned mines, and had flagrantly misused natives in those mines.[9]

The crown reacted vigorously to the bishop's report and sent several *cédulas* forbidding priests from either directly owning mines or holding mines through intermediaries. Any priest already guilty of this offense was to be removed from the province for having set a bad example.[10] In 1725 the Spanish monarch prohibited Indian labor in the mines of New Granada.[11] But time dulled the effectiveness of at least the first part of these reforms, and in the late 1750's priests once again owned mines in the province.[12] In the 1770's Governor Nicolás Clausens believed the situation to be worse and asked the crown to give the old order new strength by repeating it.[13]

The close church-state relationship in the Spanish Empire meant that priests held both important and favored positions. Special exceptions could be made to many regulations concerning clerics, and the royal order restricting priests from owning mines is but one example. The usual procedure for legally avoiding a royal order was to petition the crown for an exemption. One such case occurred in 1731, when Nicolás de Hinestrosa, a priest in Tadó, petitioned to be permitted to retain his mine in that area, stating that: (1) he had spent a great deal of his money to establish the mine and slave gang, (2) he used no Indians but worked the mine entirely with his own Negro slaves, (3) he personally received no income from the mine, since all the profits went to support his widowed sister and her children, one of whom was a theological student in Popayán, and (4) he had a *mayordomo* for the mine, and thus he devoted his full attention to ministering to the Indians in his district. King Philip V noted that, although Hinestrosa's continued ownership of a mine clearly was contrary to royal desires, circumstances made this a unique case. The *audiencia* in Santa Fe de Bogotá was ordered to gather further testimony and decide on the merits of the priest's petition.[14]

The Spanish judicial system also favored priests accused of mistreating the natives. In 1743, Fray Francisco Gutíerrez of Lloró was denounced for murdering an Indian. Indians charged that the unfortunate victim died as a result of a lashing after he refused to attend mass. The priest contended that the man had been sick before the whipping and that the illness was the real cause of death. Spanish witnesses agreed that the lashing itself could not have caused death, and the priest was declared not guilty. He was, however, transferred to another site.[15] No one seemed to argue on behalf of the dead Indian, who, if he really was sick, perhaps had a legitimate reason for not attending mass. In any case, the priest was not reprimanded for negligence or poor judgement.

Although they were ineffective, the bishops of Popayán continued to exercise jurisdictional powers over ecclesiastical matters in the Chocó and to maintain surveillance over the region. A *visita* report written in 1736 by Bishop Diego Fermín concluded that the spiritual condition of the Indians had not improved since their conquest. The bishop blamed both priests and corregidors for their lack of of advancement. He sadly reported that most of the officials and pricsts in chargc of thc Indians were lazy and corrupt, living off wealth produced by the natives. Only a few priests had learned to speak the Indian languages, and in several of the *corregimientos* he visited not a single person could recite mass. Corregidors overworked the Indians, "paying them late, poorly, or never with old clothes or wine valued at unrealistically high prices." The Indians' reaction to this treatment was, according to the bishop, drunkenness or flight.[16]

Another *visita* conducted in 1742 by Bishop Francisco de Figeredo y Victoria to Noanamá, Nóvita, and Sipí (San Agustín) uncovered irregularities similar to those reported in 1722 and 1736. Bishop Francisco, however, concluded that the fault lay entirely with the corregidors. Corregidors ignored religious instruction and failed to construct or repair churches in their districts. Priests could not minister to the Indians when there were no churches or when Indians were continually outside the villages on work projects. The bishop suggested that corregidors who did not correct these abuses be punished with stiff fines.[17]

Unfortunately, the behavior of the corregidors did not improve. They evaded prosecution without difficulty, and greater profits were to be made through exploitation than through Christian love. In 1755, following yet another *visita*, the bishop of Popayán proposed that the *corregimiento* system be abolished in the Chocó. Nothing, he pronounced, could be done to correct the excesses of the corregidors for even if one was removed, another, often worse, replaced him. Priests were unable to minister to the natives because the corregidors kept the Indians so occupied in jobs away from the villages that religious instruction was too infrequent to be of any value. Corregidors had also placed mulatto and mestizo *mayordomos* among the Indians to oversee work projects. The bishop believed this to be both illegal and cruel, for the *mayordomos* did not hestitate to use harsh methods of control. Corregidors, the bishop noted, had become very wealthy. The system had been so lucrative that many of the corregidors had made over 50,000 pesos during their short tenures in the Chocó. But every day the Indians fell further and further from the true religion.

Since the system had not been effective in Christianizing the natives, and in the bishop's opinion never would be, he asked that the *corregimientos* be abolished and the Indians placed in mission districts administered solely by clerics. The bishop admitted that Indians provide a labor force necessary for the prosperity of the province but concluded that it was important for this force to be a Christian one. Tributes could be collected by employing the natives in a *mita* system similar to that used in Peru. The priests in charge of the new mission districts could lend Indians to mine owners (receiving the Indians' wages) and oversee crop production. Never more than half the Indians would be taken away from their villages for work projects, and the other half would receive lengthy lessons in religious indoctrination. Thus work would be accomplished, and at the same time the Indians would receive the fundamental lessons of the Christian religion.[18] The plan, which seemed ideal to the bishop, would probably have suffered the same fate as the earlier Jesuit mission scheme. The profit motive outweighed humane idealism; great fortunes could be amassed through the exploitation of the Indians. The *corregimiento* system, with all its faults, continued.

The large profits gained by the corregidors came principally from three sources. First the corregidors received part (usually one-third) of the tribute (head tax) paid by all male Indians between the ages of fourteen and fifty. Second, the corregidors had the right to sell, or control the sale of, goods to the Indians in their *corregimientos*.[19] Clothes, liquor, tools, and food were distributed by the corregidors in return for work or sold for the cash the Indians sometimes earned. The system naturally created large profits for the corregidor since he could fix prices and compel the Indians to accept the products he wanted to distribute. The apportionment of unwanted supplies and the prices charged on these goods always constituted one of the Indians' major grievances. Third, corregidors made money through the direct labor of the Indians, by using them as *cargueros* (cargo carriers), renting them to mine owners, or employing them within the *corregimientos* to build canoes and harvest crops, which were then sold to the mine owners. Complaints that the corregidors monopolized food production in the region were common. Corn and *plátanos* (plantains) were absolute necessities for the *cuadrillas*, and many mine owners had to pay the corregidors' asking price if they were to feed their slaves. If the corregidor rented Indians from his district to Spanish mine owners in the area, he received at least one peso a day for their labor, and then paid the Indians four *reales* a day in goods.[20] The corregidor thus made a double profit, since he made four *reales* directly from the Indian labor and then more on the goods he forced them to accept in return for their work.

The arrangement led to widespread corruption, especially since the corregidors were appointed for only short terms. Fortunes could be made, but they had to be made quickly. Governor Josef Michaeli, writing in 1793, observed that corregidors serving for periods of two or five years realized they would have to drive the Indians pitilessly if they were to ensure their fortunes. The corregidors discovered, the governor advised, that they could treat the Indians as they pleased. The *corregimientos* were simply too isolated, officials who might correct wrongdoings too few, and the products of the Indians' labor too necessary for the crown officials to rectify any but the most glaring offenses. Governor Michaeli contended that, while he did not wish to condemn all the corregidors, he felt that the serious decline in the Indian population in the last twenty-five years (he estimated a drop from six thousand to three thousand) could be directly attributed to abuses and overwork by the corregidors.[21]

Although complaints continued to emanate from the Chocó concerning the mistreatment of the Indians during the last half of the eighteenth century,[22] the Indians had a greater chance of being heard. In the 1780's a crown official called the "protector of the Indians" was appointed. The protector defended the rights of the Indians and in several cases was instrumental in having a corregidor removed.

One such case, in 1787, involved the corregidor of Los Brazos. The charges were typical. The protector of the Indians, Joaquín Diego López, discovered that the corregidor, Roque de Ugalde, who was also the lieutenant governor of Nóvita, forced the Los Brazos Indians to make repeated trips to the mouth of the San Juan River to bring up products, paying them little in return. Ugalde did not allow the natives free time to tend their own crops, and they were on the verge of starvation. The church in Los Brazos was in such a shambles that it could not be used. In fact, the over-all treatment of the Los Brazos Indians was so bad that over half of them had run away.[23] López, in summing up the accusations against Ugalde, said that the lieutenant governor was guilty and that he had demonstrated both ignorance and malice in his handling of the Indians.[24]

A *fiscal* of the *audiencia* removed Ugalde from his post and ordered the former lieutenant governor brought to Santa Fe de Bogotá to stand trial. Ugalde had to return to the Los Brazos Indians a total of 2,256 pesos in reparations, and help pay for the reconstruction of the village church.[25] It should be noted that, although Ugalde was punished, in similar cases of the same period corregidors successfully argued their way clear of allegations.[26] Ugalde had been too flagrant in his mismanagement of the Indians, and, living in one of the most populous regions of the Chocó, his transgressions were easily noticed. Besides, he had used Los Brazos Indians to monopolize the transportation of goods up the San Juan River and in so doing had angered merchants in Nóvita and elsewhere who wanted to employ other Indians from Noanamá and Tadó. Ugalde, in his position as lieutenant governor of Nóvita, granted licenses for carrying products upriver from the mouth of the San Juan, and he awarded them only to merchants who agreed to use his Indians as *cargueros*. Naturally he charged high rates for this transportation.[27] Had he not been excessively greedy, angering the merchants of the area, he might never have been brought to trial.

The Indians, for the most part, accepted their roles within the *corregimiento* system. Some did run away either to the mountains or to the Cunas in the north, and occasionally they helped lead raiding parties against the *vigía* of the Atrato, or settlements in the region.[28] They also developed a form of resistance used by enslaved peoples in many parts of the world—they deliberately worked inefficiently. In 1784 the corregidor of Bebará, Luis Díaz Pizarro, reported that he had been forced to withdraw some of his Indian charges from a construction project because in four months they had completed virtually nothing and what work they had done was unacceptable. The mine owner who had requested the Indians,

Bartolomé Polo, sent them back and refused to pay the corregidor wages. Díaz explained that, if he paid the Indians badly, it was because they did nothing to earn wages.[29]

In 1797, however, Indian resentment against forced labor and tribute paying developed into a potentially dangerous problem. Indian rebellions had recently occurred in Ecuador, and the Chocó Indians somehow learned of the uprisings. Governor Michaeli was informed by several reliable *vecinos* (inhabitants) in Quibdó that the Indians had planned an armed revolt for Easter Thursday. The governor alerted the militia and ordered armed parties to patrol the streets of Quibdó during the Easter holidays. As a result, only a few incidents involving drunken Indians were reported. Nonetheless, Governor Michaeli believed that only quick action had averted a serious encounter. Then Michaeli, upset that information concerning the Ecuadorian Indian revolts had filtered into his region, angrily denounced those who had, through "harmless" gossip, made the news available to the Indians. The irate governor informed the viceroy that reports of revolts in other areas would always present dangers in the Chocó where Indians and slaves vastly outnumbered the whites. Michaeli recommended that messages of this sort be prohibited in private letters.[30]

As the colonial period drew to an end, the effects of the *corregimiento* system on the Indians of the Chocó became apparent. The arrangement had been profitable for the corregidors and had helped supply miners with needed food stuffs, but had it in any way benefited the Indians? In 1808, Governor Carlos Ciaurriz sent the viceroy a lengthy report about the province, which included information on the conditions of the Indians. The Indians, Ciaurriz confided, had not been converted to Christianity and still clung to many primitive beliefs. Their lives revolved around superstition and witchcraft. The Indians believed that every animal sound they heard, whether the cry of the guaco bird or the roar of a tiger, was an omen of events to come. They had no understanding of the Christian religion, did not fear for their sins, and had difficulty distinguishing between the king and God. Their houses contained no crucifixes or statues of saints, and they never spoke the "sweet name of Jesus or Mary." Heathen in their dress, they wore only loin cloths and loved to paint their faces red and wear large gold nose rings, necklaces, and bits of gay-colored ribbon.

Governor Ciaurriz reported that the Indians' dominant vice was drunkenness but also said that they had very "uncivilized" ideas concerning marriage. The Indians preferred experimentation with love to discover whether they could remain faithful to each other before they entered into a marriage contract—a pact bound more by tribal regulations than by Christian precepts. The Indians recognized no difference between illegitimate and legitimate children, but once they did marry, adultery occurred rarely (again because of tribal laws). Ciaurriz further wrote that few Indians spoke Spanish, which in great part accounted for their poor understanding of the Christian religion. Schools needed to be built to instruct them in Spanish, and then they could begin to understand the meaning of Christianity.[31] Obviously, in 150 years the *corregimiento* system had been unsuccessful in "civilizing" the indigenous inhabitants.

With the Wars of Independence, the Indian in the Chocó gained new paper freedoms. In March, 1820, Simón Bolívar ordered that Indians be treated with special attention and given land whenever possible, that schools be set up to educate them, and that the use of Indians as a labor force without strictly regulated pay was prohibited.[32] In 1821 the military and political commander of the Chocó, Lieutenant Colonel José Cancino, asked that a special protectorate be set up for the Indians and that the tribute be used to help pay for the organization of the protectorate. A congressional commission, after reviewing the request, concluded that the idea of a protectorate should indeed be implemented but that it would have to be financed by some other means since the Indian tribute had been abolished.[33] But when the Indians were no longer forced to live within specified settlements, they left their old villages and retired to isolated locations, where they lived off subsistence agriculture. They contributed nothing to the industry and development of the Chocó in the Republican period.[34]

Indians were the victims of an overprotective father when the Spanish crown forced them to live within carefully defined settlements, where they performed tasks for the corregidor in return for religious instruction, protection, and moral guidance. The Indians almost always complied with their part of the arrangement, but rarely did they receive just compensation. Religious instruction was careless or nonexistent, and the corregidors so mercilessly exploited the Indians that the need for protection from forces outside the system was scarcely conceivable. The attempt to enforce the crown's laws in the Chocó, where the obvious goal was the rapid accumulation of wealth, proved extremely difficult and in many cases impossible. Corregidors acted as miniature dictators in their own districts, and experience proved that, even if their actions provoked complaints, they could argue themselves free, or at worst expect a reprimand or removal. Cases involving the mistreatment of Indians showed that, while Indians were permitted to testify in their own behalf, any opposing white testimony was considered of more value. Indians had recourse to justice, but the Spanish legal system usually decided in favor of the descendants of those who had made the laws.

By the close of the colonial period the Indians still lived in a state of semisavagery. They had not been Christianized, educated, or civilized. The corregidors were of course primarily responsible for this failure to enculturate the Indians, but the church had also failed in its 150-year mission. The Indian was no more ready for citizenship in the new republic than he would have been at the time of his conquest. The Indian had been important, but only for the product of his labor, not as an individual. Like his laboring black counterpart, the Indian, though not a slave, had in fact been used as such. His only consolation was that he did not suffer the indignity of being called one.

7

The Black: His Presence

As the Indians disappeared—because of disease, flight, or conquest—it became increasingly apparent that without the black the economic exploitation of the Chocó would be impossible. In the minds of many, blacks had already proved their capacity for hard labor in the tropics, and since the 1540's they had worked New Granadan gold fields in Antioquia, the Cauca Valley, and elsewhere. There were additional advantages with regard to black slave labor: since neither the church nor Spanish law disapproved of the slavery of the black—as they did of the Indian—and Africans continually arrived at the nearby port of Cartagena, which had become a major slave depot. By the second decade of the eighteenth century most of the miners in the Chocó during the last decades of the seventeenth century were *bozales* (blacks directly from Africa), and most came from Cartagena by way of the Atrato River. In 1692, Felipe de Velasco Rivagueiro, a resident of Santa Fe de Bogotá and a mine owner in the province of Citará, reported that the blacks in the province were all *bozales* working in the mines. While justifying Indian service to build houses and canoes, grow crops and serve as *bogas* (boatmen), he explained that *bozales*, being "foreigners," did not understand these complicated occupations, although they easily adjusted to labor in the placer mines.[1]

Bozales doubtless could have learned the "complicated occupations" (blacks later became proficient in all these endeavors—especially the freedmen) without difficulty had the early owners been willing to sacrifice potential profits by taking them out of the mines. But slaves, unlike the Indians, required a capital investment and were employed in tasks which produced quick monetary returns.

Owners generally did not engage *bozales* in mining ventures for at least a year following their arrival. The rigors of the middle passage and transportation to the labor site often left the *bozales* ill or weak. Prudent owners took the time to nurse the *bozales* back to good health. Some slaveholders, of course, wanting or needing immediate returns on investment, employed their *bozales* after a minimal rest period of only two to four months.[2]

Since Cartagena served as the major slave port for New Granada, most slaveowners in the Chocó purchased their slaves in that city, conducting them to the Chocó via one of several routes. Whenever possible, slaves were imported directly from Cartagena by way of the Atrato River. But restrictions prohibiting navigation of the Atrato and the importation of slaves along the San Juan made these river highways illegal entrances for slaves during most of the eighteenth century. Hence slaves had to enter the region through overland trails leading from Antioquia or the Cauca Valley. *Bozales* from Cartagena arriving in the Chocó frequently passed through Panama, Buenaventura, and Cali, or were shipped up the Magdalena River, which bisects the center of Colombia, and then journeyed westward into the Chocó. These legal routes were time-consuming, and transportation costs were expensive.

There was also the risk that owners who relied on the overland routes from Cartagena would suffer considerable losses. Slaves faced a difficult trek of several hundred miles intermittently through lowland jungles and then over towering ranges of the Andes. As a security precaution many blacks—male and female— were chained together by the hand or neck and forced to walk single file. Food was often scarce, and provisions, together with blankets, medicines, and other supplies had to be carried. Dysentery, very common among *bozales*, frequently caused delays and even death. Mortality rates often exceeded 20 per cent on these overland treks.[3]

Owners unwilling to pay the costs of overland transportation or sustain the losses involved resorted to the illegal shipment of slaves into the Chocó by one of the prohibited water routes. Some of those found guilty of receiving contraband blacks—without the king's mark or a *guía* of legal importation—were not apprehended until they transferred their *cuadrillas* (slave gangs) to sites outside the region.[4] Had they kept their slaves in the Chocó, at least during the early years of the eighteenth century, detection would have been difficult. The sheer distance of the Chocó from watchful colonial officials would have guaranteed their safety. However, those persons unlucky enough to be caught often presented alibis that allowed them to escape serious punishment.

In 1723, for example, authorities discovered that Jaciento de Mosquera had a number of unbranded slaves working his mines near Tadó. In this instance a personal enemy of Mosquera had informed the *audiencia* of the slaveholder's illegal possessions. Mosquera admitted owning some unmarked slaves, but he claimed to have purchased them from José Caicedo (who was by then dead) without noticing at the time of the transaction that the slaves did not bear the king's brand. Mosquera had to pay the regular taxes on imported slaves but received no further penalty.[5] The few cases involving those caught with illegal slaves undoubtedly constituted but a small fraction of those actually guilty of the offense. Thus an accurate accounting of the exact number of slaves introduced into the Chocó, and the blacks' point of entry, is impossible.

As the mines prospered during the first part of the eighteenth century, it was not uncommon for a master, or several masters, to retain an agent in Cartagena to purchase slaves. The agents served as middlemen, working either on a commission or on a salary basis. Prices in black cargoes rose steadily, and in 1718 an individual could purchase slaves in Cartagena at 225 pesos a person and sell them in Cali for double that amount.[6] Many of the owners in the Cauca Valley who purchased these slaves sent them to their mines in the Chocó.* The volume of slaves sent to the region during

* Because of the additional journey from Cali to the Chocó prices were generally

113

the early years of the eighteenth century was so large that the population working the mines soon outstripped the amount of food produced by the Indians. In 1717, following the moratorium on shipping along the San Juan River, some mine owners transferred slave *cuadrillas* out of the Chocó.[7]

Wealthy Chocó mine owners easily purchased slaves in Cartagena as several nations—including England with the famous *asiento* awarded to the South Sea Company in 1713—supplied that port with *bozales*. Slave inventories for the Chocó during the first half of the eighteenth century show that a high percentage of the slaves were *bozales*. The Spanish usually retained the *bozales'* African tribal names, or their place of origin in Africa, as the blacks' surnames. Second-generation slaves might retain this African surname but usually either had no surnames, took the surnames of their masters, or were designated *criollos* (born in America). In 1725 a slave gang owned by Jaciento de Mosquera demonstrated the use of this custom. The inventory included the names Salvador, Joaquín, and Domingo Mosquera (listed as *criollos* of the province of Chocó), Agustín Mina, Josef Bomba, Felipe Arara, Francisco Mina, and others described as having been purchased in Cartagena.[8] Other inventories showed slaves with the surname Criollo. This denomination became more common as the eighteenth century progressed.[9]

African names remained in use throughout the colonial period although the frequency of these surnames diminished after the 1780's. It was not unusual for slave gangs in the first half of the eighteenth century to be composed almost entirely of *bozales*,[10] and two excellent slave enumerations for the entire Chocó in the 1750's recorded a large number of African surnames.[11] Of the 3,918 slaves registered in the slave census of 1759 nearly 40 per cent had only first names. Most of them were under the age of fifteen. Roughly half the remaining slaves had the surname Criollo. The rest had

---

higher in the Chocó than in the Cauca Valley (see Table 10). The high mortality rate of the trek and the demand for slaves were the major reasons prices were so high in the interior.

either African tribal or regional surnames. Those most commonly inscribed were Mina (139 slaves), Congo (80), Arara (47), Carabali (45), Chamba (30), Chala (25), Zetre (23), Mandingo (21), Popo (17), and Tembo (10). Other African surnames included Lucumi, Nango, Vivi, Bomba, Longo, Catanguara, and Caraba. A few slaves had Spanish surnames, but they proved to be the exception in this census.[12] Actually, blacks were more likely to assume their owners' surnames following manumission than while they remained in captivity.

Because capital was invested in little else in the Chocó, the number of slaves a citizen owned demonstrated his worth and to a certain extent determined his social position.[13] Slave gangs often numbered in the hundreds. In 1759, over 90 per cent of the slaves in the Chocó (3,578 out of 3,918) existed in *cuadrillas* of thirty or more slaves. Most of the larger mines were owned by a small coterie of families—principally the Arboledas, Caicedos, Arroyos, Hurtados, Mosqueras, Morenos, and Gómezes. Members of these "golden dynasties" resided in interior New Granada—often Popayán—intermarried, and in time dominated the entire economic life of the Chocó and the Cauca Valley.[14] Capital accumulated in the Chocó mines thus found its way to Popayán, where (especially in the latter part of the eighteenth century) it was reinvested in various businesses or used to maintain the residences of the slaveholders.[15] Money spent in the Chocó went almost entirely toward the maintenance of *cuadrillas*, the purchase of more slaves, or the opening of new mines. As a result, by the 1750's the Chocó had a number of large slave gangs engaged in mining, and there was virtually no economic diversification.

Most of the slaves were kept in the province of Nóvita, and the 1759 slave census showed that 35 whites owning property in that province had large slave gangs. Sergeant Major Salvador Gómez de la Asprilla y Novoa had 567 slaves at his mines near Nóvita; Francisco Gómez de la Asprilla y Novoa owned a *cuadrilla* numbering 192 slaves at his mines of Saltó and Yalí; the priest Francisco Gerónimo Mondragon worked 125 blacks in his mines near San

Agustín (Sipí); Joseph de Mosquera y Figueroa owned 133 slaves in his mines at Santa Rita de Iró; Cristóbal de Mosquera y Figueroa held 179 blacks at Santa Barbara de Iró; and Francisco Xavier de Mosquera y Figueroa kept 110 slaves at his mine in San Joaquín de Iró. Almost all of these owners are listed as residents (*vecinos*) of Popayán. Many smaller slave gangs numbering between 30 and 80 were held in such places as Opogodó and Tadó.

The province of Citará did not compare either in the total number of slaves nor in the number of owners with the province of Nóvita. But the 1759 slave census recorded 23 whites owning more than 5 slaves apiece in the Citará region, and several—Ignacio Renteria, Josef Leonardo de Cordoba y Velásco, Clemencia de Caicedo, and Francisco Gonzáles de Trespalacios—owned *cuadrillas* that totaled over 100. Although the province of Nóvita contained 2,685 slaves and the province of Citará, 1,233, not all these slaves were used for work in the mines. Almost two-fifths of the slaves listed (1,569 out of 3,918) were registered as *chusma* (nonworking, useless)* because of age, injury, or illness.[16]

Mine owners were the power elite in the Chocó, but they seldom exerted much direct influence on administrative changes. The mine owners' guild which developed (*gremio de mineros*) was essentially a closed corporation. Although no one could be prohibited from owning or working a claim in the region, membership in the miners' guild was definitely limited. One qualification for membership stipulated that a member own at least five slaves.[17] This requirement kept most of the small miners, mainly free blacks and *mazamorreros* (independent prospectors, white or black), from joining the guild. Many of the mine owners who qualified for membership did not actually reside in the Chocó and were not, therefore, vitally concerned with local problems.

Although it could not initiate any kind of legislation, the *gremio de mineros* did occasionally make suggestions to the crown. The

---

* Most of the slaves designated as *chusma* were children. Even seventy-year-old slaves worked in the mines providing they were healthy. It was rare to assign more than a few slaves to attend the mine's agricultural holdings or serve as hunters, blacksmiths, and so forth.

increase in slaves in the Chocó in the 1750's undoubtedly resulted from the owners' and the crown's desire to increase production in the mines. The Spanish king asked the miners' guild to send a delegate to Spain to discuss methods of increasing gold production,[18] and in 1750 the crown permitted slaveholders in New Granada to purchase slaves directly from a foreign colony, provided they paid the proper duties on the slaves they imported.[19] James Ferguson King, a historian of the slave trade to New Granada, asserted that, after 1750, Spain, for the first time in her history, began to pursue a policy which recognized the "Negro traffic primarily as a means of stimulating the wealth and productivity of her colonies, rather than as a direct source of revenue itself."[20]

Slaveholders in the Chocó quickly took advantage of the crown's liberalized policy. Carlos de Andrade, the selected delegate from the miners' guild in the Chocó, said that owing to the new crown policy the number of slaves had increased so rapidly that by 1756 famine was once again a major problem.* Andrade's solution to developing food problems, however, was not to limit slave importation but rather to break the corregidors' stranglehold on food production and Indian labor in the Chocó.[21]

The number of slaves in the Chocó continued to increase, and by 1778, 5,756 blacks were held in bondage. But many of the most robust slaves had been able to gain freedom (by methods to be discussed in Chapter 8). Almost one-third of the blacks in the Chocó were freedmen in 1778.[22] Many of the blacks who remained in bondage were too young or too old to be very productive. Therefore, in 1777, Chocó mine owners petitioned for direct importation of *bozales*, stating that newly imported blacks were best suited for work in the mines and were more obedient. The mine owners asked for the immediate importation of two hundred *bozales* through Port Chirambirá, and at least one hundred more every two years. They sought *bozales* between the ages of fifteen and twenty from

---

* Food prices did increase, and it is interesting to note that rates of profit on investments and total bullion production began to decline at about this time despite the increased number of slaves (see Chapter 10).

the Congo and Carabali tribes, whom they characterized as better workers and less likely to rebel. They also asked to be given at least two years to pay for the new slaves. A member of the *audiencia* reviewed the petition. He sympathized with the mine owners' labor needs but advised that for the present the viceroy could not permit the importation of blacks by way of Port Chirambirá. He promised to send a report to Spain and pledged the *audiencia* to seek other methods of aiding the Chocó mine owners.[23]

In 1786, after Francisco Chabaneau perfected the method of refining platinum, the Spanish crown—in a series of confidential letters to the viceroy of New Granada—ordered the collection of all platinum in the country. The Chocó, as the major region of the viceroyalty containing the newly valued metal, received increased attention from the Spanish authorities in Santa Fe de Bogotá. A *fiscal* for the *audiencia*, Vicente Yáñez, recommended among other things that the viceroy purchase 1,500 *bozales* from foreign sources on the king's account and sell these blacks to mine owners in the Chocó. Each *bozal* should be sold for three to four hundred pesos, depending upon age and condition, and the mine owners should have five years to pay.[24]

Viceroy Antonio Caballero y Góngora appointed Yáñez *visitador* to the Chocó, and in 1788, while resident there, he again asked the viceroy to ship *bozales* to the Chocó.[25] Since the Atrato River had been reopened to trade and navigation in 1782, no legal obstacle remained regarding direct importation of blacks from Cartagena. *Bozales* were sent, and one account book in Nóvita from September 1, to December 1, 1789, documented the sale of 387 *bozales* to Chocó mine owners. Although the usual price for a prime slave was the 300 pesos Yáñez recommended, many slaves brought lower prices (140 to 180 pesos) because of illness. On one list recording the sale of 52 *bozales*, 27 were designated as ill or unfit. Ages ranged from ten to forty years and although bills of sale listed no children under the age of ten, several of the *bozal* women had infants (*con cría*) or were pregnant.[26]

Bozales who entered the Chocó in the late 1780's and early 1790's comprised the last substantial number of blacks brought directly from Africa. The crown's liberalization of the slave trade laws reached its zenith in 1791, when any Spaniard was permitted to journey to any foreign colony to procure slaves. Even foreigners could bring slaves to New Granada without restrictions. King Charles IV granted this privilege for a six-year period, stating that he hoped the measure would help increase agricultural and mineral production in his American colonies.[27]

The free trade in blacks did have one limitation, however: slaves could be introduced only through Cartagena. But this posed no hardship on the Chocó slaveholders, for, with the Atrato River reopened to commerce, slaves could easily and cheaply be carried to the region by an all-water route. Large organized shipments of blacks were no longer necessary, since individual mine owners could purchase slaves in Cartagena when and in the number they desired. When the six-year time period elapsed, the crown renewed the original concession, stating that Spaniards could continue importing blacks for another twelve years, and foreigners for another six. The orders also granted Spaniards the right to introduce certain products from the foreign colonies (tools, engineering instruments, and knives) if they could not "purchase blacks."[28]

Free trade in slaves ostensibly meant that an unlimited number of blacks could be imported into New Granada. Although many ship captains took advantage of provisions permitting them to import trade goods rather than blacks, slaves were imported,[29] and prices for slaves dropped noticeably in the Chocó toward the end of the eighteenth century. Prime slaves in 1797 brought only 250 to 300 pesos,[30] and by 1817 a gentleman from Cartagena who tried to sell slaves in the Chocó complained that no one was interested and that prices on slaves were very low.[31]

Although slave prices fluctuated in the Chocó, a pattern emerged whereby slave values clearly reflected the laws of supply and demand. Slave prices were high in the first half of the eighteenth century because bullion production was high. Owners sought to exploit the Chocó gold fields rapidly and were willing to pay pre-

mium prices for slaves. Slaves valued at 200 or 300 pesos in Cartagena early in the eighteenth century were worth double that
amount in the Chocó.* A 1711 evaluation of the Chocó slaves
owned by Nicolás de Mosquera showed that forty-five prime slaves
(male and female) were worth 22,575 pesos, or 525 pesos each.[32]

Despite the large number of blacks available in Cartagena, and
the increasing size of the *cuadrillas* in the Chocó, slaves continued
to bring high prices, doubtless because bullion production and the
transportation costs of slaves and supplies remained high. In 1725
slaves between the ages of fifteen and thirty-five in good physical
condition (prime slaves) brought an average of 517 pesos, and in
1741 a group of prime slaves numbering 84 were worth 520 pesos
each. As late as 1779 owners evaluated most prime slaves at 500
pesos.

Table 10 shows the average value of prime slaves in the Chocó
during the eighteenth century and lists the number of observations.
These average values were derived from representative *cuadrillas*
and bills of sale and include all prime slaves irrespective of sex.
Although a few slaves with special skills, such as ability to handle
canoes (*canoero*) or cure snake bites (*curandero de viboras*), or
slave bosses (*capitanejos*) were evaluated as high as 600 pesos,[33]
the normal value for prime slaves from the years 1700 to about 1765
was between 500 and 525 pesos. The average value of prime slaves
declined gradually from 1741 until sometime after 1779, when
prices plummeted to 305 pesos for a prime slave.†

The figures in Table 10 represent only the average prices for

---

* The closing of the Atrato River in the 1690's had an effect on slave prices in the
Chocó. It should be noted, however, that the late seventeenth century was a period
of general increase in the number of *bozales* transported to the Americas as the
British and Dutch became established in the transatlantic slave trade with such
companies as the Dutch West Indian Company and the Royal African Company.
Many of the *bozales* shipped by the British and Dutch merchants entered the
Spanish colonies (often illegally). One of the original motives for closing the
Atrato River to maritime commerce was to prevent this trade.

† In 1788 the shipment of *bozales* purchased on the king's account by *visitador*
Vicente Yáñez arrived at Quibdó. Prime slaves sold for 300 pesos whether purchased
from the crown or from individuals. See AHNC, Esclavos 1, fols. 472–82, 485–92,
501–31 (1789).

prime slaves. Average values for all slaves in the Chocó were considerably lower, since they include slaves who were ill, children, and older slaves. The prices listed in Table 11 reflect the average worth of slaves in the Chocó irrespective of age, sex, or condition.

Average values were higher at the beginning of the eighteenth century because high bullion production created an immediate demand for slaves. This demand was not easily fulfilled owing to import restrictions on available routes into the Chocó. As the century progressed, *cuadrillas* also became more balanced and included children and other slaves, and the average value of all slaves declined.*

Slaves normally increased in value as they approached working or childbearing age. Blacks were judged prime slaves (according to price) between the ages of fifteen and thirty-five—but forty-five-year-old slaves could still be worth as much as 400 pesos. Slave children only several months old were worth 25 to 50 pesos, and by age eight months to a year their value had increased to 75 to 100 pesos. Between the ages of eight and ten values were 250 to 300 pesos, even though children of that age were rarely productive members of the *cuadrilla*. Of course a slave who was ill or had a handicap did not bring as high a price (see Table 12).

Although prime slaves were the most valuable and productive members of the *cuadrillas*, slaves performed important services well past the age of thirty-five. Only the foolish or vindictive owner seriously abused his slaves, since continued service paid better returns in the long run. Mining involved some strenuous labor, but it was not extremely dangerous (there was no shaft mining in the region), and many hours were employed in panning and separating the gravel product of the sluice washings. Older slaves, both male and female, became expert at these and other tasks and thus remained valuable. Forty- to fifty-year-old slaves were worth an average of 382 pesos in the 1760's and 1770's, and slaves in their

* At the end of the seventeenth century it was not uncommon for *cuadrillas* to be composed entirely of prime slaves. See AHNC, Minas del Cauca 5, fols. 358–65 (1690). The profitability of slavery also had an impact on the value of slaves (see Chapter 10).

fifties were evaluated at over 200 pesos. Even slaves in their sixties retained more than a nominal value. Only when slaves reached the age of eighty were they usually listed as *sin valor* (without value).

Table 12 shows the average price of slaves, based on the observations of representative *cuadrillas* in 1768 and 1779, and provides a breakdown for 247 slaves by age and sex. Prices differed for males and females at most ages because of the condition of the individuals involved, but total values for 123 males and 124 females were identical—301 pesos. Throughout the colonial period female slaves brought prices roughly equivalent to those paid for male slaves. This may be attributed to their reproductive capacities,[34] and because they performed many of the same chores as males in the mining operations.

The two representative *cuadrillas* in Table 12 present important information about the makeup of slave gangs in the Chocó. The first *cuadrilla*, owned by Francisco de Rivas Santavilla and Juan de Bonilla y Delgado, represents a balanced slave gang. The male-to-female ratio was almost equal (sixty-nine males and sixty-seven females), and there were fifty-five children (aged fourteen and under); forty-five slaves of prime working age (fifteen to thirty-four); and thirty-six slaves over the age of thirty-five. Thus older slaves lent stability and performed some work, one-third of the *cuadrilla* was of prime working age, and a number of children were on hand to provide the labor force of the future.[35]

The second *cuadrilla*, owned by Francisco Gonzáles de Trespalacios, was also a fairly balanced slave gang—but with several significant differences. While there were fifty-four males and fifty-seven females, there were also thirty-five slaves over the age of fifty (32 per cent of the *cuadrilla*). The percentage of children (35 per cent) and slaves of prime working age (28 per cent) was slightly lower than desirable, but the proportion was still respectable.

However, only 5 per cent (6 slaves) of the *cuadrilla* were between the ages of thirty-five and fifty.[36] Additional information concerning the Gonzáles slave gang disclosed that the *cuadrilla* declined from 136 members in 1746, to 111 in 1779.[37] Many of the missing members of the *cuadrilla* had purchased their own freedom and would have been in the thirty-five-to-fifty age group.[38] Thus Gonzáles supported a large number of slaves who were marginal workers—either children or old slaves—while at the same time losing slaves through manumission during their prime working years.

The Gonzáles slave gang was at a dangerous point of transition and would have to be carefully administered in order to maintain a reasonable balance between working and nonworking slaves. Gonzáles died in 1779 and the administrator selected by his heirs permitted the trend to accelerate. During the next decade more prime slaves bought freedom, and the burden of supporting the old slaves and children became too great for those prime slaves who remained. In 1789 the Gonzáles de Trespalacios estate was declared bankrupt.[39]

The decline in the value of prime slaves is partly attributable to the opening of the Atrato River to maritime commerce in 1782. Miners could deal directly with the slave market in Cartagena; agents did not have to be retained; transportation costs were cut in half; and, because of the faster, easier route, mortality rates among slaves making the journey also diminished. However, except for the sale of *bozales* in 1788 and 1789—made especially attractive by liberal time payments—there is no evidence that slaveowners bought many slaves from outside the Chocó during the last decades of the colonial period.

The slave population of the Chocó declined from 7,088 in 1782 to slightly under 5,000 in 1808. Economic priorities had changed, and investiments became holding actions rather than expanding enterprizes. The absentee mine owners showed little interest in reinvesting in the Chocó after 1780, and they did not purchase new slaves to replace members of their *cuadrillas* who died, fled, or were manumitted. The failure to acquire *bozales* is perplexing because they were available in Cartagena, and potential purchasers had been offered many new advantages and opportunities to buy them.

The lack of demand on the part of the Chocó mine owners can be explained. Although bullion production dropped in the 1750's and

1760's (Table 9), it took several decades for slaveholders to adjust to the new situation. For a time they continued to believe that more slaves meant greater productivity. *Bozales* were still desired in the 1750's and 1760's, and prices remained high until sometime in the 1780's. But when production did not increase despite more slaves (which meant higher costs), demand suddenly disappeared. Slave values dropped sharply, as did new purchases. The decision not to purchase *bozales* reflected a response, slightly delayed by the optimism that production would improve, to the profitability of slavery in the Chocó.[40]

Not unlike Brazil and the islands of the Caribbean, slavery in the Chocó depended heavily upon African importation for maintenance and growth of the slave population. But the conclusion should not be drawn that slaves had a high mortality rate or a low rate of reproduction.[41] Procreation among Chocó slaves is evidenced by the percentage of children in the region. In 1759 more than one-third of the slaves in the Chocó were children,[42] and with the two representative *cuadrillas* of Table 12 the proportion of children was 38 per cent.

Procreation among slaves was in part the result of the male-to-female ratio. From 1778 to 1808 females never constituted less than 45 per cent of the total slave population, and in 1808 the ratio of male-to-female slaves was almost equal—2,540 males and 2,428 females (Table 13). There is also every indication that the Chocó slaveholders preferred family units to single slaves;[43] and marriage, encouraged and sanctioned by the Roman Catholic church, was common during the latter part of the colonial period. In 1782 almost one-third (32.05 per cent) of the slaves were married (2,273 out of 7,008), and many of the nonmarried slaves were children in family situations.[44] Pregnant slaves received extra rations and special privileges, and so procreation was rewarded.[45]

One excellent example of the continuing procreation among slaves can be found in the *cuadrilla* owned by Francisco Gonzáles de Trespalacios. In 1746 his slave gang numbered 136; 100 slaves were over the age of 14, and 36 were children.[46] In 1759, when his *cuadrilla* totaled 125 slaves, there were 90 adults and 35 children.[47] Finally, in 1779 (the year Gonzáles died), his estate included 111 slaves in the following age categories: 0 to 9, 26 slaves; 10 to 19, 22 slaves; 20 to 49, 32 slaves; 50 to 69, 8 slaves; and, surprisingly, 70 to 90, 23 slaves. There were 54 male slaves and 57 female slaves.[48]

The Gonzáles' inventories not only list the number of children, males and females, and ages but also trace some individual slaves for a period of thirty-three years. In 1759, 80 slaves are identifiable by name with blacks on the 1746 *cuadrilla*. The number of original members still remaining was larger, but most of the children on the 1746 list were not named and cannot be matched on the 1759 census. Twenty years later the 1779 inventory included 36 original members of the *cuadrilla*, and 37 more who appeared in the 1759 census. Of the 31 slaves between the ages of 50 and 90, all but 2 were original members of the slave gang.

Although slaves left the *cuadrilla* from 1746 to 1779, the decline in numbers was not always through death. Four slaves in 1779 are recorded as runaways[49] and a number of others purchased their freedom. The exact number of manumitted slaves cannot be determined, but in 1780 nineteen *mazamorreros* (free independent prospectors) from around Cértegui—where Gonzáles de Trespalacios maintained his *cuadrilla* and owned his mines—had the surname Palacios.[50] Twelve of the nineteen so named had been members of the Gonzáles *cuadrilla* in 1759, and the other seven probably included some of the unnamed children of the 1746 inventory. In addition, because few freedmen registered as *mazamorreros*, the number of slaves manumitted by Gonzáles from 1746 to 1779 doubtless exceeded nineteen.

Because of the frequency of manumission it is impossible to calculate mortality rates for the Chocó. However, the large number of older slaves enumerated on Gonzáles' 1779 inventory is evidence that blacks could and did survive the rigors of mining in the Chocó in surprising numbers. And, although the slave population did not increase rapidly through natural causes, the black population did. Between 1782 and 1808, when the slave population declined by a yearly average of 1.3 per cent (7,088 to 4,968), the number of freedmen increased by an annual rate of 5.7 per cent (3,899 to 15,184). The total black population in the Chocó almost doubled, increasing at an annual rate of 2.45 per cent from 10,987 to 19,968. Since few *bozales* were imported during the period from 1782 to 1808, black birth rates exceeded death rates.

When the Chocó frontier opened late in the seventeenth century, mine owners quickly became dependent upon black slave labor. By the 1720's blacks had replaced Indians in the mining operations and the number of slaves increased steadily until the 1780's. Then, despite new advantages offered by the crown to potential slave buyers, the numbers of slaves, but not blacks, in general declined. Manumission, death, and flight contributed to the numerical decline of slavery, but profitability also played a significant role. As investments in the Chocó became less attractive, the purchase of *bozales* all but ceased. Children resupplied manpower for the *cuadrillas*, and by the end of the colonial period most slaves in the Chocó were native-born as is evidenced by the virtual disappearance of African surnames. The rapid slave expansion of the early nineteenth century had been reversed, although mine owners still believed that slavery was the most efficient and profitable method of exploiting their holdings.

8

Slavery in the Chocó: Law and Reality

Frank Tannenbaum argued that the tradition of slavery in the Iberian Peninsula meant that the black slave became "the beneficiary of the ancient legal heritage."[1] Long before blacks arrived in the Chocó, the Spaniards established a series of slave laws that guaranteed slaves certain rights and expected of them certain obligations. Slavery in the New World was first based upon the juridical concepts of the famous *Ley de Siete Partidas,* compiled in the thirteenth century by King Alfonso the Wise of Castile. The *Ley de Siete Partidas* regulated many aspects of slavery, such as manumission, the marriages of slaves, the status of children born of slaves, punishments that could be inflicted upon slaves, and specific instances when slaves could testify against their masters.[2] But conditions in the Americas differed greatly from those in Spain, and many of the established laws were changed, misunderstood, or ignored.

During the colonial period the Spanish monarchs proclaimed hundreds of specific *cédulas* (laws) designed to regulate the system of slavery in the Spanish colonies. Slave legislation was included in the *Recopilación de las leyes de los Reynos de las Indies* in 1680. Some of the regulations set forth by the Spanish kings admonished slaveowners to treat their blacks with more kindness, and others severely chastised slaves who misbehaved.

Contradictions over a period of several centuries were inevitable, and by the time the Spaniards conquered the Chocó, only a well-trained lawyer could determine whether a *cédula* prohibiting castration as a form of punishment for runaway slaves[3] carried more weight than one passed a few decades later permitting it.[4] It was not until 1789 that the crown for the first time promulgated a comprehensive slave code;[5] and even then, as one investigator of New Granadan slavery noted, copies of the code were rare and difficult to find.[6] Since there is no mention of the 1789 code in any document originating from the Chocó, it is unlikely that the slaveowners had access to it. Thus the first problem concerning slavery, law, and mores in the Chocó is that Spanish legislation and law regarding slavery was not generally known.

Even if the laws were known, slaves in the Chocó could not expect much help from governmental officials who purportedly protected them from abuse. Despite the region's importance because of its gold production, the population was always too small to justify the expense to the crown of the many minor administrators and military men who generally composed the broad lower base of Spanish bureaucracy. During the eighteenth century the Chocó was administered by a governor, two lieutenant governors, and thirteen corregidors. Communication among these officials was poor, since they were separated from each other by several days' travel. Governmental authority and power resided, therefore, in the hands of relatively few individuals. The physical isolation caused by mountains, rivers, and jungles meant that each white—miner, merchant, overseer, cleric, or official—was his own master.

The Spaniards did devise a system in which officials retained contact with the people of their regions and heard complaints. By law governors and lieutenant governors had to visit each mine and population center within their jurisdiction at least once during their tenure of office. One of the important duties assigned to these officials, the *visita*, supposedly assured the fair treatment of slaves in the mines, Indians in the *corregimientos*, and the population in general, by checking on such things as scales and weights and measures of the various merchants.[7] In *visitas* to the mines slaves were asked a series of questions relating to the nature of their labor, the amount of time they worked, the danger involved, the rations and free time allotted, and the Christian education they received.[8] The *visita*, although a method of control employed by the crown to correct flagrant abuses, rarely uncovered serious problems. This does not mean that problems did not exist, but rather that the method of interrogation did not reveal them. Officials talked to selected individuals, such as mine owners, overseers, corregidors, and the slave bosses (whose position depended upon the good will of the overseer or master). Forewarned of impending *visitas* by officials who wanted to be properly entertained, owners could easily transfer slaves with legitimate complaints. Absence of voiced discontent was also due to the fact that many officials did not want to create potential enemies by questioning possible lawbreakers too carefully. Governors and lieutenant governors also had a keen interest in amassing wealth in as short a time as possible, and many were themselves involved in contraband trade. There was no profit in offending mine owners and corregidors who might then inform on their own behavior. *Visitas* became *paseos* (pleasure trips), returning extra money for those officials who conducted them.*

There is a striking contrast between the Chocó and the urban centers Herbert Klein described in Cuba. The several officials in charge of *visitas* in the Chocó were often corrupt, and slaves with legitimate complaints had little or no access to other authorities. The towering Cordillera Occidental effectively blocked off slaves from the centers of Spanish justice in New Granada. Many slaves in Cuba—or elsewhere in New Granada for that matter—had more direct approaches to justice, and it was perhaps more difficult for owners to evade existing Spanish regulations.[9] Thus, whether or not Spanish law was an ameliorating influence on the harshness of slavery elsewhere, it was not a factor in the Chocó.

Tannenbaum also asserted that alongside the law another powerful institution existed to help temper slavery in Latin America. The role of the Roman Catholic church is often stressed in explaining

---

* One of the reasons owners were informed of projected *visitas* was to assure that proper arrangements could be made. Early in the 1750's the miners' guild complained that the expenses they sustained accommodating the governors' official parties could be as high as four hundred pesos. AHNC, Minas del Cauca 5, fols. 996–1000 (1751).

relationships between masters and slaves. Certainly religion formed a common denominator between exploiters and exploited. In the eyes of the church all men were equal before God, and masters were admonished to protect the moral welfare of their slaves and see to their spiritual instruction. But the church did not condemn slavery, and few churchmen spoke against the institution. On occasion individual clerics protested to the king when slave laws were evaded, but they did not argue against slavery. In 1770, for example, the bishop of Popayán complained that some mine owners forced their slaves to work on Sundays and religious holidays. On November 10, 1771, the king instructed the viceroy to remedy this violation of the law.[10]

Priests working with the *cuadrillas* in the mining camps were in a position to view incidents of misuse, and indeed they did sometimes report owners who seriously abused their slaves.[11] But this potential safeguard against maltreatment was never very effective in the Chocó—perhaps because there were so few clerics. In 1782 there were only eighteen priests in a total population of 17,898—one priest for every 1,000 inhabitants.[12] And the curates in the Chocó were responsible primarily for the salvation of the remaining Indians. In 1720 the governor of the Chocó reported that there was not a single padre in the province of Quibdó to serve the spiritual needs of blacks and mulattoes.[13]

The scarcity of priests in the Chocó becomes significant when it is compared to other slaveholding regions of Spanish America. For example, in 1778 in Cuba—where Klein emphasized the role of the church in adjusting relationships between masters and slaves—there were 1,063 priests in a total population of 179,484—one priest for every 168 people.[14] Even in other sections of New Granada the ratio of priests to total population was markedly better. Just to the east of the Cordillera Occidental, in the province of Popayán (also a region of slavery and gold mining) in 1779 there was one priest for every 261 inhabitants (382 priests, 99,879 inhabitants).[15]

In the Chocó the climate and the pattern of settlement made the priests' task a difficult one. Since they often had to travel over dangerous and rough terrain to minister to isolated slave gangs, they could visit few mines more than once a year.[16] Too, many of the secular clergy were not zealous in their missionary work and spent their time in efforts to enrich themselves. Many priests owned mines and slaves in the region, devoting much of their time and energy to supervising their holdings rather than to performing religious duties. In 1722, as a result of this "scandalous behavior," the crown prohibited clerics from owning or benefiting directly from a mine. Several priests who had been particularly notorious in their conduct were expelled from the area, and the king commanded the bishop of Popayán to enforce the regulations.[17] Despite royal wishes, however, individual clergymen and religious orders continued to own mines and slaves in the Chocó.[18]

Even those curates not directly involved in mining received ample monetary rewards for their services. Priests garnered part of the Indian tribute for ministering to the Indians, and slaveowners paid a stipend (one to two pesos a year) for each working slave confessed in their *cuadrillas*.[19] Church accounts for the province of Nóvita in 1780 reveal that the return from these stipends was indeed substantial.[20] Mine owners did not object to paying the fees, and they evinced considerable concern for the religious welfare of their *cuadrillas*. With few exceptions whites in the Chocó viewed the church as an important and necessary part of their lives.

The church commanded the respect and spiritual subjugation of the inhabitants of the Chocó. But its role in helping guarantee slaves' rights was limited both by the number of clerics actively involved and by the priests' desires to attain earthly rewards. As an institution the church was not a factor in the treatment of Chocó slaves.

Small slaveowners and *mazamorreros* administered their own slaves, but large slaveholders (who were generally absentee owners) delegated the management of their *cuadrillas* to *mayordomos*. No intelligent owner wittingly entrusted his *cuadrilla* to an overseer who tyrannized slaves, failed to provide proper rations or make other food arrangements, or let costs get out of hand. Owners continually checked on their hired employees and removed some for theft or mismanagement.[21]

Unfortunately for the owners, the results of poor management in handling a *cuadrilla* or not properly tending to a mine's agricultural holdings might not become evident for several years. The unsuspecting absentee owner might continue to receive profits for some time until suddenly production dropped, a large percentage of slaves became ill, and expenditures increased rapidly. It could take years to repair the damage done by a careless overseer. New agricultural lands had to be cleared, new tools purchased or made, and slaves nursed back to health. An example of this occurred late in the eighteenth century at the Cértegui mine, which had belonged to Francisco Gonzáles de Trespalacios. The mine, which had been prosperous for years, lost money for over a decade while it recovered from not one, but several administrators' mistakes.[22]

The overseers selected several slaves to serve as bosses (*capitanejos*), if the *cuadrilla* numbered over thirty, who helped run the slave gang and oversee the mining operations. As a safeguard against theft from both slaves and *mayordomos*, the *capitanejos* also had to be present when the heavy gold-bearing sand collected by the slaves received its final washing. The *capitanejos* remained slaves, but they had special privileges—their own homes, better food, and their pick of the slave women.[23] Little is said about the selection of the the black bosses, but they must have been slaves whom the rest of the members of the *cuadrilla* respected—or feared —and whom the *mayordomos* could trust.

Supplying food for the *cuadrillas* was a serious problem, especially during the first part of the eighteenth century. Whites arrived as masters and exploiters. None of the early whites were interested in farming. So recklessly did they pursue their golden dreams that they frequently failed to establish supply lines or even food sources. The grim specter of famine was a common companion in the Chocó. The Indians' way of life had been totally disrupted, and, although they had once produced enough to feed 60,000 people, by 1717 they could not supply one-fourth that total. When the crown closed the

San Juan and Atrato rivers to commerce, slaveowners estimated that more than three hundred slaves perished from hunger. Some owners were forced to transfer their slaves from the region.*

Those owners who remained devised new methods of supply. They often forced slaves to forage for themselves, and provisions were purchased from interior New Granada at high prices. In addition, corregidors realized high profits by overworking the surviving Indians to produce corn and *plátanos*. In time the production of staples became more regularized, and it is clear that owners tried to provide proper food, clothes, and medicine for their slaves.

The basic diet of slaves was corn and *plátanos* grown by the Indians or by members of the slave gangs.[24] The weekly ration consisted of eight hands of *plátanos* (eight to a hand), or one *almud* (ten kilos) of corn,† and some salt.[25] Children and slaves who no longer worked in the mines (those slaves designated as *chusma*) received half rations. Meat was expensive and not usually included in the rations. Slaves who were ill or pregnant, however, often received this precious commodity. Honey, rice, wine, sugar, *aguardiente*, oil, and extra salt were also granted as incentives or given to children and older slaves.[26]

The rations provided by the owners—corn, *plátanos*, salt, and occasional special foods—lacked variety or balanced nutrition. Many slaves raised vegetables, fruits, and sugar cane during their free time. Sugar cane was a favorite crop not only because of its sweetness but also because of its alcoholic by-product. Administrators of the royal *aguardiente* monopoly charged that slaves grew sugar cane, established illegal stills, and produced their own liquor.[27] Drinking must have been a serious problem, considering the ease with which spirits could be distilled. Slave inventories, which include descriptions of the slaves, frequently listed individuals as drunkards (*borrachos*).

Slaves also supplemented their diets by hunting and fishing.

* This was the period immediately following the embargo along the San Juan River in 1717.

† Corn and *plátanos* are still sold in the Chocó by the *ración* (64 *plátanos*) and the *almud*.

Hunters used dogs, and they were also permitted the use of fire-
arms. This is somewhat surprising, since Spanish law prohibited
the possession of weapons by slaves. However, meat was so scarce
and expensive that many owners overlooked the regulation.[28] Deer,
wild pigs, tapirs, turkeys, parrots, and jaguars were hunted in the
Chocó. Fishermen used nets and worked individually or in groups.
The prize catch was the manatee—a large mammal which lived in
the Atrato River. The manatee, which grows to thirteen feet in
length and weighs over five hundred pounds, was so extensively
hunted that it had become rare by the end of the colonial period.
Its importance, however, has been remembered in folk stories
and songs, where it is affectionately referred to as "Tío (Uncle)
Guachupecito."*

Some slaves—usually on the smaller *cuadrillas*—received no rations but they had three days off every week to provide for their
own food.[29] On the larger *cuadrillas*, where rations were provided,
slaves had less free time. Even these slave gangs, however, were
given free time on Sundays, special religious holidays (Christmas,
Easter, and important saints' days), and usually Saturdays as well.
Mine owners in the 1720's reported that slaves worked 269 days a
year,[30] and *visita* reports in 1784 and 1804 showed the number of
work days as 260 a year.[31] The five-day work week (or less) maintained in the Chocó is remarkable when compared to other areas
of the Americas. Slaves in most other regions labored six or seven
days a week, but were usually provided with more nearly complete
rations.[32]

The tradition of slaves providing part or all of their own provisions began early, when food sources were limited and owners
could not provide sufficient rations. Owners trimmed maintenance
costs by allowing slaves to work for themselves and made some
income by selling products to their slaves. Many slaves chose to pan

---

* Although references are still made to Tío Guachupecito, few in the Chocó now
realize that the name was given to the once-numerous manatee. One of the most
beautiful folk songs of the Chocó relates a fisherman's affection for Tío Guachupecito
and his sorrow at having to kill him. The song has been recorded by Leonor Gonzáles
Mina (*Cantos de mi Tierra y de mi Raza*, Medellín, Sonolux).

gold during their time off, and they purchased extra or special foods from the overseers with the money they earned. Although the shortened work week limited production in the owners' mining operations, it should be remembered that slaves did not pan gold continuously. Considerable time was spent locating and preparing ground sluices and pit placers. During the slack time slaves were frequently rented out or else contracted to work independently. They were expected to pay *jornales* to the owner. In any case, an efficient overseer arranged the work schedule to maximize efforts during the final washing stages.

It might be argued that slaves given days off instead of balanced rations were not afforded generous treatment, since they were forced either to work during their free time or starve. The system could have been particularly unfortunate for those slaves too ill or too old to provide for themselves. However, the extra food supplements alloted to these slaves shows that owners accepted the responsibility of providing a more balanced diet for slaves who could not work advantageously during their free time. It is also probable that the healthier slaves helped the less fortunate. Actually, the *visitas* revealed that slaves preferred more free time to more food.[33] Gold was plentiful, and slaves working for themselves had opportunities to earn and save money. These savings became a significant source of income for slaves attempting to purchase their own freedom.

Because the provisions slaves grew, caught, killed, or purchased were seldom recorded, it is difficult to determine—as Robert W. Fogel and Stanley L. Engerman have done for North American slavery—whether a slave's basic diet was balanced and nutritious or provided a sufficient caloric intake.[34] It is probable, however, that, without supplements provided through personal labor, a number of slaves would have been undernourished.

Sick or old slaves were not usually required to labor in the mines, and they received attention, special foods, and medicine. Slaves did not usually perform dangerous tasks, such as moving heavy boulders or felling trees.[35] Owners rented Indians from corregidors to undertake these chores, and occasionally slaveholders hired free blacks. Accidents did of course occur in the mining operations, and the work was arduous and long—usually from sunup to sundown five days a week—when a ground sluice or pit placer was being worked. But the fact that the black population increased naturally and that many slaves survived to old age is partial proof that *cuadrillas* were properly and fairly maintained.

The owners' concern for the physical welfare of slaves may not demonstrate any humanitarian motivation, since economic factors were involved. Nevertheless, whether motives were pragmatic or benign, owners did attempt to maintain their slaves. In fact, physical abuse of slaves was remarkably rare. Although archival data cannot be entirely trusted on this subject, primary sources—including governors' reports, *visitas*, travel accounts, and personal letters—seldom include any evidence concerning the deliberate mistreatment of slaves.

Unfortunately, several owners did administer severe and inhuman punishments. One of the few examples of harsh handling occurred in 1788, when a mistress whipped a slave so severely that a doctor later testified that the slave's back had been a festered, open sore. Even worse, the mistress had tortured the slave by placing hot oil and burning chili sauce (*ají*) on his genitals. The slave reacted by stunning the mistress and then hacking her to pieces with an ax. The slave then fled but was soon recaptured. The Spanish officials agreed that, even though the slave had not acted in defense of his life (the only possible legal justification for his actions), the mistress had behaved so as to provoke her own murder. However, further discussion convinced the officials that the death penalty had to be ordered, since anything less might encourage similar acts of violence among the large slave population and endanger the lives of the white inhabitants in the region. Authorities had the murderer hanged and his right arm severed and placed on a pole as a warning to other slaves who might strike their masters.[36] It should be stressed that this case was the exception and not the rule.

Personal and domestic servants often received good treatment, as well as affectionate friendship,[37] but because few owners maintained residence in the area and because urban centers did not exist, the number of slaves employed in domestic service was small in comparison to that of those working in the mines. In most of the larger mines several slaves were assigned to perform household chores for the owner or overseer. Since there were no butlers, bootblacks, or coachmen, most of the personal servants were women or children.[38] Occasionally the owner had a personal manservant,[39] but normally there was a minimal loss in manpower from the mining operations.

Close proximity to their owners and overseers meant that the domestic servants were carefully watched, and they were occasionally accused of crimes. In one incident, which occurred in Quibdó in 1748, a female slave was accused of having tried to poison a Spaniard. The case, although amusing and inconsequential, illustrated both the tensions inherent in the master-slave relationship and the fact that slaves, in an urban environment at least, could be declared innocent through the process of Spanish law. When a distinguished visitor became ill, the lieutenant governor in whose house the guest lodged summoned a slave well known for her curative arts. She was ill, and another servant, a *bozal* Negro woman named Marta, arrived in her place. She was instructed to prepare a medicine made from sugar cane and salt, but somehow she bungled the concoction. Carrying the foul-smelling mixture to the kitchen, the lieutenant governor discovered what appeared to be a frog in the bottom of the kettle the inexperienced *bozal* had used to prepare the medicine. Witnesses were called, and Marta was taken to jail, where authorities tried to force a confession. The confused servant continued to maintain her innocence. A crime could not be proved, even though several witnesses testified that they had seen some sort of animal (which looked like a frog) in the pot. Despite the serious nature of the suspected crime,* the judge re-

* Had it really been a frog in the pot there would indeed have been reason for concern. The Indians of the Chocó extract a deadly poison for their darts from a small green frog common in the area.

viewing the testimony dismissed the case for lack of evidence. Indeed, he stated that, even if there had been a frog in the medicine, the woman might well have been innocent. Frogs, the judge commented, apparently in all seriousness, were famous as jumping animals, and, besides, the object probably was an unpeeled potato as several witnesses had suggested.[40]

Marta was lucky to escape punishment, for domestic servants who were convicted of crimes such as theft were given fifty lashes and then sold for work in the nearby mines.[41] The Spaniards and slaves obviously considered labor in the mines arduous and undesirable, since it was viewed as a form of punishment for recalcitrant servants. The mere threat of labor in the gold fields doubtless prevented many household servants from committing petty crimes.

One of the rights guaranteed to slaves under Spanish laws was the opportunity to seek protection against mistreatment, and, when a case reached the courts, slaves had a good chance of winning.* But masters found guilty of seriously mishandling their slaves received little more than a mild rebuke. One Spaniard in the town of Tadó, Joaquín García de la Flor, pitilessly punished his female slave Agustina on the pretext that some candles and meat were missing from the kitchen. Agustina was pregnant at the time (later testimony contended that García was the father of the unborn child), and her master kicked and whipped her so ruthlessly that she aborted and nearly died. Since the incident occurred in a settled region, several of Agustina's friends informed the corregidor and the local priest. García later argued that both these individuals were his personal enemies, which may explain why they prodded

* Norman Meiklejohn argued that, because law cases involving slaves often resulted in favorable judgments for slaves, Spanish slave legislation was effectively enforced. See Meiklejohn, "Negro Slave Legislation"; and Meiklejohn, "The Implementation of Slave Legislation in Eighteenth Century New Granada," in *Slavery and Race Relations in Latin America*, 176–203.

Cases involving slave mistreatment in New Granada, however, were not numerous. In the Chocó, in over a hundred years, there were only five such cases—an unbelievably low number. Two conclusions for this are possible: either slaves were well treated and had little reason to use the courts, or those cases involving mistreatment were not usually brought to justice. It is likely that masters evaded prosecution and that Spanish laws were not effectively enforced.

the governor to inaugurate proceedings against him. The subsequent investigation found García guilty of mistreating his slave, but the only penalty prescribed by Spanish law was that he had to sell Agustina to another master.[42] Public opinion doubtless condemned him as a cruel master, which may have harmed him socially, but he did not even suffer a financial loss as a result of his crime.* Other cases involving mistreatment show that the maximum benefit a persecuted slave could hope for was sale to a different master.[43] Justice was possible, but scarcely evenhanded.[44]

Not knowing the exact regulations that supposedly governed their behavior, most owners devised slave codes of their own. Such personally designed slave codes may be the best evidence for testing the Tannenbaum thesis in the Chocó. Those codes, perhaps even more than deeds that may have been irrational reactions to the circumstances of the moment, should reflect the influences of the owners' cultural and traditional values and the necessities of the frontier.

Slave codes demonstrate that, while Chocó owners attempted to treat their slaves with a degree of kindness and to instruct them in the precepts of the Catholic religion, they also placed a number of restrictions upon the slaves. One typical code ordered the overseer to instruct the slaves carefully in religious matters, to encourage slaves to marry (other slaves), to keep slave families united, to attend the sick, and to provide medication, sufficient food, and clothing. The owner cautioned that good relations between the overseer and the slaves would result in greater productivity. However, slaves were to be immediately punished with a minimum of fifty lashes for any disobedience, dishonesty, or blasphemy. They (not even slave families) could not have their own homes, but were to live together as a group so that they could be closely supervised. Under no circumstances were members of the *cuadrilla* to communicate with free blacks or even with members of other slave

---

* However, it is likely that, because of the punishment Agustina received, she did not command as high a selling price as normal. In this respect García did suffer a minor financial penalty for his actions.

gangs.[45] A similar code, written two decades later, also emphasized the need for religious indoctrination, the desirability of married slaves, the importance of proper food, and the necessity of keeping slaves separated from freedmen.[46] Many other documents reveal that these instructions constituted the customary basis for the treatment of slaves in the Chocó.

It might be argued that the treatment designed for slaves in the Chocó followed the pattern described by Tannenbaum and Klein, even though the Spanish legal system and the church were not directly involved. Details about the number of lashes given for offenses differed from Spanish law and from region to region, but in general the emphasis on religious instruction, marriage of slaves, and proper physical care reveals common concerns.

However, the codes demonstrate that the limits of "good" treatment were almost entirely physical. Only the simple survival and continued good health of their slaves were of concern to the owners. Slaveholders exhibited almost total disregard for the "moral personality of the slave." Families were not always permitted to live together (although family units were preferred), and communication between slaves and other blacks in the region was strictly prohibited. The role of the father or husband was limited. Slaves who resisted the authority of the owner were flogged. Stanley Elkins, Eugene D. Genovese, and many others have already noted the difference between physical welfare and "treatment" in the sense of opportunities for development or freedom. Few humanizing aspects were included in the Chocó slave codes.

Slaves suffered abuse under the system of slavery, and they clearly resented their position. Owners and overseers who employed what they considered fair treatment were perplexed when slaves rebelled or escaped.[47] One overseer admitted that in spite of his best efforts the slaves worked with indifference; and, most mystifying to him of all, only one black on the entire *cuadrilla* seemed to enjoy his work.[48]

Far from exhibiting humane, legal, or religious values, the Chocó slave codes were very pragmatic. Religion has been described as a tool of discipline within slave systems when it stressed obedience as a Christian virtue. Marriage among slaves was likewise considered proper Christian behavior, and it kept slaves more closely bound to the *cuadrilla*. A slave with family ties doubtless thought twice before attempting to rebel. Escape was more difficult with a wife and children. Slaves needed to be fed properly not only to maintain their health and productivity for the owner but also, as one owner explained, to eliminate needless grumbling.[49]

The owners had still other motives. One of the reasons owners stressed proper maintenance was to limit grievances that might lead slaves to escape or rebel. Since slaves vastly outnumbered whites (by almost twenty to one in 1782), there was always the threat that the enslaved majority would initiate acts of physical violence. Slave rebellions were a major concern of the white inhabitants of the Chocó. Following one particularly violent rebellion near Tadó in 1728, the king admonished slaveowners to improve conditions and afford "better treatment to the blacks." Only in this way, the king warned, would there be peace and prosperity in the region.[50] Thus owners tried to limit causes for escape or rebellion and they vigorously pursued those who resisted or fled.

Finally, economic determinism was a factor in helping shape the behavior of slave owners in the Chocó.[51] The Spaniards settled the region for one reason—to exploit the gold fields. In the Chocó, as elsewhere in Latin America, slaves were valuable property, which, if in good condition, could return a handsome profit for the master.

It is interesting that nowhere in the Chocó slave codes were there any provisions for manumission. Under the Spanish legal system any owner could free his slaves without restriction, either during his lifetime or in his will. Over a period of years the number of *libres* (freedmen) normally increased as masters granted freedom to more slaves. The masters probably hoped to avoid the issue, but manumission in the Chocó was not only possible but occurred. In 1778, 35.44 per cent of the black population was free (3,160 of 8,916).[52] Although the ratio of slave to free was not as high in the

141

Chocó as elsewhere in Latin America in 1778,[53] slavery had existed
in the Chocó for only one hundred years. Time certainly worked
on the side of slaves seeking freedom. During the next thirty years
the free black population increased by a remarkably constant 5.7
per cent a year.[54] By 1808, 75.34 per cent of the black population
in the Chocó was free.

Although owners in the Chocó emancipated slaves voluntarily,
the most common method of manumission was self-purchase. Although it was rare in many parts of Latin America, self-purchase
was not unique to the Chocó.[55] In Cuba, for example, the famed
system of *coartación* was extensive and worked to the benefit of
urban wage-earning slaves.[56] Rural slaves, however, were normally
excluded from the system of *coartación*, for they lacked the opportunities available to their city-dwelling counterparts to earn and
save money. In the Chocó the reverse was true. Cities and their
opportunities did not exist, but rural slaves laboring in the mines
had a source of ready income from the placer deposits. Slaves could
work in the placer fields during their "free time," including religious
holidays following mass, and keep what they earned.* Owners
hoped slaves would use this money to buy extra food, tobacco, and
liquor which they sold to their slaves at high prices. But, with luck
and hard work, slaves working in the Chocó could save enough
money to buy their own freedom.

Few *notarial* records relating to the colonial period exist for the
Chocó. Thus, it is difficult to determine exactly how many slaves
purchased their own liberty. However, a rough estimate for the
rate of manumission from 1782 to 1808 can be calculated by sub-
tracting the annual rate of increase of the total black population
(2.45 per cent) from the annual rate of increase for the free black
population (5.7 per cent). The difference, 3.25 per cent, is the
annual rate of manumission.†

* To work the owner's mine during "free time," the slave had to have the express
permission of the owner. But slaves could locate and work their own claims with
no legal problems.
† It is possible that the birthrate for free blacks was slightly higher than for slaves.
However, because of the large percentage of children listed in the slave inventories

This rate of manumission becomes more significant in light of the findings of Fogel and Engerman, which stressed the role of incentives in North American slavery as crucial to the structure of that institution. In essence, slaves were offered a form of the carrot and the stick. They could adapt to the system (this does not mean becoming a Sambo) and receive benefits in return,[57] or they could resist—in which case they did not receive the rewards of greater productivity or were castigated. But incentive in the United States rarely included manumission. By at least 1830 it was very difficult for slaves in the United States to benefit from the incentive of freedom.

In the Chocó not only could slaves work to improve their physical comforts but they also had the incentive of possible self-purchase from slavery. Most of the cases of manumission through self-purchase were recorded for slaves in their prime working years, and men and women were manumitted with almost equal frequency. Therefore, slaves working in the Chocó had a high manumission potential through self-purchase up to the age of thirty-five, but their possibilties decreased every year after that age.[58] It would appear that slaves unable to save money during their prime working years were less likely to do so in their older age. On the other hand, voluntary manumission was more likely to involve older slaves because of their "faithful" service to the master.*

Most owners had to accept the self-purchase arrangement,[59] and it appears to have been one of the few Spanish laws that blacks in the Chocó both knew about and took advantage of.[60] Knowledge of the law must have been passed from slave to slave; there is no indication that owners or overseers ever publicized the regulation.

By at least the 1780's some slaves had made arrangements with their owners to pay for their freedom in installments.[61] These slaves (between 33 and 38 per cent), the difference was probably minimal. The manumission may have been slightly higher than 3.25 per cent since a 2.45 per cent birthrate for blacks is higher (by about 0.25 per cent) than that calculated by Fogel and Engerman (*Time on the Cross*).

* The 1789 slave code prohibited the manumission of old slaves who were not able to provide for themselves. This was designed as a humanitarian measure to prevent masters from freeing sick or old slaves who had become a liability.

(called *libertos*) were considered freed from service to their masters once they submitted a specified part of their value (the amount varied from 20 to 50 per cent), but they were expected to continue payments on a regular basis.[62] Thus, following a down payment some slaves were free to seek their own employment and work full time on their own accounts.[63]

One of the most difficult problems faced by slaves attempting to purchase freedom was finding a safe place to keep their savings. There was no secure hiding place in the slave quarters. Because of the warm climate, slaves were scantily clad, and it was difficult and dangerous to conceal gold dust on their persons. Slaves stole from one another, and the *capitanejos* could not be trusted. Some slaves gave their savings to their masters or overseers for safekeeping. While most owners and overseers handled these sums honestly, some slaves were sadly deceived.[64] Complaints to Chocó officials of this deception resulted in favorable decisions for the slaves, providing they could prove that they had given money or produce from their crops to the owners or overseers.[65] The lack of security for funds earned by slaves may well have been one of the reasons for the installment-payment system.

Naturally some owners objected to slaves' rights to manumission. Occasionally a relative or heir contested a will freeing slaves, but it was to no avail.[66] Even verbal testimony was accepted if there was no will to prove that the deceased owner's intent had been to manumit a certain slave or slaves.[67] A few owners bitterly disputed their slaves' rights to purchase freedom because they feared that freeing slaves would lead to a drop in production in their gold mines. Slaveholders who challenged this form of manumission usually claimed the slave had either stolen the money (a charge that had to be proved conclusively) or simply wished to cause trouble.[68] One owner from the Chocó recommended to the *audiencia* that slaves be forced to prove they had not stolen the money they presented to purchase freedom, thus reversing the due process of law.[69]

A typical example of an owner's objection to self-purchase occurred in 1728, when Isidoro, a slave owned by Francisco Josef de Arboleda, brought six hundred pesos to the lieutenant governor of Nóvita and claimed his freedom.* Arboleda contested the claim, stating that Isidoro must have stolen the money—after all, he argued, everyone knew that slaves stole from the mines and then later pretended to have mined the gold during their free time.† Testimony, however, supported the slave. Witnesses said that Isidoro worked efficiently, labored long and hard on his own time, and had collected a considerable amount of gold (exact amount unknown). No witnesses offered any proof that the money had been stolen. Arboleda lost the suit, and the slave gained his freedom, but Arboleda angrily predicted the ultimate ruination of the province, arguing that slaves would now openly steal from their masters in order to buy freedom.[70]

Another equally bitter owner, forced to liberate a fifteen-year-old slave, argued that his private-property rights were being violated. Since he did not have to sell furniture or other property against his wishes, surely he did not have to part with slaves simply because they had money. The *fiscal* for the *audiencia* reviewing the case ignored the dehumanizing aspects of the argument and openly sympathized with the distraught owner. However, the *fiscal* concluded that the law was quite clear. He had no recourse but to declare the slave free.[71]

It is likely that disgruntled slaveholders hoped to intimidate the slaves into forfeiting their legal rights to freedom, for they doubtless realized that the slaves able to buy their own liberty were the best-qualified or hardest workers. Although the system was open

---

* The value of a slave was legally set by one of the Spanish officials in the region (usually the governor or the lieutenant governor), and the owner had to accept this price regardless of what the slave was worth in terms of skills or other qualifications. The prices set, however, were usually the maximum. Isidoro's value, for example, was 83 pesos higher than the average value of prime slaves at the time (see Table 10).

† Unquestionably slaves stole from their masters, and even if actual theft was not involved, other tactics that benefited the slaves at the expense of the masters were employed. For example, it was possible to pass over rich deposits in the mines during work days and return to extract them during fiesta days. The *mayordomos* and *capitanejos* were supposed to prevent such duplicity.

to injustice—particularly in instances where owners did not agree to manumit a slave, and the slave had to find an official willing to initiate an investigation—nonetheless, manumission laws clearly favored slaves. Thus an escape valve, the possibility of manumission, was an incentive for the more ambitious slaves.

In assessing the applicability of the Tannenbaum thesis to the Chocó, it is clear that several of the pillars upon which the argument rested were weak in this frontier region. The forces of the Roman Catholic church and Spanish law, while present, were not important in regulating slavery. The church was ineffective, and Spanish law was often ignored or unknown. Because the institutions conveying traditional mores were not strong, the implementation of these values was imperfect.

Slaves seldom had recourse to the Spanish courts in matters other than manumission. In practice slaves had to find an official willing to listen to grievances and, more importantly, to take action to correct them. Officials and clerics in the Chocó were few in number, and their primary concern was not for the welfare of the slaves, or of the Indians, but of themselves. The *cuadrillas* worked by overseers were often situated in isolated regions, and permission to lodge complaints with distant officials was not given. Slaves traveling without this permission risked the brand of runaway, which carried with it the threat of serious punishment. For the slave the only real avenue for improving his lot was hard work. This might bring increased personal comforts, food, liquor, clothing, or, if he was diligent and lucky, enough money to purchase freedom.

Visitas, which on paper helped protect Indians and slaves from mistreatment were, in fact, meaningless. The officials conducting them hesitated to stir up problems by pursuing such minor and time-consuming offenses as the maltreatment of Indians or slaves. Questions and answers were in form only, but they satisfied the requirements of the crown and Spanish law. In practice most crown regulations that might have restricted the actions of whites were simply "paper" laws that could be ignored with impunity.

In addition, the owners and officials in the Chocó had bonds of heritage, friendship, status, and a comon fear of slave revolts. They had similar motives for remaining in the Chocó, and one group seldom worked against the interests of the other. Finally, the slaves usually had no knowledge of the laws that protected them—the obvious exception being those regarding manumission. Masters did not inform the slaves of their rights. Indeed, the owners themselves were often ignorant of the laws.

The slaveholders' commitment to gold caused continual confrontations between economic concerns and legal and cultural values. On the one hand, the distinction between slaves as men and slaves as things was not important to the Chocó owners. They viewed their slaves as tools necessary to extract gold. On the other hand, the owners devised codes that stressed marriage among slaves, religious instruction, adequate food (or more free time), clothing, and medicine. Even without effective influence from church or state, safeguards against physical and psychological abuse, including the crucial right to manumission, were understood by slave and master alike. Blacks who were the strongest, and the most ambitious, could gain liberty by working for it. The safety valve of manumission relieved tensions. There was a steady stream of young, able-bodied blacks who purchased their own freedom.

Slaveholders in the Chocó understood the formula that better physical treatment resulted in healthier workers and greater productivity. Mistreatment led to dissatisfaction and possible rebellion. Profit motives helped determine slave treatment but, ironically, behavior was in general accord with the Spanish conduct Tannenbaum and Klein described.

❖❖❖❖❖❖❖❖❖❖❖❖❖❖❖❖❖❖❖❖❖❖❖❖❖❖❖❖❖❖❖❖❖❖

9

Libres, Cimarrones, and Black Resistance

The question of the *libres'* place in Spanish society has always been regarded as important, for, if Spaniards held relaxed racial attitudes, then the freedman should have benefited from a higher degree of acceptance. Indeed, Tannenbaum wrote that "endowing the slave with a moral personality before emancipation, before he achieved a legal equality, made the transition from slavery to freedom easy, and his incorporation into the free community natural."[1]

Most observers would agree that Spanish concepts of race were complex.[2] The transition from slavery to freedom was never easy, nor was incorporation into the free community as natural as Tannenbaum implied. It is true that in Cuba the large free black community received a degree of acceptance because it was essential to the Cuban economy, but that was not necessarily the assimilation Tannenbaum suggested.[3] In Brazil, because of the role of the mulatto, society was less stratified than in the United States,[4] and Frederick P. Bowser, summarizing the situation in Spanish America, judged that "the authorities undoubtedly would have been pleased had all blacks remained slaves, but once the free colored community came into existence, its recognition, and even its organization, was deemed desirable."[5]

The Chocó did not fit these patterns in assimilation, need, or organization for the free blacks. For the most part, *libres* remained individuals apart, unaccepted by the whites in the region and apparently unwilling, in turn, to accept white society. Because of the scarcity of white women in the Chocó, miscegenation was common, but it did not create a greater acceptance of blacks. Spaniards in the Chocó, perhaps unwittingly, evinced signs of enforcing the *limpieza de sangre* (purity of blood) doctrine. The *limpieza* mores originated in the Iberian Peninsula as a result of religious conflicts and were transferred to the New World in a form that assured the dominance of the European immigrants.[6] In Spain the pressure of *limpieza* doctrines came not from the upper Spanish nobles, whose position was secure, but from the lower ranks seeking elevation. J. H. Elliott wrote that the lesser members of the Spanish nobility contended that it was far better to be born of humble origin, "but of pure Christian parentage, than to be a *caballero* of suspicious racial antecedents."[7]

In Spanish America the racial rather than religious implications of the *limpieza* doctrine were stressed. Spanish observers of the colonies were sometimes astounded by the highly stratified racial system in Latin America. Jorge Juan and Antonio de Ulloa, two prominent crown inspectors in the middle of the eighteenth century, for example, commented at length on this phenomenon in Cartagena.[8]

Although the rigid racial system described by Juan and Ulloa for New Granada's north coast does not appear to have been vigorously employed in the Chocó, there was a feeling of white superiority. Colonial documentation from the Chocó included many examples of racial inequities. On many occasions blacks were openly classified as shiftless individuals whose natural tendencies led them to drunkenness and thievery.[9] At other times Spanish officials reported that blacks were completely untrustworthy and constituted a dangerous element in and around the settlements of the region.[10] A few Spaniards carried their intolerance to extremes. One, a convicted dealer in contraband articles, sent a petition to the *audiencia* objecting not so much to his imprisonment as to having to share a cell with a black.[11]

The whites' failure to accept or incorporate *libres* into Chocó society is partially due to the lack of urban development.[12] Jobs were not available in cities, because there were no cities. In fact, within the simple economic structure of the Chocó, very few skilled or semiskilled positions of any kind existed. The small number of whites in the area meant that the normally wide range of service positions were scarce or filled by slaves. Free blacks had difficulty attaining even such positions as *bogas* (canoe men) or *cargueros* (cargo carriers), laborious and undesirable jobs commonly left to them in other areas of New Granada.[13] The corregidors in the Chocó wished to retain monopolies on the carrying trade by utilizing only Indians from their *corregimientos*. Unquestionably many *libres* were unemployed or underemployed, and the term *libre vagabundo* was frequently used to describe them. Thus, in the Chocó, whites and free blacks seldom worked together or developed any sort of interdependency.

Freedmen in the Chocó did acquire a greater degree of protection before the law than slaves, but very few *libres* seem to have taken advantage of it—probably because they did not know their legal rights or were too intimidated to demand them. One of the few cases involving a freedman versus a white occurred in 1747, when a *bozal libre* complained that he had been jailed and his mine and several slaves impounded by the lieutenant governor of Quibdó. The *bozal* admitted owing fifty pesos to a Spanish mine owner for some mining rights but argued that he had not been given sufficient time to pay the debt and that the interest rate being charged was too high. The *audiencia* reviewed the case and sided with the *bozal*, agreeing that the lieutenant governor had acted hastily. The lieutenant governor was reprimanded, the plaintiff was released from jail, his property was restored, and he paid only the original sum of the debt.[14] Freedmen, like slaves, could win legal disputes with whites, but they suffered the obvious disadvantage of not knowing the law or being able to hire lawyers who did.

Official positions in the Chocó were few in number and were reserved almost exclusively for whites. Most colonial documentation carefully recorded the race of an individual, especially if he was of Indian or African ancestry. There is no evidence that a black, mulatto, or *zambo* was ever appointed corregidor, lieutenant governor, governor, or administrator of the major crown agencies in the Chocó. Nor were any of the important merchants of the region of African origin, although some freedmen doubtless operated small stores. Whites could easily have excluded blacks from most of the commercial business in the Chocó, since the contracts to carry supplies into the region were granted by Spanish officials.[15]

Libres could and did own slaves and mines in the Chocó, but very few can be classified as major owners. Of the seventy-two individuals listed in 1755 and 1759 as owners of more than five slaves, only Miguel Ibo de Tovar, with five slaves, and Miguel Soliman, with twenty, were *libres*. By way of comparison, ten Spanish slaveholders held more than one hundred slaves, and forty-four Spaniards owned slave gangs numbering more than thirty.[16]

Jobs were available in the mines, and wages were one peso a day, but few free blacks exhibited any desire to work in the slaveholders' mines. Even fewer qualified as *mazamorreros*. In the province of Citará which contained 814 *libre* males in 1782, there were only 188 *mazamorreros*[17] and some of these were Spaniards. Some *libres* tried commercial agriculture, living near the mines and villages and selling their corn and *plátanos* to the overseers of the large slave gangs.[18] Often, however, black farmers were not welcome near the Spanish communities or mines; owners feared that the *libres* would spread dissension among those who remained in bondage.

Certainly one of the most serious handicaps faced by the *libres* was the difficulty of receiving any formal education. This, prevented their holding many positions (as overseers, clerks, and so forth) that required any degree of literacy. It was not necessarily a deliberate policy on the part of the Spaniards to withhold education from blacks (although that conclusion seems justified), for schools throughout Latin America were few in number. In fact, no school of any kind existed in the Chocó until late in the eighteenth century, and that school was created specifically for Indians.[19] Blacks fended for themselves, and few could afford the expense of sending a child to school outside the province as did many of the whites. Finally, institutions of higher learning were exclusive, and advanced training as doctors, lawyers, or scribes was almost always denied blacks. Most university charters allowed entrance only to those of pure Spanish descent,[20] and the Spanish crown frowned on black enrollment in universities.[21]

One of the few prestigious occupations open to a free mulatto or black was a position in the colonial militia. In many regions of Spanish America, including Cuba and the Caribbean coast of New Granada, a number of free blacks, with crown approval, joined the militia in the eighteenth century. They served well, gained certain *fueros* (special privileges), and were depended upon to help defend the colonies.[22] Except in times of dire emergency they formed segregated regiments. By 1761 a company of *mulatto libres* had been formed in Nóvita,[23] and in 1774 the viceroy ordered the governor of the Chocó to form a company of mulattoes in Quibdó.[24]

The crown did not always approve the formation of colored militia units in the Chocó. In 1779, for example, Governor Manuel de Entrena requested permission to establish several companies of militia that would include free blacks, citing the increased size of slave gangs, the developing conflict with England, and the threat of an English–Cuna Indian invasion as his reasons.[25] The viceroy denied his request, stating that the threat of an English invasion of the Chocó did not appear likely and that there was a dual problem involved in enlisting blacks in the militia in the Chocó. First, the viceroy explained, blacks were needed in the mines to ensure the continued production of gold (this reason does not appear valid in light of the data concerning *libres* involved in full-time mining). Second, he said, although there was a need for militia units, blacks were not entirely trustworthy, and some feared that arming them might actually lead to rebellion.[26] Thus, although militia units including *libres* were established in the Chocó, they were never very important.

Membership in the militia did not depend entirely upon skin color, but color was indeed a factor in becoming a military officer. Officers received certain *fueros*, and these positions were highly sought by some members of the black community. However, special privileges and recognition for freedmen in the Chocó were rare and contrary to prevailing policies in the region. As a result, there were few black officers, even within the mulatto regiments. One free mulatto, Juan Antonio de Lasprilla, was named captain and commander of the mulatto *libre* company of Nóvita in 1761. But, significantly, Governor Ponce de León, who made the appointment pending approval from Santa Fe de Bogotá, assured the viceroy that Lasprilla was of honorable character, was of light complexion, and would derive no *fueros* from the commission, "nor any distinction whatever other than carrying a cane, which here is much admired."[27] A separation between whites and freedmen in the Chocó was carefully maintained.

Unaccepted and restricted by white society, hundreds of *libres* left the Spanish settlements, retreating to inaccessible locations in the jungle. Freedmen were not forced to leave the settled communities because of lack of available land. The whites, as extensive as their holdings were, did not monopolize all the gold-mining terrain nor all of the good agricultural land along the riverbanks. The *libres* fled because they desired to be free in spirit as well as in law.[28]

The independent status of the mulatto and the free black in the Chocó was possible in part because survival was relatively easy. In the warm climate there was no need for expensive clothing or shelter, and food, though not plentiful, was easy to grow or catch in the jungle. Freedmen reared their families, produced their own food through primitive agriculture, and mined enough to supply themselves with basic necessities.[29] Contact between whites and free blacks in the Chocó was never as extensive as elsewhere in Latin America.

Interestingly, there is little evidence that the free black population ever formed anything approaching a free colored community in the Chocó. Only in rare instances did the freedmen demonstrate any signs of interest-group orientations. On two occasions freedmen presented petitions complaining about high prices and their inability to participate in commercial matters. The first series of complaints, in 1766, ultimately led to a confrontation between *libres* and whites in the province of Citará.[30] The second petition, in 1809, resulted when a newly arrived governor, Juan de Aguirre, sought to remove the lieutenant governor of Nóvita, Francisco Antonio Caycedo. Governor Aguirre tried to prove that Caycedo resisted his authority, monopolized commerce in the region, and acted in a manner prejudicial to the welfare of the province. Aguirre, unable to rally white support, turned to several unlikely allies including *libres*. The freedmen, therefore, were "used" to corroborate his position. This proved to be a highly unpopular move, and the governor ultimately asked to be transferred.[31]

There was, of course communication among *libres*, but they lived almost as independently from each other as from the whites. A few families might cluster together, but black villages did not develop except for a few isolated *palenques* (runaway-slave settlements).[32] The basic unit was the immediate family, and this unit doubtless would have been difficult to maintain had it not been for the ratio of black males to black females. The slave population was roughly equal with regard to male and female (a phenomenon that was decidedly not the case in many other slave areas of the New World),[33] and in 1782 there were nine more *libre* women *de various colores* than *libre* men—1,954 females and 1,945 males (see Table 14).

In the Chocó women were able to take equal advantage of manumission; they had considerable free time and knowledge of many mining procedures.[34] There is also evidence that females received monetary gifts in return for sexual favors,[35] but there is no way to determine whether prostitution was common. Probably it was not as common as in other slaveholding areas of the New World because of the male-to-female ratio among the blacks.

The isolation of *libres* in the Chocó, and their rejection of Spanish society during the colonial period, made possible the survival of African music, customs, and folktales in the area. Many freedmen in the Chocó were first- or second-generation immigrants who retained memories or firsthand accounts of their past homeland. A Colombian expert on music and folklore, Enrique de la Hoz, has said that the Chocó provides one of the most interesting sources of folklore in the country.* Leonor Gonzáles Mina ("La Negra Grande de Colombia") collected many of her songs from the Chocó, and several contain direct references to Africa.[36] Witchcraft and magic are commonly practiced† and folk stories of animals (in the same tradition as the Uncle Remus stories) are very popular.[37] Rogerio Velásquez in particular collected many Chocoano folkstories relating to black remembrances and explanations of their environment.[38] Thus, because of its colonial heritage, the Chocó provides a fertile field for modern anthropoligists, folklorists, and musicologists who wish to examine aspects of African influence in the New World.[39]

Census reports listed the Chocó's large number of *libres* but did not include the considerable number of *cimarrones* (runaways). Perhaps one of the reasons owners attempted to treat their slaves decently was to limit grievances that might lead slaves to escape. Blacks took advantage of the terrain and the isolation of their *cuadrillas* by fleeing to escape bondage or mistreatment. The jungles and mountains provided natural hiding places, and *cimarrones* congregated in areas where their recapture would be difficult. Some *cimarrones* from the Chocó even fled as far south as the Putumayo region near Ecuador, where they formed a *palenque* and built a fortress.[40]

Carl Degler argued that the most important requirements for successful, long-term escape and the development of runaway set-

* "Hay un interesantísimo venero folklórico en el Chocó, la más característica zona de color de Colombia." "Música contemporánea de Colombia," *Cuadernos Hispanoamericanos*, XXXII (1957), 346. Colombians have recently come to appreciate the unique flavor of Chocoano music and dance. In recent years the dance troop from the Chocó has won several national *Ballet Folclórico* awards and they receive enthusiastic welcomes throughout the country. I attended one such performance in Bogotá in 1971 with a group of Chocoano friends and was impressed both at the reception and the obvious African influences of the dances they presented.

† There are many *brujas* (witches) in the Chocó renowned for their cures of various ailments. One of the most famous *brujas* in Colombia lived in Tadó, where I worked as a Peace Corps volunteer. People came from hundreds of miles to confer with "la bruja Pacha."

tlements were a sparse population and a warm climate.[41] In the Chocó, settled communities and mining camps were situated along the major rivers and streams and were easily avoided. Because of the climate shelter and clothing were not major problems, and food could be grown or hunted in the jungle. Family life was even possible because females appear to have fled as readily as males.[42] Certainly women—especially those without young children—had the same opportunities to escape as males.

Because of the terrain recapturing small groups of *cimarrones* was virtually impossible. If *cimarrones* banded together in large groups, however, seeking protection in number, they were actually more vulnerable to attack. In 1788 a *palenque* in the Chocó was destroyed by Spanish troops from Cartago, who were informed of the settlement's location. The captured runaways were thrown in jail and sentenced to two hundred lashes. Their owners had to pay the expenses of their recapture.[43]

Usually the *cimarrones* retreated before the forces sent to defeat them. In the beginning of the nineteenth century, for example, slaves from the Chocó, Barbacoas, and the Cauca Valley formed a *palenque* just south of the Chocó. Expeditions sent against this settlement were met by deserted houses as the blacks slipped farther into the jungle. A foray led by the governor of Micay in 1819 finally succeeded in capturing a few of the *cimarrones* in this group and temporarily stopped raids on mines in the region. But he admitted that further problems would probably arise.[44]

Runaway slaves posed a real threat to their owners' prosperity in the Chocó not only because of the example they set but also because they sometimes returned to the mines and villages on raiding parties, looting and burning, stealing women, and raping and killing the inhabitants.[45] Owners tried to recapture *cimarrones*, but there were few direct economic benefits to be gained. Captured runaways were often seriously injured or punished and thus of little further use to the owner, and slaves who had fled once were likely to escape again.

Bushwhacking expeditions formed in the Chocó, composed of

armed whites and freedmen, received a fee of fifteen to twenty-five pesos per captive (regardless of condition), plus expenses.[46] On at least one occasion the royal treasury paid these costs: some of the *bozales* imported in 1789 immediately fled, and, since they had not yet been sold, they still belonged to the crown.[47]

The number of *cimarrones* in the Chocó is impossible to calculate—no one ever tried to compile statistics on them—but it must have been a vexing and continual problem. Throughout the eighteenth century property inventories, letters from overseers to owners, and documents written by Chocó officials enumerate expenses for the recapture of runaways or mention that slaves had escaped from the *cuadrillas*.

Certainly purchasing freedom or fleeing from the forced labor of the slave gang were forms of black resistance, and they could cost the owner capital investment or future profits in his mine. But these problems were of little consequence compared with the threat of black aggression. The slave insurrections which occasionally erupted in the Chocó were expected, but it is especially significant that they occurred in this region of Spanish America. Blacks everywhere resisted slavery, but rarely did they have the Chocó's legal opportunities to escape bondage. Slavery could be ended through legal channels. Opportunities to make money in the gold fields and the possibility of manumission were safety valves. Armed revolt, on the other hand, was a serious crime, and any large rebellion was inevitably doomed to failure and perhaps death. No slave or group of slaves could prevent the continued exploitation of men and metals in the Chocó. But confrontations did occur and showed the frustrations and impatience blacks experienced in their captivity.

Individual slaves reacted to mistreatment by fleeing or committing minor acts of obstruction or sabotage. Sometimes, of course, their hatred exploded into violence. When only one or two slaves rebelled and remained in the area, the Spanish easily recaptured them and inflicted harsh penalties—usually death by hanging.[48] But because so few Spaniards resided in the region, major insurrections were much more difficult to handle. Fortunately for the Chocó mine owners, such confrontations were few in number, and, when they occurred, help was available from the neighboring Spanish provinces. The first such altercation took place in 1684, when a score of runaway slaves joined over a thousand Chocó Indians in rebellion against the Spanish. They were defeated in 1685 by troops sent from the Cauca Valley.[49]

The largest slave revolt in the region took place in 1728 near the town of Tadó. Forty blacks, who had been badly treated by a harsh overseer banded together and killed the offending Spaniard. Not satisfied with this single act of vengence, they raided other isolated mines in the area, killing fourteen more whites and enlisting other followers. The white inhabitants of Tadó were terrified that the slaves would attack the town itself, and with only a handful of Spaniards and few weapons they thought themselves doomed. But, instead of making a direct assault on the town, the blacks scattered, attempting to persuade slaves from other *cuadrillas* to join them in a mass rebellion.

The slaves, having few weapons, believed that safety lay in large numbers. The tactic backfired, however, when the initial outburst of the rebellion dwindled into inaction and gave the Spaniards time to send reinforcements to the region. The governor of Popayán, fearful lest an organized slave revolt spread into the Cauca Valley, immediately sent an armed expedition to Tadó. Peace was restored to the area when the military commander of the Spanish expedition, Lieutenant Julián Trespalacios y Mier, deceived four of the rebel leaders by promising to discuss grievances under a flag of truce. Trespalacios violated the truce, captured the rebels, and executed them. The remaining blacks, although a significant group, were powerless without leadership, and most of them returned to their owners. Some remained hidden as *cimarrones* along the jungle streams, but they posed no immediate threat to Spanish domination.[50]

However, the 1728 rebellion had provided the slaves with a precedence for violent resistance. A number of slaves had firsthand experience as participants in an open rebellion against their masters. *Cuadrillas* throughout the Chocó learned about the revolt. Despite the effective countermeasures taken by Lieutenant Trespalacios, tension remained high. In 1737 the governnor of the Chocó concluded that the situation had again reached an explosive stage, and he claimed that another mass slave revolt was being planned. He ordered the lieutenant governor of Nóvita to collect all weapons in the possession of slaves. The lieutenant governor complied with his instructions, even commanding the slaveowners to gather all mining tools at the end of each working day on pain of a one-thousand-peso fine.[51] These measures were a combination of common sense and preventive action, but they imposed hardships on the slaveowners and were counter to the customary procedures of the region.* The governor's orders reflected the continuing fear by Chocó officials of the growing slave population.

Disturbances continued in the area, and a number of small revolts on the fringes of the province involved blacks from the Chocó.[52] Chocó governors repeatedly warned the viceroy that uprisings could easily occur, but these warnings did not refer to any specific actions of slaves in the region. In 1803, Governor Carlos de Ciaurriz wrote that, although the Indians in the Chocó were peaceful, slaves in the area increasingly disregarded authority and needed constant surveillance. He said that he had required all mine owners to report any disorders to him immediately.[53]

Three years later, in 1806, Ciaurriz concluded that the situation had definitely deteriorated. The Chocó slaves, he warned, knew of the recent horrible events on the island of Santo Domingo (Haiti) and planned similar terrorism. The governor believed that blacks throughout the Chocó were discussing the violent methods by which Haitian blacks had not only overthrown their white masters, but also driven them from the island. Slaves refused to work and

* Although Spanish law prohibited slaves from possessing weapons, enforcement of this law was usually lax. In the Chocó, with food supply a problem, it was common practice to designate several members of the *cuadrilla* as hunters, provide them with weapons, and assign them the task of supplying fresh game. The collection of mining tools at the end of each work day was without precedent in the Chocó.

insulted their masters; even *libres* were noticeably more insubordinate. Governor Ciaurriz asked for some Spanish regulars because, although violence had not yet erupted, signs of growng unrest were everywhere.[54] The governor perhaps overestimated the widespread nature of the dissatisfaction; there is no corroborating evidence for his statements. Nonetheless, troops were sent from Cartagena. No insurrection occurred.

Black freedmen also initiated several serious incidents, and the threat of their involvement in seditious acts increased with their numbers. Limited in their opportunities, and often resentful of Spanish authority, the *libres* constituted a large and potentially disruptive group. In 1766 free mulattoes in Bebará, disgusted with the high prices of *aguardiente* and food and with the conduct of Spanish officials in the Chocó, broke into the royal warehouse in the town, stealing all the liquor on hand. After consuming large quantities of *aguardiente,* they marched on the corregidor's house. Armed with stones, sticks, and a few knives, they raised their own flags and openly insulted the corregidor. The unruly mob presented a list of grievances that began, "Long live the king and down with bad government!" Although the blacks took no further action at the time, they controlled the town, and the corregidor was powerless to prevent their continued defiance of Spanish authority.[55]

News of the incident quickly reached both the black inhabitants and the Spanish officials in Quibdó. A number of citizens informed Governor Nicolás Díaz de Perea that the *libres* in Quibdó planned similar events. Blacks outnumbered the whites ten to one in the city, and the governor, believing that he did not have sufficient forces to defeat a full-scale rebellion,[56] called for a meeting with all the town's blacks. Striding before the crowd that gathered, Díaz stated that he knew of the plot to break into the *aguardiente* warehouse and royal treasury. Alone, unaided, and obviously not intimidated, the governor continued with a stern lecture concerning the king's policy toward those who violated his agencies or harmed his officials. Any who rebelled would be punished to the limit of the law. The only hope the would-be rebels had was to hand over

The owner of this property has at his doorstep plátanos *and onions (grown on stilts to prevent them from being washed away). His wife is drying clothes on the rocks in front of the house.*

161

Children try to trap small fish near Cértegui while domesticated
ducks share the stream.

Two schoolteachers in Tadó play the role of Pied Pipers on market
day.

Two young Chocoano miners disagree about who will use the barra *(crowbar) and the shovel.*

School children gather near the Mungarra River during a community development project.

163

Market day offers few food choices other than bananas and plátanos.

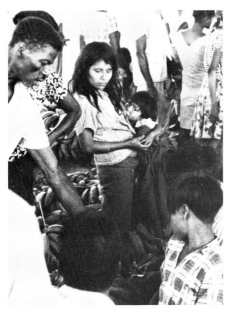

An Indian family sells
plátanos *on market day.*

A *young Chocoano carries a
half ration* of plátanos *(thirty-
two) home from market.*

165

*Flooded streets are common in the towns of the central Chocó,
where rainfall averages almost one inch a day.*

Chocó Indians bring bananas and plátanos *to market by floating them downstream in dugouts or on* balsas *(rafts).*

This Indian family has just arrived in Tadó on a heavily loaded raft. They reflect one aspect of modern cultural conflict: several Indians are dressed in western clothes, while others wear loincloths.

167

A young Indian mother carries her child tied on her back.

immediately all weapons and discard all ideas of subversion. The absurdity of a solitary official demanding surrender for a deed not yet committed was not recognized. Taken by surprise, probably bewildered, and certainly aware that acts of rebellion would be avenged, the crowd submitted to the voice of traditional authority.[57] Díaz was a strong man—confident in himself and in the system he enforced—and he successfully rebuffed a potential threat from dissatisfied but unorganized blacks.

However, the *libres* in Bebará were still to be dealt with. After organizing the "loyal vassals" of Quibdó, an expedition was sent to Bebará. The group was small in number and poorly armed, and the lieutenant governor who headed it, Juan Jiménez, expressed private doubts about some of the members because of their color. Despite these disadvantages, the foray successfully restored the governor's authority in Bebará, and twenty-nine mulattoes were taken prisoner.[58] Some who escaped tried to flee to Antioquia. The leader of the rebels, Hipólito de Viera, was later taken captive and sent for trial to Santa Fe de Bogotá. Viera had tried to initiate acts of atrocity against the Spaniards, but he was too late.[59]

Swift action, personal bravery, and good fortune had prevented a serious altercation between whites and blacks. But the crown was informed that great potential danger still existed, for, if the *libres* did start killing whites, slaves and even Indians would probably join in the blood bath. Lieutenant Governor Jiménez recommended that Spanish regulars be sent from Cartagena and permanently stationed in the Chocó since the *libres* in the long run would only respect force. The lieutenant governor also suggested that a strong fort (replacing the *vigía*) be constructed by the Atrato River and that punishment be swift and severe for any black who committed a crime.[60]

Revolts failed, or perhaps were not begun, because many slaves concentrated their efforts on purchasing freedom rather than rebellion. But the blacks' lack of success in insurrection also proved the effectiveness of the Spanish system. The white minority maintained an uneasy but continued dominance over the colored majority.

Blacks learned to obey and work for incentives or expect punishment. Rebellion had virtually no chance of continued success because blacks relied on quick isolated acts of violence rather than on prolonged, systematically organized campaigns. Weapons, educations, and authority were Spanish monopolies. Trained leadership within the black community was not encouraged and rarely tolerated. Positions and opportunities were never equal, and acts of self-assertion were not permitted. That is the real reason so many *libres* left the Spanish settlements to retreat into inaccessible locations in the jungle. They sought not just freedom from slavery but also freedom from Spanish authority, domination, and law.

10

Mining Economics and the Profitability of Slavery in the Chocó

The question of the profitability of slavery has become of considerable importance to historians. Before the detailed study presented by Alfred H. Conrad and John Meyer, a number of North American scholars argued that slavery in the United States was not economically sound, had reached its natural limits, was inefficient and cumbersome, and within a short time would have probably destroyed itself. Conrad and Meyer refuted this contention, concluding that "slavery was profitable to the whole South."[1] Recently Robert W. Fogel and Stanley L. Engerman exhaustively reviewed the secondary and primary literature and revised estimates presented by Conrad and Meyer upward from 7 or 8 per cent interest rates to slightly over 10 per cent.[2] Fogel and Engerman argued that slavery in the United States presented an investment "that compared favorably with the most outstanding investment opportunities in manufacturing."[3]

Scholars concerned with slavery in Latin America have been remarkably remiss in treating the profit stimulated by slavery. Assuredly, many scholars have studied certain economic aspects of slavery, especially with regard to manumission movements in the nineteenth century, but rarely have they examined the economic specifics of slavery. Since the economic system of the Chocó relied so heavily on slave labor, it is important to evaluate the profitability of the system.

The examination of slave profitability in the Chocó is particularly helpful in providing explanations for fluctuations in slave importations, slave prices, rates of profit, investments, and the contraband trade. To demonstrate a comprehensive view of individual profits in the Chocó, including rates of profit, twelve separate models were selected as examples (Table 15). The individual cases are followed by a province-wide estimation of profit (Table 16). The latter discussion will include estimates of contraband trade in bullion and draw conclusions concerning the profitability of slavery in the entire Chocó.

In determining the annual net profit to slaveowners in the Chocó, and even more importantly their percentage of return on capital investment, the folowing factors were considered: first, total declared earnings; second, the exact number of slaves owned and the total value of those slaves; third, the average cost of maintaining slaves in the Chocó; fourth, circulation capital and the total value of all property, including slaves, land, equipment, and furnishings; and fifth, appropriate depreciation rates for slaves and other property. Once these factors are known, rates of profit can be computed by using the formula $Y = \frac{a-(b+c)}{x+z}$ where Y is the rate of profit; a, the declared earnings; b, the depreciation; c, the total cost of maintaining the *cuadrilla*; x, the total value of slaves, and z, other property and circulation capital. Simply stated, the rate of profit equals the net income divided by the total capital investment.

Unfortunately, the volume of data used by Fogel and Engerman in calculating the profitability of slavery in the American South cannot be duplicated for the Chocó. It is extremely difficult to determine the total proceeds from the Chocó mines because of the region's flourishing contraband trade. Much of the gold mined was never recorded with officials in the Chocó, and private ledgers were destroyed out of fear of disclosing incriminating evidence. However, existing records for individual holdings give an approximation of the profits involved, and the aspect of contraband trade has been taken into consideration in determining returns on investment for the entire Chocó.

Mine owners in the Chocó who owned slaves made money in three principal ways: first, from the gold mined by their slaves;

second, from *jornales*; and third, from the sale of slaves or other property belonging to the owner.

Production fluctuated and a mine owner might find that his work force produced several hundred pounds of gold one year but very little the next.[4] Expenses continued regardless of the amount the slaves produced, and so the owner or his administrator carefully selected the ground to be worked. Experience showed that mines located in the San Juan River district consistently yielded more gold than those along the Atrato River. Thus more slaves were kept in the region around Nóvita.[5]

The discovery of a rich pocket of gold initiated the immediate deployment of an owner's available able-bodied slaves. Not all slaves in the *cuadrilla* were available for labor in the mines. Some were working for *jornales*, and others were too old, too sick, or too young to be so employed. It was not uncommon for almost half of the slaves of a *cuadrilla* to be characterized as *chusma* (nonworking),[6] and in 1759 two-fifths of all slaves involved in mining in the Chocó (1,569 out of 3,918) were classified as such. Approximately two-thirds of the slaves designated as *chusma* were children under the age of fifteen.[7] Some of the older children undoubtedly prepared food, stitched clothes, sharpened tools, or executed the less strenuous occupations necessary for the operation of the mine. They were not, therefore, worthless (certainly not in value)—even if owners listed them as such because they did not work in the mines. Besides, these children were very important as the labor force of the future.

Mine owners not only received income from *jornales* and what the slaves produced from the mines but also received money from the sale of slaves.[8] Owners did not always desire to sell their slaves, but if a slave brought enough money to purchase his freedom, an owner had to grant it. Slaves constituted capital, and could always be sold to meet expenses if the mine lost money. Many owners, believing that selling their slaves limited future profits, resisted until liabilities increased to such a degree that there was no alternative.[9] An owner could not be forced to sell his slaves because of debt, unless it was owed to the crown,[10] but all the earnings from his mine or slaves could be attached until he paid off his indebtedness.[11] When that happened, an owner received no income until the unfavorable balance against him was corrected. The owner had the choice of keeping his slaves in the hope that their earnings would ultimately settle the debt or selling some, satisfying the claim immediately. Masters used both techniques.[12]

Slaveowners purchased their labor force or inherited it from relatives. Once slaves had been procured, it was left to the owner to administer his mines and *cuadrillas* skillfully in order to receive maximum profits—or perhaps any benefit at all—from his holdings. Careless treatment, inattention, or brutality meant that slaves would become ill, weak, or dissatisfied; it could sometimes lead to the death of a slave. Any of these conditions limited production and thus profits. Hence food, clothing, shelter, and medicine had to be provided, all of which constituted a major expense. Some masters carefully supplied most of the necessary food for their slaves, while others permitted their blacks more free time to produce their own sustenance. Those owners who offered rations (almost always owners of the large mines) either grew their own food or purchased it from corregidors or freedmen. Buying food was expensive, because sellers charged what the market would bear and transportation costs on food stuffs from outside the Chocó were extremely high. Most masters tried to produce most of their own provisions.

The documentation on expenses to maintain slave gangs is often incomplete and, therefore, difficult to evaluate. But some records exist pertaining to the costs of maintaining a *cuadrilla*. In 1739 a slaveowner, Pedro de Mosquera, calculated an expenditure of 45 pesos a year for rations for each prime slave[13]—a sum equal to 360 *reales*, or slightly under 1 *real* a day. (Mosquera's estimate is abnormally high and was the highest I discovered.) Several years later, in 1747, the former lieutenant governor of Quibdó, José Pastrana, claimed that it cost approximately 260 *reales* (32.4 pesos) a year to maintain a prime slave.[14] This figure is substantiated by the expenses for a *cuadrilla* numbering forty-eight slaves owned by

Luis de Acuña y Berrios. Provisions for Acuña's slave gang included corn, *plátanos*, sugar, salt, and meat. It cost 7,877.4 pesos to feed the *cuadrilla* from 1721 to 1725. Thus the yearly expense for each slave for nourishment averaged 32.6 pesos, or 262 *reales* a year.[15]

The examination of other specific holdings shows that even Pastrana's estimates and Acuña's expenses ranged on the high side to the norm. Acuña purchased most of his rations, and other mine owners who provided the bulk of their own provisions cut costs considerably. Francisco de Rivas and Juan de Bonilla y Delgado, for example, spent 14,060 pesos (112,480 *reales*) from 1765 to 1768 to sustain a *cuadrilla* of 200 blacks,[16] or an average of 187 *reales* a year (23.4 pesos). Salvador Gómez de la Asprilla y Novóa, who owned a large number of slaves, had virtually the same half-*real* daily expense average (22.5 pesos); he spent a total of 9,000 pesos to maintain 400 slaves in 1757.[17]

The Rivas, Bonilla, and Gómez accounts included all costs for maintaining the *cuadrillas* (rations plus medicine, stipends for the clergy, tools, and so forth). The actual cost of rations probably did not exceed 15 pesos (120 *reales*) a year for each slave. The minimum expenses for rations (in the larger *cuadrillas* that provided much of their own food) would thus be 15 pesos a year and the maximum (Mosquera's estimate) 45 pesos.

Mine owners naturally had many other expenditures. They paid stipends to the clergy for ministering to the slaves, bought tools and other equipment used in working the mines, provided medical care for the *cuadrillas*, and paid *visita* expenses for local officials. Disbursement for these items varied greatly, depending upon the size, condition, and age of the *cuadrilla*. The larger slave gangs that included children and older slaves cost more in stipends (one peso per slave each visit, one or two visits a year) and medical expenses, but also made their own tools instead of purchasing them. The large *cuadrillas* also constructed their own canoes and shelters, and the owners thus saved the expense of renting Indians from the local corregidors for these tasks. In most mines five to thirteen pesos a year sufficed to meet such expenses.[18]

Many owners faced one other significant disbursement—commissions to managers. Administrators and overseers managed most of the larger mines in the Chocó. Administrators handled the distribution of slaves between mines and agricultural properties, and they had to be trustworthy since they manipulated accounts for the mines. Because of their positions of importance, administrators reaped good incomes. Few if any worked on a salary basis. They received their food and lodging and a percentage of the mine's yield or a commission on the sums spent to maintain the *cuadrilla*.

In many mines the positions of administrator and overseer were combined, but occasionally an owner paid commissions to both an overseer and an administrator. When the positions were combined, the individual holding a job was entitled to either 10 per cent of the mine's yield before the deduction of the *quinto* or 10 per cent of all expenditures for the *cuadrilla*. Regardless of how managers collected their commissions, however, it averaged from three to nine pesos a year for each slave.[19] Generally speaking, the more a mine produced the greater the increment to the administrator. In the long run the interests of the manager and the owner coincided, since the income of both depended upon the continued productivity of the mine.

In determining the owners' total outlay for running a mine and a *cuadrilla* in the Chocó, the estimates shown in Table C were made. Although the range between minimum (23 pesos) and maximum (67 pesos) expenses is wide, the maximum occurred only in rare instances when the owner purchased at high prices all the food and equipment for the *cuadrilla* and mine. The records indicate that although the total cost of maintaining a large slave gang was high, it was more efficient in minimizing costs per slave since the slaves produced most of their own food, made their own tools and shelters, and sewed their own clothing. Since over 90 per cent of the slaves in the Chocó belonged to owners of large *cuadrillas* (slave gangs numbering more than thirty),[20] it is reasonable to assume that the normal expenditure for each slave was near the minimum average of 23 pesos a year.[21] The mean cost for a slave in the Chocó (90 per

Table C
Typical Annual Costs for Maintaining
Prime Slaves (per Slave)*

Expense	Low	High
Food and clothing:		
1. Where most of the food was produced by the owner and clothes were hand-sewed	15	
2. Where most of the food and clothes were purchased		45
Medical care (illness, pregnancies, etc.)	1	5
Tools and shelter	2	4
Stipends for the clergy	1	2
Visitas, diezmos	1	2
Supervision and administration	3	9
	23	67

* Costs given in silver pesos.

cent at 23 pesos and 10 per cent at 67 pesos) can be estimated at 27.4 pesos a year. As a safeguard against too low an estimate this figure has been raised in my subsequent calculations to 30 pesos for a prime slave a year.

One final factor must be considered in determining total maintenance costs. Slaveholders listed slaves either as *útil* (working) or *chusma*. *Chusma* slaves normally received only half rations and thus cost less to provision. I have classified three-fifths of each *cuadrilla* as *útil* and two-fifths as *chusma*[22] unless specific information was given to the contrary. Each *útil* slave, therefore, cost an average of thirty pesos a year to maintain, and each *chusma* slave twenty pesos.

To derive the total value of the owner's property, I have estimated assets other than slaves (tools, mines, shelters, agricultural lands, furnishings, and so forth) and added this sum to the value of slaves owned. In a number of property inventories slaves constituted approximately 75 per cent of the total property value.[23] In the larger holdings, however, they accounted for a significantly larger proportion. In 1768, in the case of one large *cuadrilla*, 212 slaves were worth 67,190 pesos, while total assets were appraised at only 78,980 pesos.[24] Land, tools, houses, and furnishings constituted only 15 per cent of the total assets for this slaveholder. On the other hand, large mine owners needed more circulating capital. Hence the 25 per cent figure is a reasonable estimate for assets other than slaves. The average value of the slaves themselves was determined from Tables 10 and 11.

The Chocó owners did not compute depreciation, but consideration must be given to this factor in order to derive net profits or rates of profit. Tools, houses, and furnishings depreciated, but, because the owners themselves rarely lived in the region (with their big houses and expensive furniture), their total worth is not of great significance. Land is difficult to evaluate, because most owners claimed large plots of ground, and mines represented only a fraction of their holdings. The alluvial nature of the gold deposits dictated the use of placer-mining techniques: when owners exhausted the gold from one small plot of land, they moved to another nearby section. The abandoned ground became worthless but that did not affect the value of a large claim. What became especially valuable was cleared agricultural land, and it usually increased in value with development. Abandoned agricultural land, however, quickly lost its value, since it returned to tropical rain forest within a few months. In no instance where it was possible to trace holdings for several generations was the land ever devalued. Nevertheless, because owners had to replace buildings and worn equipment, I have adopted a depreciation rate of 10 per cent for land, equipment, and furnishings.

More importantly, depreciation of the owners' greatest and most valuable asset—slaves—must be estimated. Although the mortality rate of slaves cannot be determined because of the frequency of manumission, all indications are that blacks did not suffer a high rate of attrition and that by at least the late 1760's birth rates exceeded death rates. In addition, the labor of prime slaves raised within the *cuadrilla* quickly paid off their master's total investment and by the age of eighteen they produced almost pure profit.[25] After the age of thirty-five slaves declined in value, but they remained productive long after that. From the slave prices presented in Table 12 it can be seen that healthy slaves were considered a contribution to the *cuadrilla* until about the age of seventy. The decrease in average value from ages thirty to thirty-four (488 pesos) to ages fifty to fifty-nine (224 pesos) represents an annual devaluation of approximately 2 per cent.

Obviously this does not constitute the total depreciation rate, because other slaves on the *cuadrillas* fled, died, or were granted freedom. *Cimarrones* (runaways) presented a continual problem, and virtually every slave inventory listed one or more slaves as having fled. However, except in 1728, there were no mass escapes, and most of the slaves who ran away in 1728 were quickly recaptured. The most common means of escape from slavery was self-purchase (*coartación*). Owners, therefore, did lose slaves, but there is no indication that even 10 per cent of a *cuadrilla* died before old age, fled, or was manumitted in any given year.[26] The depreciation rate for lost slaves (probably about 8 per cent a year) plus the decrease in value of slaves past prime working age (2 per cent) yields a total annual depreciation of 10 per cent. This estimate has been adopted in order to calculate rates of profit.

The twelve case studies reported in Table 15 were selected for three reasons: first, they spanned almost the entire period of Spanish occupation in the Chocó; second, records pertaining to these chance samples were more complete than others; and third, certain special factors made these illustrations of particular interest. Eleven of the twelve representative mines showed a net profit and the range on rates of profit varied from –5.71 per cent to 49.2 per cent. All the calculations in the formula $Y = \frac{a-(b+c)}{x+z}$ are figured on a yearly basis.

The high profits received by Francisco Arboleda Salazar were typical of the returns recorded by those early miners who ventured into the Chocó. The slaves Arboleda brought with him were all prime slaves, and thus the average value of his *cuadrilla* was figured from Table 10 (525 pesos) rather than Table 11. His maintenance costs were also higher than normal since all eighteen of his slaves were *útil.*[27] The high rate of profit Arboleda experienced (49.2 per cent) doubtless justified the risks and hardships involved in establishing a slave gang in the Chocó and encouraged other miners to enter the region.

The mine owned by Luis de Acuña y Berrios thirty years later showed a net profit of only 395 pesos a year. Although Acuña's holdings had an accretion of funds (since prime slaves cost 520 pesos in the early 1720's, and his rate of profit was only 1.51 per cent) his over-all success seems very unlikely. Acuña was in fact jailed for debt, and the many financial obligations he incurred initiated a lawsuit against his assets that continued for several years.[28]

Partnerships seem to have been common in the Chocó. However, the company formed by Pedro de Mosquera and Miguel Moreno was not a lasting one. Personal letters included with papers related to the company show that both men were wealthy and influential. Mosquera resided in Popayán and was a descendant of some of the first miners to enter the Chocó. Moreno, who lived in Mariquita, had business interests throughout western New Granada and owned several other slave gangs in the Chocó. Both partners shared equally in expenses and profits, but late in 1740 Moreno concluded that Mosquera (who was in charge of the venture) had cheated him. Mosquera denied the accusations, but Moreno argued that Mosquera deducted unreasonably high maintenance costs for the slaves in his charge from the gross product of the mine (sixty-seven pesos a year for each prime slave). The partnership was dissolved, despite the fact that the company's holdings had returned a reasonable rate of profit (10.22 per cent).[29]

Data concerning the *cuadrilla* owned by Francisco Maturana presented an example of the high earnings possible in the first half of the eighteenth century. Maturana's slave gang worked a very rich section (*playa*) and mined more than 150 pounds of gold (worth 30,000 pesos) in less than a year.[30] That fortunate owner, like Arboleda before him, could have paid for his prime slaves in less than two years' time, and the amount produced by each slave (300 pesos a year) was well above average. Maturana's rate of profit (42.69 per cent) was the second-highest recorded.

Doña María Clemencia de Caicedo's mine gave a more reliable over-all view because the information covered five years, came from an established mine, and did not rely on a lucky discovery. The mine had only fourteen washings (*cortes*) during the five-year span and profits were sent directly to the owner in Santa Fe de Bogotá.[31] No mention was made of *jornales*, but income from this source was probably included in the sums remitted to the owner. Doña María Clemencia's rate of profit (14.11 per cent) was probably typical of the established mines in the middle of the eighteenth century.

Economic information concerning the *cuadrilla* and mines owned by Manuel Gómez de la Asprilla y Novoa is unfortunately sketchy, despite the fact that the Gómez family owned several of the largest slave gangs in the Chocó.[32] In 1757 the administrator of the mine, Pedro Salviejo (son-in-law of Manuel's brother Salvador) requested payment of his salary and out-of-pocket costs for maintaining the *cuadrilla* belonging to Manuel (he also administered this father-in-law's slave gang). He claimed that the total washings of the mine amounted to 16,000 pesos during the previous year and expenses amounted to 3,500 pesos.[33] Significantly, the stated expenses are very close to the estimate derived by the calculations for maintenance costs previously described (3,440 pesos). Because of the large capital investment depreciation costs were high, but the rate of profit was still 9.03 per cent.

The *cuadrilla* owned by Agustín Perea y Salinas returned a much higher profit a slave for its owner. Perea's slaves produced a significant gain—200 pesos a slave (children included), 333 pesos a prime slave—but they may have done even better. A short and obviously incomplete record book for *quintos* paid in Nóvita was used to derive the sum of 7,000 pesos, and only one entry was given under Perea's name.[34] Even with the suspicion that Perea may well have gleaned more from his mine in 1766, he clearly had a sound investment.

In reviewing the records of individual mines in the middle of the eighteenth century, I received the impression of continued growth. One example involves the mines and slaves owned in partnership by Francisco de Rivas and the cleric Juan de Bonilla y Delgado. The data are exceptionally good for the examination of growth because Bonilla y Delgado submitted detailed copies of the partnership's balance sheets to authorities in Popayán (because of inheritance problems) following the death of Rivas.

In 1752 the two men formed a company to exploit mines near Nóvita, sharing equally in expenses and profits. The initial investment included 33 slaves worth 12,645 pesos, together with another 12,645 pesos in cash and mining supplies (one partner put up the slaves, the other an equal value in cash and equipment).[35] By 1759 they owned 98 slaves, and in 1768 (the year Rivas died) the total value of their property was 78,980.1 pesos (212 slaves valued at 67,190 pesos; mines, houses, agricultural property, and tools worth 11,790.1 pesos). Therefore, in a period of sixteen years their total assets had increased 53,690.1 pesos.

During the sixteen-year partnership, from 1752 to 1768, the gross income (production, sales, and *jornales*) from the company's holdings amounted to 118,384 pesos. Expenditures totaled 98,559.2 pesos (these costs included food, clothing, tools, taxes, *visitas*, administration, the purchase of land and slaves, medicine, loans, and interest rates on loans). Net income (because of the lengthy time period under examination and because new slaves, tools, and land were purchased, depreciation should be included in total costs) amounted to 19,828 pesos.[36] By adding net income to the increase in assets, the two partners were ahead 73,514.6 pesos, still retained their original investment, and made an average of 4,595 pesos a year.

Although it is difficult to determine the exact rate of profit on their investment—the profits and expenditures for any given year are unknown—averages can be used to approximate the rate of profit. The average amount of capital investment (using the figures 25,290 pesos in 1752, 45,733 pesos in 1759, and 78,980 pesos in 1768) was 50,008 pesos. Average net income (4,595 pesos) divided by average capital investment (50,008 pesos) yields an average annual rate of profit of 9.19 per cent. Undeniably, Bonilla y Delgado and Rivas considered their investment worthwhile and, instead of taking out all profits, they reinvested income. In sixteen years they almost quadrupled their original investment, greatly increased the size of their holdings, and earned a total profit of 73,514.6 pesos.

In 1789 Manuel Gómez became entangled in a lawsuit over the sale and ownership of several slaves. During the course of the litigation he mentioned that rentals and washings from his property at Yalí (above Nóvita) had yielded a net profit of over 80,000 pesos during the previous twenty-five years.[37] That was only the profit he declared in a lawsuit against his interests. It is reasonable to assume that after a quarter of a century he had been able to deduct all pertinent costs and that the 80,000 pesos are indications of pure profit. Some years were doubtless more lucrative than others, but for the twenty-five-year period the Yalí mine and *cuadrilla* averaged a yearly profit of 3,000 pesos.[38] However, because of the size of his slave gang, the average rate of profit on the capital invested was only 6.4 per cent. The earnings declared by Gómez may well be viewed with some suspicion. The fact that he remained in the Chocó and reinvested earnings means that profits probably exceeded those he declared.

The mine owned by Doña María Gertrudis Gonzáles de Trespalacios is significant because it demonstrates the importance of depreciation in determining rates of profit. The mine yielded a negative rate of profit (-5.71 per cent), but gross income (1,324 pesos) exceeded yearly maintenance costs (830 pesos). For several years following the death of her husband in 1779, Doña María received money from her administrator. She apparently did not suspect that her mine was in growing financial difficulties. In 1790 her mine became a declared failure.[39]

A lawsuit ensued, and Governor Manuel Junguito Baquerizo intervened, stating that the mine had been poorly supervised and administered during the decade after 1779. Most of the slaves on the *cuadrilla,* Governor Junguito said, were too old, too young, or too sick to be of any help. In addition, many slaves of prime working age had purchased freedom, and the remaining *útil* slaves did not produce enough to support the *cuadrilla.* Debts accumulated rapidly, and creditors wanted the governor to liquidate the mine's assets. Doña María, however, remembering what were termed "high profits of the past," did not wish to sell. Governor Junguito could not legally force the sale, since no debts were owed to the crown. For the benefit of all concerned, he assigned the lieutenant governor of Quibdó to personally supervise the mine.[40] The decision was correct, for a decade later the mine was once again producing profits.*

The final two models are similar in that they demonstrate a good rate of profit for the owners. In both of these cases the number of working slaves and children was specifically given: Palacios and Quintana owned nineteen *esclavos útiles*; María de la Cruz Lemus had only twelve. Not surprisingly, the formers' total production was higher by 1,140 pesos.[41]

Since the value of slaves had recently dropped, the high return experienced by Palacios, Quintana, and Doña María was necessary to sustain the loss in capital investment which resulted from the devaluation of slaves. It is significant that during the last decade of the colonial period manumission through self-purchase was common, and most of those able to purchase freedom were working slaves (male and female) in their twenties and thirties. Importantly, as late as the 1790's, slaveowners still collected 500 pesos from prime slaves who bought their freedom even though they were sold on the open market for only 300 pesos. Many owners recouped capital investment by permitting a higher number of self-purchases while at the same time making their mining operations smaller and more efficient. The large number of children present on the *cuadrillas* then replaced prime slaves who had purchased their liberty.

* Matías Palacios and Domingo Quintana (in the next sample case) were heirs of Doña María Gertrudis Gonzáles de Trespalacios.

As the twelve samples demonstrate, there was a considerable range in the sums accumulated by mine owners in the Chocó. Those with the most slaves normally made the most money but not necessarily the highest rate of profit. Depreciation was a more important factor with the larger *cuadrillas*. Food supply was also a greater problem, more prime slaves had to be kept in agricultural ventures, and, despite lower costs for each slave, earnings were generally lower. Eleven of the twelve slaveowners whose records are examined here gained income after expenditures and depreciation were deducted from their earnings, and ten of the twelve slaveowners doubtless succeeded with their ventures.

The rates of profit derived from mining ventures in the Chocó would be especially revealing if they were compared to other investment possibilities. Unfortunately no study has yet been made of the rate of return on investment for colonial New Granada. Frank Safford meticulously compiled rates of profit for the years 1831 to 1865 and estimated the profitability of various careers in central Colombia during that time. Safford stated that investors in land on the *Sabana* of Bogotá (a secure investment) could expect a return of about 5 per cent.[42] However, merchants importing products from Europe could expect a return on investment of 16 to 50 per cent, although higher risks were involved.[43] The latter figures are compatible with most of the interest rates earned in the Chocó.

Several comparative possibilities for the eighteenth century can be found. Interest rates for borrowing money during the colonial period (occasionally from the crown but usually from religious orders) ranged from 3 to 5 per cent.[44] Slaveowners in the Chocó who borrowed money (often from businessmen in the Cauca Valley) paid 5 per cent a year.[45] In Mexico at the end of the eighteenth century the more cautious businessman avoided direct mining investments, preferring to lend money at five per cent interest to nonmining ventures.[46] D. A. Brading showed that several merchants in Mexico made profits ranging from 3.2 to 9.2 per cent in the middle of the eighteenth century,[47] and haciendas returned between 3.5 and 7 per cent rates of profit.[48]

185

It is impossible to determine whether commercial and agricultural profits in New Granada were similar to those in Mexico, but, since individuals were willing to lend money to miners at 5 per cent (and doubtless believed their investments secure), it is unlikely that continued returns on the various other secure investments ranged much higher. Therefore, a profitable return on capital invested in the Chocó would have to be at least 5 per cent and, in view of the work and risks involved in establishing and maintaining a *cuadrilla*, should probably be from 7 to 10 per cent. Ten of the twelve models previously presented showed returns on investment greater than 5 per cent, and seven of the twelve had rates of profit of more than 10 per cent. These interest rates are even higher than those compiled by Fogel and Engerman for North American slavery. For most owners slavery and mining in the Chocó were indeed profitable investments.

All these investment rates represent probable minimum profits, for none of them account for the region's acknowledged and heavy contraband trade in gold dust. While estimates including the fraudulent extraction of bullion could easily be employed in the twelve case studies, it is of greater significance to consider the illicit commerce in relation to total production for the entire Chocó. *Quinto* records have already been used to derive total declared production (Table 9), and census reports for 1724, 1759, 1778, 1782, and 1804 (Table 7) enumerate the number of slaves for specific years. This information, added to total capital, depreciation, and maintenance costs—deduced as in Table 15—permits use of the formula $Y = \frac{a-(b+c)}{x+z}$ to compute rates of profit for the entire Chocó (Table 16).

In order to evaluate the effect of contraband trade, each of the selected years is divided into three categories: (1) the rate of profit at the amount of bullion legally declared; (2) the rate of profit if one-third of the gold produced was illegally exported; and (3) the rate of profit if one-half of the bullion produced was illegally exported. The difference between these rates of profit is revealing. If the Chocó miners were not involved in contraband (category 1), then as a group they lost money in 1759, 1778, and

1782. There is a negative rate of profit of –1.25 in 1759, –4.32 in 1778, and –6.03 in 1782. Moreover, as the number of slaves increased during these years, the rate of profit declined. Under category 2 the rate of profit is positive for three of the four years after 1759, but competitive to low interest rates of the time only in 1759 and 1804. In fact, in 1782 it might have been wiser to invest elsewhere even under category 3, since an investment in the Chocó yielded only 5.16 per cent.

Under 3 mining was a profitable venture producing the following positive rates of profit: 34.32 per cent in 1724; 12.69 per cent in 1759; 7.96 per cent in 1778; 5.16 per cent in 1782; and 18.87 per cent in 1804. Category 3 must have been close to the real situation. Except in 1724, the alternatives (1 and 2), while possible, are unrealistic, for they propose that slavery was an unsound investment yielding either a loss or a marginal return. Since owners continued their investments in the Chocó for almost a century, it is extremely unlikely that the rates of profit presented in the first two categories were the norm. Hence the contention that one-half the gold mined in the Chocó was illegally exported is sustained by the computation of rates of profit.

The interest rates compiled in Table 16 also help explain the decline in the number of slaves (and perhaps prices as well) in the Chocó after 1788. Slave prices and population figures show that the period of greatest mining extension in the Chocó was from about 1725 to 1785. During the first half of the century, mine owners exploited rich deposits and made good profits but had fewer slaves. Even then, however, supply problems existed. High profits encouraged the owners to reinvest heavily, and the number of slaves in the Chocó almost doubled in the brief thirteen-year span from 1759 to 1782. But the owners had overextended themselves, and by the 1780's they increasingly found their holdings less profitable.

By 1782 the region was oversupplied with slaves, return on investment declined rapidly, and the fevered activity of the previous decades abated. Once rates of profit declined, so did enthusiasm. Owners pleaded for help, and the crown responded by reopening the Atrato River to maritime commerce and providing *bozales* for sale at attractive terms. Owners helped themselves by cutting back on the number of slaves they owned (and thus on their maintenance costs), and they exploited only richer ground with a smaller number of slaves. Owners who permitted or encouraged manumission through self-purchase decreased the size of their *cuadrillas* and at the same time retained much of their original capital investment. Maintenance, food supply, and administration became easier and less expensive, and, as the *cuadrillas* became smaller, rates of profit and total proceeds once again increased.

Understanding the rates of profitability in the Chocó, however, does not completely explain why owners ceased to invest capital in the region after about 1782. A shrewd owner, for example, might have considered selling his prime slaves (through self-purchase) for 500 pesos and purchasing others on the open market for 300 pesos. Owners may also have manumitted older or sick slaves in order to curtail costs, but there is no evidence that this took place.

The reason for the decline in investments in the Chocó must remain speculative, but it is likely that during this same period (1782 to 1808) owners found alternative investments more attractive. With the advent of the Bourbon reforms and the accompanying liberalization of Spanish trade regulations in the second half of the eighteenth century, it is probable that many of the Popayán-based owners shifted a large percentage of their investments to merchant endeavors.[49]

Several sources document increased commercial activity on the part of many of the Popayán families who owned slaves in the Chocó. Both the Popayán Papers in the Southern Historical Collection at the University of North Carolina at Chapel Hill and the José María Mosquera Collection in the Archivo Central del Cauca in Popayán show that the latter part of the eighteenth century was a period of considerable commercial expansion in western Colombia. The important Popayán families could deal directly with Spain at the end of the eighteenth century (the monopoly of the Cádiz *consulado* had been broken under the Bourbon reforms), and they increased their business activities in the Cauca Valley and beyond.[50]

Popayán owners still needed the gold produced from their mining ventures to supply them with working capital, and so they did not abandon their holdings in the Chocó. But they did not eagerly reinvest earnings there. Investments in the Chocó became holding actions. The *cuadrillas*, no longer supplied with newly purchased *bozales*, dwindled in size through natural attrition and manumission.

Slavery in the Chocó, therefore, had certain economic limits. The optimum profitable number of slaves that could be engaged in the Chocó mining ventures, under the systems of labor and food supply employed, was less than 5,000. Significantly, gold production increased toward the end of the eighteenth century, even though the number of slaves declined. Whether or not subsequent investment would have again increased is unknown, because the Wars of Independence erupted and changed all commercial activities.

It might well be argued that slavery in the Chocó temporarily became cumbersome and inefficient, but slavery was in no danger of self-destruction. Precious metals remained available, and the slaveholders simply readjusted the size of their *cuadrillas* until they once again experienced a good return on investment. The profitability of slavery clearly played an important role in the Colombian Chocó.

Conclusion

Life in the Chocó centered around a gold-producing economy based on thousands of slaves, as well as several hundred independent white and *libre* prospectors who labored on small claims. Indians produced food for these miners and slaves, and they also served as transporters of goods. White merchants bought and sold various products, and the crown officials supposedly regulated commerce, prevented fraud, collected the king's duties, protected Indians and slaves from mistreatment, and oversaw the growth and development of placer mining. Everyone depended in some way upon the yield of the mines. Only escaped slaves and those Indians and freedmen who willfully separated themselves from society remained outside the gold-oriented economy.

By the end of the colonial period the Spaniards had governed the Chocó for more than a century. The crown had attempted to establish an orderly administrative system with a regular chain of government command, over 75 million pesos worth of gold had been extracted, and slavery had been a profitable venture for most mine owners.

Rates of profit fluctuated with the production of the mines, the number of slaves held, the problems of supply, depreciation, and maintenance costs. Normally mine owners made higher profits during the period from 1680 to 1750 as they exploited easily accessible rich deposits with smaller *cuadrillas*. As the century progressed, more and more slaves were imported, costs increased, and rates of profit declined. The mine owners then ceased reinvesting capital in *bozales*, and their mines became holding actions. The total number of slaves in the region declined because of manumission, flight, and death. It is also likely that the Bourbon reforms stimulated commercial activity in the second half of the eighteenth century, thus making alternative investments more attractive. Needing hard cash, mine owners did not abandon the Chocó. And, despite a lack of investment in *bozales*, the mine owners held on to the belief that slavery was the best system for exploiting the placer mines.

In spite of the fortunes made in the Chocó, in 1810 the region remained an underdeveloped area. Governor Carlos de Ciaurriz' 1808 report to the viceroy revealed that there were few roads, decent houses, official buildings, churches, or schools. The region was poorly supplied, prices were high, and, the governor continued, there was scant evidence of social refinement. Indians, mistreated and in great part "uncivilized," had not learned the rudiments of the Christian religion. Slave-dependent mining, small, isolated, and disorganized dirty villages, and contraband trade were all major problems.* Foreign travelers in the early nineteenth century confirmed the governor's analysis.

Unfortunately, many individuals who could have been influential in directing internal improvements did little or nothing. No wealthy educated group of any size resided in the Chocó. Many of the white officials and miners who worked in the area viewed their tenure as temporary and were never, therefore, vitally concerned with making changes that might limit their profits or alter the productivity of the mines. Absentee owners of the mines and *cuadrillas* likewise paid heed to what they could extract, not what they might contribute.

The whites of the Chocó, both resident and absentee, created their own laws and resented the crown's attempts to limit economic freedom. Owners and officials repeatedly violated regulations concerning gold dust and commerce, and they bitterly objected to the

---

* Governor Ciaurriz' report was the most detailed account ever written by a Chocó official. The report included *visitas*, census data, descriptions of each settlement and road, and a number of recommendations. See AHNC, Visitas del Cauca 5, fols. 273–85 (1808).

establishment of a royal smeltery in Nóvita. Finally, in 1810, the white inhabitants of the Chocó overthrew Governor Juan de Aguirre, who insisted upon strict enforcement of crown regulations, and declared independence from Spain.

It is also significant that freedmen did not aid in the development of the Chocó. Most *libres* rejected coexistence with the whites, seeking freedom from Spanish domination by moving to isolated jungle homes. The advantages of greater self-determination apparently outweighed all other considerations. Their chances of monetary or political success were few as a result of this seclusion, but in any case they were limited in their opportunities for jobs, education, or authority even when they remained in the Spanish communities.

The original occupants of the region, the Indians, did not benefit from the forced labor of the *corregimientos*. The slaves, although occupying the mining camps with a greater permanence than either the freedmen or the whites, lacked cohesiveness because of new arrivals, death, flight, and manumission. Without effective influence from either officials or the church, slaveowners devised codes that were pragmatic and consistent with their desires. The physical welfare of slaves was stressed because slaves were productive when they were present and in good health. The safety valve of manumission had an obvious impact upon slavery in the Chocó, and was a major factor in shaping behavior and attitudes of both masters and slaves. Nevertheless, the nonwhite inhabitants of the Chocó, important as they were, could do little to change the gold-oriented society they neither created nor controlled.

The strongest influence of the frontier on race relations in the Chocó involved not slavery but the role of the freedman. *Libres* did not aid in the production of wealth for the owners or officials of the region and were thus unimportant to the economic welfare of the ruling elite. In fact, freedmen were distrusted because of the example they set and because of the problems they might cause. *Libres*, by choice and necessity, remained isolated from white society. Since the region lacked urban centers, many possibilities present in other populated sections of Latin America for coexistence, assimilation, or advancement were nonexistent. Blacks never achieved the degree of social mobility in the Chocó that Frank Tannenbaum, Herbert Klein, or Carl Degler described for other areas. There is no evidence to support Tannenbaum's contention that the "Spanish acceptance of the black's moral personality" facilitated a natural incorporation into society.

Spanish occupants in the Chocó failed to diversify the economy, educate or Christianize the inhabitants, establish justice, enforce prescribed laws, encourage unity, or create effective understanding of and loyalty to the Spanish imperial system. The Spaniards chose to sacrifice these elements of development in order to maintain profits and control the nonwhite majority. As a result, the Chocó in 1810, was still a mining frontier on the edge of settled New Granada.

Certainly climate and physical isolation hindered progress in the region. Ironically, the Chocó's mineral treasure also prevented development. The only real interest of the mine owners and officials was the rapid accumulation of wealth, and quick profits could be made through mining, fraud, graft, and a misuse of power. More bullion required increased or more efficient mining rather than a diversification of the economy.

Slaveholders monopolized mining, and royal officials controlled transportation and much of the food production. There were few resident merchants or prospectors and virtually no independent farmers. No prosperous group of citizens populated the settlements or filled the gaps between the mining camps. Despite the opportunities of the gold fields, Spanish colonization rarely occurred because of geography, climate, and the need for capital and slaves.

The Chocó was a frontier mining region that reflected the gold-rush pattern of rapid expansion and exploitation. The Spaniards created a hollow frontier, weakly bound together by self-seeking miners, officials, and priests. Loyalty was pledged to self, and—even among the Indians, slaves, and freedmen—individualism was the prevailing philosophy.

Appendix

Table 1
White Population, 1778–82

Year	Province Atrato	San Juan	Total	Total Population for Chocó	Percentage of Whites
1778	174	158	332	14,662	2.26
1779	171	164	335	15,286	2.19
1781	175	161	336	16,707	2.01
1782	181	178	359	17,898	2.00

SOURCES: 1778, AHNC, Censos de Varios Departmentos 6, fol. 381; 1779, *ibid.*, fol. 481; 1781, AHNC, Miscelánea 129, fol. 106; 1782, AHNC, Censos de Varios Departamentos 6, fol. 377.

Table 2
White Population, Male and Female, 1779

Province	Male	Female	Married Male	Female	Single Male	Female
Atrato	103	61	35	19	59	42
San Juan	101	70	32	30	59	40
Total	204	131	67	49	118	82

SOURCE: 1779, Censos de Varios Departamentos 6, fol. 481.

195

Slavery on the Spanish Frontier

Table 3
Indian Population, 1660–1808

Year	Province		Total for the Chocó
	Atrato	San Juan	
1660	20,000	40,000	60,000
1763	—	—	4,732
1778	3,755	1,659	5,414
1779	3,864	1,829	5,693
1781	4,334	1,868	6,202
1782	4,445	2,107	6,552
1783	-4,415	—	—
1808	2,764	1,686	4,450

SOURCES: See Table 7. Dash indicates information unavailable.

Table 4
Indian Population by *Corregimiento*, 1782

Corregimiento	Married Males	Single Males	Married Females	Single Females	Total
Province of Nóvita (San Juan):					
Nóvita	0	0	0	0	0
Tadó	138	176	142	148	604
Noanamá	152	189	151	227	719
Los Brazos	50	75	50	56	231
Sipí	32	48	32	44	156
Las Juntas	30	57	30	23	140
Baudó	27	42	30	58	157
Cajón	0	0	0	0	0
Total	429	587	435	556	2,007
Province of Citará (Atrato):					
Quibdó	324	430	329	450	1,533
Lloró	249	318	249	375	1,191

Appendix

Corregimiento	Married Males	Single Males	Married Females	Single Females	Total
Chamí	189	364	189	320	1,062
Beté	24	21	25	36	106
Bebará	31	45	31	42	149
Murrí	46	95	46	92	279
Pabarandó	21	41	21	23	106
Cupica	30	29	30	30	119
Total	914	1,343	930	1,368	4,545
Total for Chocó	1,343	1,930	1,355	1,924	6,552

SOURCE: 1782, AHNC, Censos de Varios Departamentos 6, fol. 377.

Table 5
Black Population, 1636–1851

Year	Slaves Atrato	Slaves San Juan	Slaves Total	Freedmen Atrato	Freedmen San Juan	Freedmen Total	Total in the Chocó
1636	—	—	100	—	—	—	—
1680	—	—	41	—	—	—	—
1688	—	—	100	—	—	—	—
1704	—	—	600	—	—	—	—
1724	—	—	2,000	—	—	—	—
1759	1,233	2,685	3,918	—	—	—	—
1763	—	—	4,231	—	—	—	—
1778	2,039	3,717	5,756	1,185	1,975	3,160	8,916
1779	2,183	3,733	5,916	1,237	2,111	3,348	9,264
1781	2,180	4,377	6,557	1,611	2,001	3,612	10,169
1782	2,156	4,932	7,088	1,660	2,239	3,899	10,987
1783	2,162	—	—	1,710	—	—	—
1808	1,206	3,762	4,968	—	—	15,184	20,152
1825	—	—	4,843	—	—	—	—
1835	1,265	1,995	3,260	—	—	—	—
1843	854	1,642	2,496	—	—	—	—
1851	666	1,059	1,725	—	—	—	—

SOURCES: See Table 7. Dash indicates information unavailable.

Table 6
Black Population, Slave and Free, 1782

Town	Married Males		Single Males		Married Females		Single Females	
	Slave	Free	Slave	Free	Slave	Free	Slave	Free
Province of Nóvita:								
Nóvita	312	85	535	130	315	85	570	230
Tadó	232	85	561	214	215	72	461	157
Noanamá	2	33	4	69	2	35	2	43
Los Brazos	110	60	200	120	90	60	125	115
Sipí	130	46	310	152	130	46	286	133
Los Juntas	7	5	18	10	6	5	12	12
Baudó	0	20	0	29	0	20	0	21
El Cajón	50	26	92	47	50	25	50	49
Totals	843	360	1,720	771	808	348	1,561	760
Province of Citará:								
Quibdó	133	126	314	294	130	149	241	288
Lloró	56	47	352	82	58	47	110	79
Chamí	1	0	4	1	2	0	1	7
Beté	3	11	7	35	4	11	6	63
Bebará	102	50	232	103	102	50	173	99
Murrí	4	11	6	12	4	12	6	10
Pabarandó	18	18	78	24	17	21	53	9
Cupica	0	6	1	0	0	0	0	7
Totals	315	263	994	551	317	290	530	556
Total for Chocó	1,158	623	2,714	1,322	1,125	638	2,091	1,316

SOURCE: AHNC, Censos de Varios Departamentos 6, fol. 377.

Appendix

Table 7

Chocó Population, 1636–1856

Year	White	Slaves	Freedmen	Indians	Total for Province of Atrato	Total for Province of Nóvita	Total for Chocó
1636	—	100	—	—	—	—	—
1660	—	—	—	60,000	—	—	—
1680	—	41	—	—	—	—	—
1688	—	100	—	—	—	—	—
1704	—	600	—	—	—	—	—
1724	—	2,000	—	—	—	—	—
1759	—	3,918	—	—	—	—	—
1763	—	4,231	—	4,732	—	—	13,963
1778	332	5,756	3,160	5,414	7,132	7,530	14,662
1779	335	5,916	3,348	5,693	7,482	7,804	15,286
1781	336	6,557	3,612	6,202	8,300	8,707	16,707
1782	359	7,088	3,899	6,552	8,442	9,456	17,898
1783	—	—	—	—	8,464	—	—
1808	400	4,968	15,184	4,450	—	—	25,000
1820	—	—	—	—	—	—	22,000
1825	—	4,843	—	—	—	—	17,250
1835	—	3,260	—	—	9,669	11,525	21,194
1843	—	2,496	—	—	13,409	13,951	27,360
1851	—	1,725	—	—	22,597	21,052	43,649
1856	—	—	—	—	23,752	22,110	45,862

SOURCES: 1636, West, *Colonial Placer Mining*, 17; 116, *Geografía del Chocó*, 85 (total does not include the still hostile Cuna Indians, estimated at 30,000); 1680, AHNC, Real Hacienda 45, fol. 399; 1688, AHNC, Caciques e Indios 10, fol. 495; 1704, AHNC, Minas del Cauca 6, fol. 651; 1724, AGI, Audiencia de Santa Fe, leg., 362, Informe de José Manuel Caycedo, Santa Fe de Bogotá, July 24, 1724; 1759, AHNC, Negros y Esclavos del Cauca 4, fols. 558–90; 1763, AHNC, Mejores Materiales 2, fols. 117–124; 1778, AHNC, Censos de Varios Departamentos 6, fol. 381; 1779, *ibid.*, fol. 481; 1781, AHNC, Miscelánea 129, fol. 106; 1782, Censos de Varios Departamentos 6, fol. 377; 1783, *ibid.*, fol. 379 (only includes data for province of Citará); 1808, Data is combined for several years, 1804–1806 for slaves, 1806 for Indians, and 1808 for total, see AHNC, Visitas del Cauca 5, fols. 23–120, 145–249, 282–83; and José Manuel Restrepo, *Historia de la revolución*, I, 579, note 7; 1820, [Alexander Walker], *Colombia, Being an . . . Account of that Country . . .*, I, 376; 1825, Archivo del Congreso, Bogotá, Senado 56, Memorias de los ministros, fol. 180; 1835, AHNC, Censos Generales de Población de la República; 1843, *ibid.*; 1851, *ibid.*; 1856, AHNC (República), Gobernaciones 195, fol. 908.

199

Table 8
Carat Weight and Actual Value of Chocó Gold

	Gold Sent from the Province of Nóvita		Gold Sent from the Province of Quibdó	
	1754	1755	1754	1755
Castellanos in gold dust received	3,578.3	2,804.5	1,588.6	1,216.1
Loss through smelting (*merma*) in *castellanos*	118.0	94.5	51.6	50.1
Weight in *castellanos* after *merma*	3,460.3	2,710.0	1,537.0	1,166.0
Weight in *castellanos* at 22 carats	3,200.0	2,594.0	1,517.0	1,150.0
Value of *castellano* at 20 ½– 21 ½ carats* (in pesos)	$ 2.3	$ 2.3	$ 2.4	$ 2.4
Value *of castellano* at 22 carats (in pesos)	$ 2.5	$ 2.5	$ 2.5	$ 2.5
Value officially given of the 22-carat gold	$8,219.1	$6,498.6	$3,895.6	$2,949.3
Original value of the gold in the Chocó at $2 pesos a *castellano*	$7,156.6	$5,609.2	$3,177.2	$2,432.2
Difference between value of gold in Chocó and Santa Fe	$1,062.5	$ 889.4	$ 718.4	$ 517.1

SOURCE: Record of *quintos* received from the Chocó at the Casa de Fundición in Santa Fe. AHNC, Real Hacienda (anexo) 7, fols. 361–63 (1754–55).
* 20 ½ carats for the province of Nóvita; 21 ½ carats for the province of Quibdó.

Appendix

Table 9

Gold Mined in the Chocó on Which the *Quinto* Was Paid

Years	*Quinto* Collected in *Castellanos**	Total Gold Declared in *Castellanos**	Total Value in Silver Pesos	Average Yearly Value in Silver Pesos
1724–25	14,698	226,128	533,014	266,507
1726–30	49,719	764,902	1,788,249	357,650
1731–35	51,236	788,251	1,848,560	369,712
1736–40	53,518	823,357	1,928,379	385,676
1741–45	53,632	825,114	1,930,780	386,156
1746–50	52,479	808,023	1,883,877	376,776
1751–55	40,752	679,200	1,589,147	317,829
1756–60	34,995	582,433	1,366,134	273,227
1761–65	38,084	634,740	1,488,494	297,699
1766–70	37,193	619,878	1,453,531	290,706
1771–75	39,046	650,772	1,518,788	303,758
1776–80	24,231	596,082	1,390,922	278,184
1781–85	18,340	611,347	1,427,897	285,579
1786–90	18,874	629,120	1,467,903	293,581
1791–95	20,035	667,837	1,553,381	310,676
1796–1800	20,354	578,483	1,583,482	316,696
1801–1803	11,328	377,599	882,268	294,089
Totals, 1724–1803	578,514	10,963,266	25,634,806	320,435

SOURCES: Cuentas de la Real Hacienda de Zitará, 1693–1760, AGI, Contaduría, leg. 1603; Cuentas . . . de Zitará 1761–1788, AGI, Audiencia de Santa Fe, leg. 901; Cuentas . . . de Zitará, 1788–1802, AGI, Audiencia de Santa Fe, leg. 902; Cuentas de la Real Hacienda de Nóvita, 1724–1760, AGI, Contaduria, leg. 1580; Cuentas de Nóvita, AGI, Audiencia de Santa Fe, leg. 881; Cuentas de . . . Nóvita, 1788–1802, AGI, Audiencia de Santa Fe, legs. 882, 883; AHNC, Minas 3 (parte II), fols. 127–207 (1803).

* The assayed value of the *castellano* from Quibdó was 2.4 pesos, from Nóvita, 2.3 pesos. Proceeds from Nóvita and Quibdó have been combined in this account. It should also be remembered that the *quinto* collected did not remain constant but dropped as the century progressed.

Slavery on the Spanish Frontier

Table 10

Average Value of Prime Slaves

Year	Average Value in Silver Pesos	Number of Observations
1711	525	43
1725	517	47
1741	520	84
1744	500	19
1752	508	19
1761	500	12
1768	490	79
1779	481	51
1788–89	305	128
1797–98	300	103

SOURCES: 1711, ACC, Signatura 9757; 1725, AHNC, Minas del Cauca 6, fols. 169–75; 1741, AHNC, Minas del Cauca 5, fols. 824–30; 1744, ACC, Signatura 9983; 1752, ACC, Signatura 10362, fols. 103–105; 1761, AHNC, Minas del Cauca 6, fols. 578–81; 1768, ACC, Signatura 10362, fols. 37–42; 1779, AHNC, Minas del Cauca 3, fols. 11–14, AHNC, Minas del Cauca 5, fols. 11–30; 1788–89, Protocolos 17 (Notaría del Chocó), fols. 10–70 and AHNC, Esclavos I, fols. 479–531; 1797, AHNC, Protocolos 16 (Notaría del Chocó), fols. 42–142 and AHNC, Contrabandos 19, fol. 97.

Table 11

Average Value of All Slaves

Year	Average Value in Silver Pesos	Number of Observations
1711	415	76
1725	407	69
1744	380	85
1752	383	33
1761	370	27
1768	327	212
1779	293	137
1788–89	238	427
1797–98	240	193

SOURCES: See Table 10. The year 1797 includes AHNC, Miscelánea 119, fols. 578–92 (1798).

202

Appendix

Table 12

Average Value of Slaves by Age and Sex, 1768, 1779 (in Silver Pesos)

	Male		Female			
Age	Average Value	Number of Observations	Average Value	Number of Observations	Average Value	Total Observations
Under 5	145	18	146	24	146	42
5–9	244	15	240	17	241	32
10–14	356	8	351	12	353	20
15–19	489	9	500	8	494	17
20–29	486	15	453	19	467	34
30–34	500	13	475	12	488	25
35–39	480	5	467	3	475	8
40–49	393	7	375	10	382	17
50–59	234	12	204	6	224	18
60–69	147	3	158	2	151	5
Over 70	75	18	44	11	63	29
All slaves	301	123	301	124	301	247

SOURCES: 1768, ACC, Signatura 10362, fols. 37–42, 136 slaves; 1779, AHNC, Minas del Cauca 5, fols. 10–30, 111 slaves.

Table 13

Male- and Female-Slave Ratios

	Male		Female		
Year	Number	Per Cent	Number	Per Cent	Total
1778	3,054	53.1	2,702	46.9	5,756
1779	3,145	53.2	2,771	46.8	5,916
1781	3,585	54.7	2,972	45.3	6,557
1782	3,872	54.7	3,216	45.3	7,088
1808	2,540	51.2	2,428	48.8	4,968

SOURCES: 1778, AHNC, Censos de Varios Departamentos 6, fol. 381; 1779, *ibid.*, fol. 481; 1781, AHNC, Miscelánea 129, fol. 106; 1782, AHNC, Censos de Varios Departamentos 6, fol. 377; 1808, AHNC, Visitas del Cauca 5, fols. 124–42, 250–72.

Table 14

Male and Female Black Population, 1782

Class	Male	Female	Total
Slave	3,872	3,216	7,088
Freedmen	1,945	1,954	3,899
Total	5,817	5,170	10,987

SOURCE: AHNC, Censos de Varios Departamentos 6, fol. 377.

Table 15
Representative Models for Profits from the Chocó Mines

Name	Time-Span Date	No. of slaves owned	*Util* slaves	*Chusma* slaves	Average value of slaves (x)	Value of *cuadrilla* (x)	Value of other property (z)	Total investment (x+z)
Francisco Arboleda Salazar	1690 (6 mos.)	18	—	—	$ 525	$ 9,450	$ 3,150	$12,600
Luis de Acuña y Berrios	1721–25 (5 yrs.)	48	29	19	$ 407	$19,536	$ 6,512	$26,048
Pedro de Mosquera and Miguel Moreno	1739–40 (16 mos.)	45	27	18	$ 395	$17,775	$ 5,925	$23,700
Francisco Maturana	1745 (1 yr.)	100	60	40	$ 390	$39,000	$13,000	$52,000
María Clemencia de Caicedo	1752–56 (5 yrs.)	80	48	32	$ 383	$30,640	$10,213	$40,853
Francisco de Rivas and Juan de Bonilla	1752–68 (16 yrs.)	114	68	46	$ 329	$37,506	$12,502	$50,008
Manuel de la Asprilla	1756 (1 yr.)	132	80	52	$ 375	$49,500	$15,500	$66,000
Agustín Perea y Salinas	1766 (1 yr.)	35	21	14	$ 332	$11,620	$ 3,873	$15,493
Manual de la Asprilla	1764–89 (25 yrs.)	125	75	50	$ 300	$37,500	$12,500	$50,000
María Gertrudis Gonzáles	1784–89 (5 yrs.)	32	19	13	$ 270	$ 8,640	$ 2,880	$11,520
Matías Palacios Domingo Quintana	1803 (1 yr.)	30	19	11	$ 240	$ 7,200	$ 2,400	$ 9,600
María de la Cruz Lemus	1803 (1 yr.)	30	12	18	$ 240	$ 7,200	$ 2,400	$ 9,600

Table 15 (Continued)

Depreciation (10 per cent) (b)	$ 1,260	$ 2,605	$ 2,370	$ 5,200	$ 4,085	—	$ 6,600	$ 1,549	—	$ 1,152	$ 960	$ 960
Maintenance costs (c)	$ 540	$ 1,250	$ 1,170	$ 2,600	$ 2,080	—	$ 3,440	$ 910	—	$ 830	$ 790	$ 720
Depreciation plus Maintenance costs (b+c)	$ 1,800	$ 3,855	$ 3,540	$ 7,800	$ 6,165	—	$10,040	$ 2,459	—	$ 1,982	$ 1,750	$ 1,680
Amount produced by mine (a)	$ 4,000	$21,249	$ 7,949	$30,000	$59,648	—	$16,000	$ 7,000	—	$ 6,621	$ 4,540	$ 3,400
Amount produced per year	$ 8,000	$ 4,250	$ 5,962	$30,000	$11,930	—	$16,000	$ 7,000	—	$ 1,324	$ 4,540	$ 3,400
Amount produced per slave per year	444	89	132	300	149	—	121	200	—	41	151	113
Net profit of mine a–(b+c)	$ 6,200	$ 1,974	$ 3,229	$22,000	$28,823	$73,515	$ 5,960	$ 4,541	$80,000	–$ 3,290	$ 2,790	$ 1,720
Net profit of mine per year	$ 6,200	$ 375	$ 2,422	$22,000	$ 5,765	$ 4,595	$ 5,960	$ 4,541	$ 3,200	–$ 658	$ 2,790	$ 1,720
Rate of profit (Y)	49.2%	1.51%	10.22%	42.69%	14.11%	9.19%	9.03%	29.31%	6.4%	–5.71%	29.06%	17.92%
$Y =$	$\dfrac{8,000-1,800}{12,600}$	$\dfrac{4,250-3,855}{26,048}$	$\dfrac{5,962-3,540}{23,700}$	$\dfrac{30,000-7,800}{52,000}$	$\dfrac{11,930-6,165}{40,853}$	$\dfrac{4,595}{50,008}$	$\dfrac{16,000-10,040}{66,000}$	$\dfrac{7,000-2,459}{15,493}$	$\dfrac{3,200}{50,000}$	$\dfrac{1,324-1,982}{11,520}$	$\dfrac{4,540-1,750}{9,600}$	$\dfrac{3,400-1,680}{9,600}$

$$Y = \frac{a-(b+c)}{x+z}$$

Table 16
Rate of Profit on Total Investment in Chocó

	1724	1759	1778	1782	1804
Number of slaves in the Chocó	2,000	3,918	5,756	7,088	4,968
Util slaves	1,200	2,351	3,454	4,253	2,981
Chusma slaves (for c)	800	1,567	2,302	2,835	1,987
Average value of slaves	$ 407	$ 375	$ 295	$ 270	$ 240
Total value of Chocó slaves (x)	$ 814,000	$1,469,250	$1,698,020	$1,913,760	$1,192,320
Value of other property (z)	$ 271,333	$ 489,750	$ 566,007	$ 637,920	$ 397,440
Total investment in the Chocó (x+z)	$1,085,333	$1,959,000	$2,264,027	$2,551,680	$1,589,760
Depreciation (10 per cent) (b)	$ 108,533	$ 195,900	$ 226,403	$ 255,168	$ 158,976
Maintenance costs (c)	$ 52,000	$ 101,870	$ 149,660	$ 184,290	$ 129,170
Depreciation plus maintenance costs (b+c)	$ 160,533	$ 297,770	$ 376,063	$ 439,458	$ 288,146
Amount produced by mines (a):					
If all was legally exported	$ 266,506	$ 273,227	$ 278,184	$ 285,579	$ 294,089
If one-third was illegally exported	$ 399,759	$ 409,840	$ 417,276	$ 428,369	$ 441,134
If one-half was illegally exported	$ 533,012	$ 546,454	$ 556,368	$ 571,158	$ 588,178
Rate of profit for entire Chocó					
If all was legally exported	9.76%	-1.25%	-4.32%	-6.03%	3.74%
If one-third was illegally exported	22.04%	5.72%	1.82%	-.04%	9.62%
If one-half was illegally exported	34.32%	12.69%	7.96%	5.16%	18.87%

$$Y = \frac{a-(b+c)}{x+z}$$

If all gold produced was legally declared:

	1724	1759	1778	1782	1804
	$Y\ \dfrac{266,506-160,533}{1,085,333}$	$Y\ \dfrac{273,227-297,770}{1,959,000}$	$Y\ \dfrac{278,184-376,063}{2,264,027}$	$Y\ \dfrac{285,579-439,458}{2,551,680}$	$Y\ \dfrac{294,089-288,146}{1,589,760}$

$$Y = \frac{a-(b+c)}{x+z}$$

If one-third of gold produced was contraband:

	1724	1759	1778	1782	1804
	$Y\ \dfrac{399,759-160,533}{1,085,333}$	$Y\ \dfrac{409,840-297,770}{1,959,000}$	$Y\ \dfrac{417,276-376,063}{2,264,027}$	$Y\ \dfrac{428,369-439,458}{2,551,680}$	$Y\ \dfrac{441,134-288,146}{1,589,760}$

$$Y = \frac{a-(b+c)}{x+z}$$

If one-half of gold produced was contraband:

	1724	1759	1778	1782	1804
	$Y\ \dfrac{533,012-160,533}{}$	$Y\ \dfrac{546,454-297,770}{}$	$Y\ \dfrac{556,368-376,063}{}$	$Y\ \dfrac{571,158-439,458}{}$	$Y\ \dfrac{588,178-288,146}{}$

Notes

PREFACE

1. *Anuario Colombiano de Historia Social y Cultural*, Vol. I, No. 1 (1963), 3–62.
2. *The Journal of Negro History*, Vol. LVI, No. 2 (1971), 105–18.
3. Ph.D dissertation, University of California, 1939.
4. Ph.D. dissertation, Columbia University, 1969.
5. Ph.D. dissertation, Tulane University, 1972.
6. David Paul Pavy, "The Negro in Western Colombia" (Ph. D. dissertation, Tulane University, 1967); Norman E. Whitten, "An Analysis of Social Structure and Change: Profile of a Northwest Ecuadorian Town" (Ph.D. dissertation, University of North Carolina, 1964).

INTRODUCTION

1. W. J. Cash, *The Mind of the South*, 9.
2. Frank Tannenbaum, *Slave and Citizen: The Negro in the Americas*.
3. For example, Herbert Klein, *Slavery in the Americas: A Comparative Study of Virginia and Cuba*; Stanley Elkins, *Slavery, A Problem in American Institutional and Intellectual Life*; Luis M. Díaz Soler, *Historia de la exclavitud negra en Puerto Rico*; Norman Meiklejohn, "The Observance of Negro Slave Legislation in Colonial Nueva Granada;" and David Chandler, "Health and Slavery: A Study of Health Conditions among Negro Slaves in the Viceroyalty of New Granada and its associated Slave Trade, 1600–1810," present studies which support and even expand Tannenbaum's original conclusions. On the other hand, David Brion Davis, *The Problem of Slavery in Western Culture*; Marvin Harris, *Patterns of Race in the Americas*; Stanley Stein, *Vassouras: A*

Brazilian Coffee County; A. J. R. Russell-Wood, "Colonial Brazil," in *Neither Slave Nor Free: The Freedman of African Descent in the Slave Societies of the New World*, ed. by David W. Cohen and Jack P. Green, 84–133; C. R. Boxer, *The Golden Age of Brazil, 1695–1750*; and Carl Degler, *Neither Black Nor White: Slavery and Race Relations in Brazil and the United States*, include evidence that is often critical of the Tannenbaum thesis.

4. Tannenbaum, *Slave and Citizen*, 43–69.

5. Harris, *Patterns of Race in the Americas*, 81–96.

6. Summaries of the various issues and arguments may be found in Eugene Genovese, "Materialism and Idealism in the History of Negro Slavery in the Americas," in *Slavery in the New World: A Reader in Comparative History*, 238–55; Davis, *The Problem of Slavery*, 225 *et passim*; Frederick P. Bowser, "The African in Colonial Spanish America; Reflections on Research Achievements and Priorities," *Latin American Research Review*, Vol. VII (Spring, 1972), 77–94; Degler, *Neither Black Nor White*, 25–92.

7. Davis, *The Problem of Slavery*; Eugene Genovese, *The World the Slaveholders Made*; Russell-Wood, "Colonial Brazil," in *Neither Slave Nor Free*, 84–133; Boxer, *The Golden Age of Brazil*.

8. Eric Williams, *Capitalism and Slavery*; Davis, *The Problem of Slavery*; Genovese, *The World the Slaveholders Made*.

9. Gilberto Freyre, *The Masters and the Slaves*; Donald Pierson, *Negroes in Brazil: A Study of Race Contact at Bahia*.

10. Degler, *Neither Black Nor White*, 224–25.

11. Klein, *Slavery in the Americas*, 147, 158–63, 184–227.

CHAPTER 1

1. *Geografía económica de Colombia*, VI, *Chocó*, 515.

2. Antonio B. Cuervo, ed., "Descripción de la provincia de Zitará y curso del Río Atrato (1753)," *Colección de documentos inéditos sobre la geografía y la historia de Colombia*, 4 vols., I, 323.

3. Robert Cooper West, *The Pacific Lowlands of Colombia: A Negroid Area in the American Tropics*, 11; Enrique Ortega Ricaurte, ed., "Relación del Chocó, o de las provincias de Citará y Nóvita . . . 1780," *Historia documental del Chocó*, 224.

4. *Geografía del Chocó*, 50.

5. *Technical Paper for the Atrato-Truandó Geophysical Survey*, 25–27; West stated that the average rainfall for Quibdó exceeded 400 inches a year (*Pacific Lowlands*, 25).

6. AHNC, Miscelánea 42, fols. 591–95 (1817).

7. West, *Pacific Lowlands*, 57–67; *Atrato-Truandó Survey*, 32–34.

8. Robert Cooper West, *Colonial Placer Mining in Colombia*, 14–15.

9. ". . . un abismo y orror [sic] de montañas, ríos y ciénagas." AHNC, Caciques e Indios 10, fol. 495 (1688).

10. For detailed descriptions of the Chocoano houses see *Geografía del Chocó*, 152–55; West, *Pacific Lowlands*, 114–25.

11. AHNC (República), Gobernación del Chocó 15, fols. 76–77 (1854); Augustín Codazzi, "Report to the governor of the province of the Chocó, Nóvita, March 22, 1853," *Jeografía física i política de las provincias de la Nueva Granada . . .* IV, 323; John C. Trautwine, "Rough Notes on an Exploration for an Inter-Oceanic Canal Route by way of the Rivers Atrato and San Juan, in New Granada, South America," *Journal of the Franklin Institute*, Vol. LVII (1854), 364.

12. Luis Ospina Vásquez, *Industría y protección en Colombia, 1810–1930*, 23–24.

13. AHNC, Poblaciones del Cauca 2, fol. 937 (1793); José Rafael Mosquera, representative from Nóvita to the Colombian Congress, wrote on June 12, 1823 that, although the governors of the Chocó had been legally required to reside in Nóvita, many of them had lived in Quibdó where they had engaged in contraband trade on the Atrato River. See Archivo del Congreso de Colombia, Bogotá, Camara de Representantes (Informes de Comisión), 45, fol. 163.

14. AHNC, Visitas del Cauca 5, fol. 274 (1808).

15. AHNC, Miscelánea 42, fols. 584–91 (1817).

16. AHNC, Visitas del Cauca 5, fol. 274 (1808).

17. *El Ensayo* (Quibdó), December 16, 1908.

18. *El Chocoano* (Quibdó) January 10, 1899.

19. Charles Stuart Cochrane, *Journal of a Residence and Travels in Colombia during the Years 1823 and 1824*, 2 vols., II, 446–47.

20. *El Cabildo de Quibdó a la nación y al Congreso*, Quibdó, July 17, 1851 (Cartagena, 1851). After 1803 Quibdó became the unofficial capital of the Chocó, see *idem*.

21. AHNC (República), Gobernaciones 166, fols. 502–504 (1851).

22. Codazzi, *Comisión corográfica*, 323.

23. Trautwine, "Exploration," 363. However, Trautwine was not overly impressed with Quibdó, *idem.*, 361–63.

24. AHNC, Miscelánea 72, fols. 215–16 (1806); AHNC, Visitas del Cauca 5, fol. 273 (1808).

25. Ricaurte, "Relación del Chocó . . . 1780," 232. The assumption that Cupica was abandoned is mine. I found no mention of Cupica in any document after 1791.

26. AHNC, Poblaciones del Cauca 2, fols. 854 (1793), 935 (1793).

27. AHNC, Visitas del Cauca 5, fol. 282 (1808).

28. AHNC, Aguardientes del Cauca 5, fol. 75 (n.d.); AHNC (República), Gobernación del Chocó 16, fols. 375–76 (1820).

29. AHNC, Impuestos Varios 1, fols. 143–45 (1778); AHNC, Milicias y Marinas 60, fol. 810 (1802).

30. AHNC, Censos de Varios Departamentos 6, fol. 377 (1782).

31. *Ibid.*, fols. 375–76 (for the year 1779).

32. AHNC, Reales Cédulas 8, fols. 290–91 (1725).

33. *Geografía del Chocó*, 85.

34. AHNC, Contrabandos 10, fols. 673–74 (1749).

35. AHNC, Censos de Varios Departamentos 6, fol. 381 (1779).

36. *Ibid.*, fol. 377 (1782).

37. AHNC, Contrabandos 18, fol. 332 (1783); AHNC, Problaciones del Cauca 2, fol. 936 (1793); AHNC, Historia Eclesiástica 11, fols. 47–51 (1802); AHNC, Alcabalas 17, fols. 861–63 (1807).

38. AHNC, Mejores Materiales 17, fols. 821–24 (1799); AHNC, Milicias y Marinas 124, fol. 1098 (1806); in 1804, almost 15 per cent of the tribute-paying Indians in the Chocó were listed as having fled (167 of 1195). See AHNC, Censos de Varios Departamentos 8, fol. 663 (1804).

39. AHNC, Caciques e Indios 23, fol. 955 (1708).

40. AHNC, Contrabandos 18, fol. 332 (1783). For a complete discussion of the health conditions encountered by blacks in New Granada see David L. Chandler, "Health and Slavery."

41. AHNC, Estadística 11 (parte I), fols. 221–22 (1808).

42. Robert Cushman Murphy, "Racial Succession in the Colombian Chocó," *Geographical Review*, Vol. XXIX (1939), 461–71; Norman Meiklejohn, "Negro Slave Legislation," 98.

43. William Paul McGreevey, *An Economic History of Colombia, 1845–1930*, 22; Eduardo Posada and Pedro M. Ibáñez, eds., "Relación

del . . . Arzobispo Obispo de Cordoba . . . 1789," in *Relaciones de mando*, 242.

CHAPTER 2

1. Robert Cushman Murphy, "The Earliest Spanish Advances Southward from Panama along the West Coast of South America," *Hispanic American Historical Review*, Vol. XXI (1941), 19; Francisco Cordoba, *Nociones de geografía e historia del Chocó*, 26; Joaquín Acosta, *Historia de la Nueva Granada*, 58–61; Kathleen Romoli, *Balboa of Darién: Discoverer of the Pacific*, 18–19, 30, 34.

2. Romoli, *Balboa*, 154.

3. One typical account of conquest ending in failure is told by Pedro Cieza de León, *The Travels of Pedro Cieza de León, A.D. 1532–50.* . . , 106–107.

4. Jorge Alvarez Lleras, *El Chocó*, 20–21; Antonio Olano, *Popayán en la colonia*, 26.

5. *Geografía del Chocó*, 220. At this early stage of the conquest the crown received none of this money. See AHNC, Caciques e Indios 10, fol. 533 (1693).

6. Cordoba, *Nociones del Chocó*, 51; Enrique Ortega Ricaurte, ed., "Descripción del río Atrato y sus afluentes . . .," *Historia documental del Chocó*, 101–105.

7. Fray Gregorio Arcila Robledo, *Apuntes históricos de la provincia Franciscana de Colombia*, 190–93.

8. *Ibid.*, 194.

9. AHNC, Empleados Públicos del Cauca 22, fol. 311 (1688).

10. Arcila Robledo, *Apuntes Franciscanas*, 194.

11. AHNC, Real Hacienda 45, fols. 395–99, 405–406 (1680).

12. *Ibid.*, fols. 397–99 (1680).

13. AHNC, Empleados Públicos del Cauca 22, fol. 311 (1688).

14. AHNC, Reales Cédulas 4, fol. 142 (1685); see also AHNC, Minas del Cauca 6, fol. 649 (1702).

15. AHNC, Caciques e Indios 23, fols. 849–53 (1686).

16. AHNC, Caciques e Indios 10, fol. 605 (1695).

17. AHNC, Minas del Cauca 6, fol. 651 (1702).

18. Olano, *Popayán en la colonia*, 45; *Geografía del Chocó*, 101.

19. Olano, *Popayán en la colonia*, 35; Jorge Mendoza Nieto, *Geografía ilustrada del Chocó*, 11.

20. Archivo Central del Cauca (hereafter cited as ACC), Popayán, Signatura 1831 (1689); ACC, Signatura 1933 (1691).

21. AHNC, Caciques e Indios 14, fol. 222 (1702).

22. AHNC, Minas del Cauca 6, fols. 653–66 (1702).

23. *Ibid.*, fols. 656–58 (1702); ACC, Signatura 2561 (1703); see also AHNC, Caciques e Indios 14, fols. 299–302 (1703). This 1702 invasion by the British was not directly connected with the ill-fated Scots colony of the Darién (1699–1701). The Scots settlement at Caladonia, however, did draw attention to the area and may have indirectly contributed to the invasion of the Chocó and Antioquia in 1702. See Francis Russell Hart, *The Disaster of Darién: The Story of the Scots Settlement and the Causes of its Failure, 1699–1701*; and John Prebble, *The Darién Disaster: A Scots Colony in the New World, 1698–1700*.

24. AHNC, Minas del Cauca 6, fol. 658 (1702). Although the Spanish officials continually referred to the invaders as the "English enemy," obviously men from other nations also participated.

25. AHNC, Caciques e Indios 14, fols. 237–41 (1703).

26. AHNC, Minas del Cauca 6, fols. 658–59 (1702).

CHAPTER 3

1. Juan Friede, ed. and comp., "Título de gobernador al licensiado Pascual de Andagoya para Río de San Juan (December 12, 1538)," *Documentos inéditos para la historia de Colombia*, 10 vols., V, 79–82.

2. *Geografía del Chocó*, 220–21.

3. AHNC, Empleados Públicos del Cauca 22, fols. 309–12 (1688).

4. AHNC, Contrabandos 5, fols. 448–54 (1695).

5. Although this information was not included in the *visitador's* report, other sources describe the trips and time involved. See for example AHNC, Visitas del Cauca 5, fols. 852–53 (1787).

6. AHNC, Contrabandos 5, fols. 448–54 (1695).

7. AHNC, Mejores Materiales 2, fols. 12–15 (1720); AHNC, Contrabandos 5, fols. 120–21 (1732); AHNC, Miscelánea 95, fols. 357–58 (1753); Alexander de Humboldt, *Political Essay on the Kingdom of New Spain*, 4 vols., III, 392.

8. Informe de José Manuel Caycedo, Santa Fe de Bogotá, July 24, 1724, Archivo General de Indias (hereafter cited as AGI) Sección 5, Audiencia de Santa Fe, leg. 362; AHNC, Contrabandos 17, fols. 262–63

(1732); AHNC, Miscelánea 139, fols. 510–12 (1755); Francisco Silves-tre, *Descripción del Reyno de Santa Fe de Bogotá* . . . *1789*, 73.

9. Elizabeth Donnan, *Documents Illustrative of the History of the Slave Trade to America*, 4 vols., II, xxxvn.

10. AHNC, Caciques e Indios 10, fol. 532 (1692).

11. AHNC, Contrabandos 5, fols. 448–50 (1695).

12. AHNC, Caciques e Indios 38, fol. 725 (1784). This valuable docu-ment includes a review of all the decrees issued by the *Real Audiencia* and the crown concerning navigation of the Atrato River.

13. AHNC, Contrabandos 5, fol. 451 (1695).

14. Autos sobre la fundición del castillo y forteleza nombrado San-tiago del río de Atrato, de la provincia del Zitará, AHNC, Gobernación del Chocó, Miscellaneous Boxes (1712).

15. *Ibid.*

16. Philip V to Governor Francisco de Ibero, AHNC, Contrabandos 22, fol. 1041 (1726); AHNC, Miscelánea 107, fols. 801–805 (1766); AHNC, Real Hacienda 43, fol. 249–54 (1786).

17. AHNC, Contrabandos 22, fol. 1039 (1779) and fol. 1042 (1780); AHNC, Real Hacienda 12, fols. 557–59 (1784).

18. AHNC, Caciques e Indios 10, fols. 628–30 (1715).

19. ACC, Signatura 8174 (1717).

20. *Ibid.*

21. AHNC, Archivos 4, fols. 489–91 (1719); Informe de Antonio de la Pedroza y Guerrero, April 29, 1720, Santa Fe de Bogotá, AGI, Sección 5, Audiencia de Santa Fe, leg. 362.

22. AHNC, Mejores Materiales 2, fols. 11–16 (1720).

23. AHNC, Reales Cédulas 7, fols. 94–95 (1724).

24. *Ibid.*

25. Informe de Antonio de la Pedroza y Guerrero, March 8, 1721, Santa Fe de Bogotá; Informe de José Manuel Caycedo, July 24, 1724, Santa Fe de Bogotá; Informe de Antonio de la Pedroza y Guerrero, Madrid, August 9, 1724. AGI, Sección 5, Audiencia de Santa Fe, leg. 362.

26. AHNC, Reales Cédulas 7, fols. 94–95 (1724).

27. ACC, Signatura 3362 (1726).

CHAPTER 4

1. AHNC, Minas del Cauca 1, fols. 120–21 (1751).

2. AHNC, Miscelánea 38, fols. 782, 784–89 (1705).

3. The major mining code used in the Chocó had been issued by the governor of Antioquia, Gaspar de Rodas, in 1587. The Rodas' mining code may be found in Vicente Restrepo, *Estudio sobre las minas de oro y plata de Colombia*, 2d ed. (1888), 249.

4. AHNC, Minas del Cauca 5, fols. 740–42 (1744); AHNC, Minas del Cauca 3, fols. 988–96 (1791).

5. See for example AHNC, Minas del Cauca 6, fols. 325, 370 (1734); AHNC, Minas del Cauca 3, fols. 177–83 (1792).

6. Bill of sale for mining rights sold to Marcelino de Mosquera y Figueroa, Buga, 1776, Archivo de la Compañía Minería Chocó Pacifico, Andagoya, Chocó (2,400 pesos); ACC, Signatura 6233 (1784) (5,141 pesos).

7. ACC, Signatura 6233 (1784); AHNC, Minas del Cauca 5, fols. 352–65 (1690).

8. AHNC, Minas del Cauca 5, fols. 352–65 (1690).

9. AHNC, Minas del Cauca 1, fols. 27–31 (1737).

10. AHNC, Minas del Cauca 5, fols. 847–50 (1741–47).

11. *Ibid.*, fols. 847–49 (1747).

12. West, *Pacific Lowlands*, 176.

13. AHNC, Visitas del Cauca 5, fol. 282 (1808).

14. West, *Pacific Lowlands*, 176.

15. AHNC, Minas del Cauca 6, fol. 898 (1728).

16. Ignacio Mosquera to José María Mosquera, Nóvita, February 10, 1782, ACC, José María Mosquera Collection.

17. West, *Pacific Lowlands*, 176–78; *Geografía del Chocó*, 337–40.

18. See for example AHNC, Minas del Cauca 6, fols. 940–64 (1721–23); AHNC, Empleados Públicos del Cauca 5, fols. 262–64 (1747); AHNC, Minas del Cauca 5, fols. 76–81 (1786) and 89–91 (1790); ACC, Signatura 10362, fols. 55–57 (1768).

19. This slave paid the significant sum of 1,634 pesos to his owner Luis de Acuña. He did not have to pay rental for ninety-six days each year which were considered holidays. See AHNC, Minas del Cauca 5, fols. 288–89 (1730).

20. AHNC, Minas del Cauca 1, fols. 482–85 (1719).

21. See for example, AHNC, Minas del Cauca 5, fols. 288–89 (1730) and 200–201 (1800); ACC, Signatura 10362, fols. 47–59 (1768).

22. AHNC, Minas del Cauca 5, fol. 200 (1800) and 284–85 (1804).

23. Posada and Ibáñez, "Relación de . . . Antonio Caballero y Góngora,, 1789," *Relaciones de mando*, 737.

24. AHNC, Minas del Cauca 5, fols. 314–20 (1730); AHNC, Minas (parte II), fol. 100 (1773).

25. AHNC, Minas del Cauca 1, fol. 997 (1787).

26. Restrepo, "Noticias sobre la platina," *Estudio sobre las minas*, 120.

27. AHNC, Mejores Materiales 2, fols. 15–16 (1720).

28. West, *Pacific Lowlands*, 178.

29. Restrepo, *Estudio sobre las minas*, 113. Few miners in the Chocó used mercury in the first half of the eighteenth century and some of those who did complained that it was extremely difficult to purchase and not very effective. See AHNC, Minas del Cauca 1, fol. 8 (1726).

30. AHNC, Minas del Cauca 1, fol. 1 (1720).

31. Restrepo, *Estudio sobre las minas*, 113.

32. AHNC, Milicias y Marinas 142, fols. 196–99 (1748).

33. AHNC, Minas del Cauca 1, fol. 997 (1761).

34. Restrepo, *Estudio sobre las minas*, 119n.

35. AHNC, Minas del Cauca 5, fols. 803–805 (1787).

36. AHNC, Minas del Cauca 1, fol. 988 (1786).

37. Viceroy Antonio Arzobispo . . . to Marqués de Sonora, Santa Fe de Bogotá, August 21, 1786, AGI, Sección 5, Audiencia de Santa Fe, leg. 835.

38. AHNC, Minas del Cauca 5, fol. 820 (1786).

39. *Ibid.*, fol. 823 (1786); Confidential report from Governor Carlos Smith to Viceroy Caballero y Góngora, Nóvita, AHNC, Milicias y Marinas 111, fols. 39–40 (1786).

40. Restrepo, *Estudio sobre las minas*, 119n.

41. AHNC, Minas del Cauca 5, fols. 803–805 (1787).

42. Instrucciones reservadas de Virrey Antonio Caballero y Góngora a visitador Vicente Yáñez, Cartagena, December 1, 1787, *ibid.*, fols. 859–62.

43. AHNC, Minas 3 (parte I), fols. 296–97, 304 (1788).

44. AHNC, Miscelánea 59, fol. 92 (1788).

45. AHNC, Minas 3 (parte II), fol. 125 (1802).

46. Restrepo, "Noticias sobre la platina," *Estudio sobre las minas*, 117–18.

47. *Ibid.*, 114.

48. AHNC, Miscelánea 79, fol. 96 (1778); see also AHNC, Impuestos Varios 1, fols. 729–30 (1781).

49. AHNC, Impuestos Varios 1, fols. 117–18 (1779), 704–705, 719 (1780).

50. *Ibid.*, fols. 729–30 (1781).

51. *Ibid.*, fols. 740–41 (1783).

52. *Ibid.*, fols. 809–14 (1792).

53. AHNC, Minas del Cauca 6, fols. 430–34 (1793); see also AHNC, Impuestos Varios 18, fol. 309 (1795).

54. ". . . parece que se puede asegurar que nada ha a favor de su conservación." AHNC, Impuestos Varios 18, fol. 309 (1795).

55. AHNC, Impuestos Varios 1, fols. 804, 809–14 (1792).

56. *Ibid.*, fols. 796–97 (1792).

57. *Ibid.*, fols. 842–43 (1794).

58. *Ibid.*, fols. 776–79 (1785).

59. *Ibid.*, fols. 306–307, 860–67, 870–74 (1795).

60. AHNC, Impuestos Varios 8, fols. 347–48 (1805).

61. AHNC, Impuestos Varios 1, fols. 776–79 (1785), 870–74 (1795).

62. AHNC, Impuestos Varios 8, fols. 347–48, 377–81, 417–19 (1805), 457–59 (1806).

63. AHNC, Impuestos Varios 1, fols. 778–79 (1785).

64. AHNC, Impuestos Varios 8, fols. 417–19 (1805), 457–59 (1806).

65. AHNC, Impuestos Varios 24, fols. 389–94 (1806).

CHAPTER 5

1. Juan Friede, ed. and comp., *Documentos inéditos para la historia de Colombia*, 10 vols., V, 87; see also Clarence H. Haring, *The Spanish Empire in America*, 255–60.

2. Informe de Virrey Antonio de la Pedroza y Guerrero, March 8, 1721, Santa Fe de Bogotá, AGI, Sección 5, Audiencia de Santa Fe, leg. 362.

3. AHNC, Minas del Cauca 5, fol. 291 (1730); AHNC, Miscelánea 19, fols. 484, 487, 489 (1730).

4. The usual duty was 1½ per cent, see AHNC, Minas del Cauca 6, fol. 432 (1792); Haring, *The Spanish Empire*, 260; The ⅝ figure is derived from the fact that in 1792 officials at the foundry collected 5

Notes

tomines per 100 *castellanos* on the gold smelted, see AHNC, Impuestos Varios 1, fols. 829–32 (1794).

5. AHNC, Impuestos Varios 8, fol. 347 (1805).
6. See for example AHNC, Impuestos Varios 1, fols. 829–32 (1794).
7. AHNC, Real Hacienda (anexo) 7, fols. 361–63 (1755).
8. AHNC, Minas del Cauca 6, fols. 413–14 (1793).
9. AHNC, Mejores Materiales 2, fol. 13 (1720); AHNC, Reales Cédulas 9, fol. 271 (1734); AHNC, Contrabandos 5, fol. 115 (1762); Haring, *The Spanish Empire*, 260.
10. AHNC, Miscelánea 95, fols. 363–66 (1752).
11. "Relación del estado . . . de Arzobispo Obispo de Cordoba, 1789," *Relaciones de mando*, (ed. and comp. by Eduardo Posada and Pedro M. Ibáñez) 750. For other accusations see Informe de José Manuel Caycedo, July 24, 1724, AGI, Sección 5, Audiencia de Santa Fe, leg. 362.
12. AHNC, Contrabandos 18, fols. 325–44 (1783).
13. *Ibid.*, fol. 347 (1784).
14. Auto sobre Don Felipe Valencia, 1743–1752, AGI, Sección 5, Audiencia de Santa Fe, leg. 837.
15. Expediente seguido entre Don Domingo Carvajal y Don Juan Bonificio Roman, Citará, 1722–1731, AGI, Sección 5, Audiencia de Santa Fe, leg. 381.
16. AHNC, Minas del Cauca 6, fol. 414 (1793); AHNC, Minas 3 (parte I), fols. 296–97, 299, 304–305 (1788); Sergio Elias Ortíz, ed. and comp., *Escritos de dos economistas coloniales*, . . . , 145.
17. Official account books recording *quintos* paid show that most gold brought in did not come directly from the mines. In 1803, for example, Lieutenant Governor Ventura Salzas Malibran collected the *quinto* on 43,543.4 *castellanos* of *oro en polvo* in Quibdó. He listed 26,728.4 *castellanos* as having come from *rescates* (trading, collections). See AHNC, Minas 3 (parte II), fols. 127–207 (1803).
18. AHNC, Minas del Cauca 6, fol. 414 (1793).
19. AHNC, Contrabandos 5, fols. 158–59 (1719).
20. AHNC, Juicios Criminales 151, fols. 992–94 (1738).
21. *Descripción del Reyno de Santa Fe de Bogotá, escrita en 1789 . . .*, 73. William McGreevey noted that there was considerable discrepancy in estimates concerning contraband and he tended to accept the higher estimates. See *An Economic History of Colombia, 1845–1930*, 28–29.
22. See for example AHNC, Minas del Cauca 1, fols. 482–85 (1719).

217

Testimony in this document from a number of slaveholders shows that they earned between one and two pesos a day per slave working in the mines. This is generally a higher return than owners in the second half of the eighteenth century recorded.

23. This was the general practice throughout the Spanish Empire. In 1717 it was officially decided that the church did not have to pay the *quinto* on any gifts or stipends received for services in the Chocó. See AHNC, Contrabandos 5, fols. 172–74 (1717).

24. Restrepo, *Estudio sobre las minas*, 2d ed. (1888), 104.

25. ACC, Signatura 3372 (1727); AHNC, Contrabandos 27, fol. 323 (1734); AHNC, Caciques e Indios 67, fols. 762–64 (1761); AHNC, Contrabandos 25, fols. 208–11 (1764); AHNC, Contrabandos 3, fols. 252–54 (1797); AHNC, Contrabandos 20, fols. 505–507 (1799).

26. AHNC, Caciques e Indios 67, fols. 733–41 (1730).

27. AHNC, Miscelánea 135, fols. 992–93 (1744).

28. AHNC, Real Hacienda 36, fols. 445–56 (1757); AHNC, Mejores Materiales 2, fols. 335–36 (1780).

29. AHNC, Mejores Materiales 2, fols. 335–36 (1780).

30. *Ibid.*, fols. 44–47 (1762).

31. *Ibid.*, fols. 117–18 (1763).

32. *Ibid.*, fols. 117–24 (1763).

33. AHNC, Caciques e Indios 67, fols. 762–64 (1761); AHNC, Contrabandos 22, fol. 795 (1764).

34. AHNC, Contrabandos 23, fols. 768–70 (1760).

35. AHNC, Contrabandos 5, fol. 159 (1719); AHNC, Real Hacienda 25, fols. 976–77 (1732); AHNC, Contrabandos 24, fols. 990–91 (1799).

36. AHNC, Real Hacienda 25, fols. 976–77 (1732); AHNC, Real Hacienda 43, fols. 534–35 (1805). The purpose of the attachment of a defendant's property was to guarantee the crown received any fine that might be imposed.

37. AHNC, Reales Cédulas 9, fols. 76–77 (1730).

38. AHNC, Contrabandos 17, fols. 262–63, 271, 294 (1732).

39. The lieutenant governor of Quibdó and several other merchants from that city were also prosecuted. See AHNC, Real Hacienda 25, fols. 976–77 (1732).

40. *Ibid.*; AHNC, Reales Cédulas 9, fol. 271 (1734).

41. Governor Junguito's six associates included Melchor de Varona y Betancur, Francisco de Lloreda, Juan Martí, José Gaez, Antonio Joaquín

Froes, and Ignacio Soto, AHNC, Contrabandos 19, fols. 7–15 (1797). All of these men were wealthy influential individuals. The property of Varona, for example, was valued at over 100,000 pesos (AHNC, Contrabandos 5, fols. 406–409 [1805]), and that of Lloreda at 41,350 pesos (AHNC, Contrabandos 19, fols. 96–98 [1797].)

42. AHNC, Real Hacienda 48, fols. 191–202 (1797); AHNC, Contrabandos 5, fols. 433–35 (1808).

43. AHNC, Contrabandos 5, fols. 433–35 (1808); Melchor de Varona paid a fine of 1,500 pesos. The actual fine paid by Governor Junguito was not recorded in the testimony, but he spent over 4,000 pesos on his defense. See AHNC, Contrabandos 17, fols. 888–90 (1801–1803).

44. AHNC, Miscelánea 18, fols. 104–105 (1747); AHNC, Reales Cédulas 10, fols. 131–32 (1748); AHNC, Contrabandos 18, fols. 347–50 (1784); AHNC, Juicios Criminales 133, fols. 928–30 (1797); AHNC, Real Hacienda 29, fols. 944–46 (1805).

45. Archivo del Congreso de Colombia, Bogotá, Camara de Representantes (Informes de Comisiones) 45, fol. 163 (1823).

CHAPTER 6

1. AHNC, Reales Cédulas (anexo) 664, fols. 63–66 (1713); Informe de Joseph López de Carvajal y Cortes, October 1, 1713, AGI, Sección 5, Audiencia de Santa Fe, leg. 362.

2. AHNC, Real Hacienda 42, fols. 437–40 (1714).

3. *Ibid.*

4. AHNC, Minas del Cauca 2, fol. 684 (1720).

5. *Ibid.*, fols. 684–86 (1720).

6. *Ibid.*, fols. 687–88 (1720).

7. *Cédula Real*, June 30, 1720. AGI, Sección 5, Audiencia de Santa Fe, leg. 411.

8. AHNC, Reales Cédulas (anexo) 664, fols. 149–50 (1722).

9. AHNC, Reales Cédulas 7, fols. 745–48 (1722).

10. *Ibid.*, AHNC, Caciques e Indios 59, fols. 266–68 (1727).

11. AHNC, Reales Cédulas 8, fols. 290–91 (1725).

12. AHNC, Negros y Esclavos del Cauca 4, fols. 574–75 (1759).

13. AHNC, Historia Eclesiástica 9, fols. 524–25 (1776).

14. AHNC, Minas del Cauca 6, fols. 837–47 (1731); AHNC, Reales Cédulas 9, fols. 173–74 (1731).

15. AHNC, Reales Cédulas 10, fol. 90 (1743).

16. Informe to the Audiencia de Santa Fe de Bogotá from the Bishop of Popayán (Diego Fermín), Citará, November 3, 1736, AGI, Sección 5, Audiencia de Santa Fe, leg. 411.

17. AHNC, Reales Cédulas 10, fols. 657–61 (1742).

18. AHNC, Miscelánea 141, fols. 332–38 (1755).

19. AHNC, Reales Cédulas 17, fols. 461–64 (1768). This cédula stated that the corregidors of the Chocó had held the right to sell goods to the Indians in their *corregimientos* since the end of the seventeenth century.

20. AHNC, Visitas del Cauca 5, fol. 277 (1808).

21. AHNC, Poblaciones del Cauca 2, fol. 936 (1793).

22. AHNC, Visitas del Cauca 5, fols. 308, 341–43 (1784), 852–54 (1787).

23. AHNC, Visitas del Cauca 5, fols. 852–53 (1787); AHNC, Caciques e Indios 26, fols. 906–907 (1788).

24. AHNC, Visitas del Cauca 5, fols. 891–93 (1789).

25. AHNC, Visitas del Cauca 5, fols. 880–82 (1788), 875 (1789).

26. *Ibid.*, fols. 341–42, 354–56 (1784).

27. *Ibid.*, fols. 852–53, 857–61 (1788).

28. AHNC, Milicias y Marinas 52, fols. 283–98 (1757).

29. AHNC, Visitas del Cauca 5, fols. 354–56 (1784).

30. AHNC, Caciques e Indios 23, fols. 151–54 (1797).

31. AHNC, Visitas del Cauca 5, fols. 275–78 (1808).

32. Jesús María Henao and Gerardo Arrubla, *History of Colombia,* 341.

33. Archivo del Congreso de Colombia, Bogotá, Senado (Informes de Comisiones) 44, fols. 29–31 (1821).

34. *El Atratense* (Quibdó), September 9, 1880.

CHAPTER 7

1. AHNC, Caciques e Indios 10, fols. 519–20 (1692).

2. Chandler, "Health and Slavery," 144–45.

3. *Ibid.,* 106–19.

4. ACC, Signatura 2761 (1710).

5. ACC, Signatura 3124 (1723).

6. Gustavo Arboleda, *Historia de Cali desde los origines de la ciudad*

hasta la expiración del periodo colonial, 3 vols., II, 22–23.

7. ACC, Signatura 8174 (1717); ACC, Signatura 3144 (1725).

8. ACC, Signatura 3144 (1725).

9. AHNC, Negros y Esclavos del Cauca 4, fols. 558–90 (1759).

10. AHNC, Minas del Cauca 5, fols. 824, 830 (1741); AHNC, Miscelánea 132, fols. 181–84 (1744).

11. AHNC, Negros y Esclavos del Cauca 2, fols. 961–64 (1755); AHNC, Negros y Esclavos del Cauca 4, fols. 558–90 (1759).

12. AHNC, Negros y Esclavos del Cauca 4, fols. 558–90 (1759).

13. "Relación de . . . José de Ezpeleta, 1796," *Relaciones de mando*, 339; James J. Parsons, *Antioqueño Colonization in Western Colombia*, 50; José Rafael Arboleda, S.J., "La historia y la antropoligía del negro en Colombia," *Universidad de Antioquia*, No. 157 (April–June, 1964), 244.

14. Restrepo, *Estudio sobre las minas*, 87; AHNC, Negros y Esclavos del Cauca 4, fols. 558–90 (1759).

15. See the Popayán Papers which cover a span of 250 years from 1640 to 1890. These papers demonstrate that several families controlled the business interests in the Popayán region from Cali to Quito.

16. AHNC, Negros y Esclavos del Cauca 4, fols. 558–90 (1759).

17. AHNC, Visitas del Cauca 5, fol. 283 (1808).

18. *Cédula real* dated August 3, 1751, in AHNC, Mines del Cauca 1, fol. 991.

19. AHNC, Minas del Cauca 1. fols. 972–73 (1750).

20. "Negro Slavery in the Viceroyalty of New Granada," 138.

21. AHNC, Minas del Cauca 1, fols. 93–97 (1756).

22. AHNC, Censos de Varios Departamentos 6, fol. 381 (1778).

23. AHNC, Minas del Cauca 2, fols. 453–59 (1777).

24. AHNC, Minas del Cauca 5, fols. 807–15 (1787).

25. *Ibid.*, fols. 863–64 (1787); AHNC, Minas 3 (parte I), fols. 311–14 (1788).

26. AHNC, Esclavos 1, fols. 485–90, 492–98, 477–82, 501–31 (1789).

27. AHNC, Reales Cédulas 35, fol. 629 (1804).

28. "No encontrasen negros," *ibid.*, fols. 630–31 (1804).

29. Philip Curtin estimated that between 1774 and 1807 roughly 30,000 *bozales* entered the viceroyalty of New Granada. See *The Atlantic Slave Trade: A Census*, 30.

30. AHNC, Protocolos (Notaría del Chocó) 16, fol. 18 (1797).

31. AHNC, Minas 3 (parte II), fols. 381–83 (1817).

32. ACC, Signatura 9757 (1711).

33. ACC, Signatura 10362, fols. 37–42 (1768); AHNC, Minas del Cauca 5, fols. 21–27 (1779).

34. This was generally true throughout New Granada and one of the ways a buyer could annul a sale was to prove that a female he had purchased could not reproduce. See Chandler, "Health and Slavery," 104.

35. ACC, Signatura 10362, fols. 37–42 (1768).

36. AHNC, Minas del Cauca 5, fols. 11–30 (1779).

37. AHNC, Miscelánea 132, fols. 181–82 (1746).

38. See p. 125.

39. For greater detail concerning the economics of this case see pp. 183–84.

40. The aspect of profitability and its relationship to slave prices and rate of purchase are discussed in chapter 10.

41. Philip Curtin calculated that New Granada received only 2.1 per cent of all slave imports to the Americas but by 1950 contained 7.2 per cent of all Americans of African descent. The increase in black population as compared to slave imports is second only to the United States of America. See *The Atlantic Slave Trade*, 89–91.

42. AHNC, Negros y Esclavos del Cauca 4, fols. 558–90 (1759). Both Robert Cooper West (*Colonial Placer Mining in Colombia*, 86–87) and David Chandler ("Health and Slavery," 149–50) missed some of the significance of the word *chusma* as it was used in the Chocó. Both imply that many of the *chusma* slaves were adults working in other ventures and they fail to note the number of children so designated.

43. Slave codes written by Chocó owners show that masters instructed their overseers to encourage marriage between slaves in great part to prevent illicit relationships. See for example AHNC, Minas del Cauca 1, fols. 948–50 (1783); AHNC, Minas del Cauca 6, fols. 283–85 (1804).

44. AHNC, Censos de Varios Departamentos 6, fol. 377 (1782).

45. See p. 133.

46. AHNC, Miscelánea 132, fols. 181–82 (1746).

47. AHNC, Negros y Esclavos del Cauca 4, fol. 588 (1759).

48. AHNC, Minas del Cauca 5, fols. 21–27 (1779).

59. *Ibid.*

50. AHNC, Minas 3, (parte I), fol. 38 (1780). A number of other

mazamorreros on this list are also identifiable with individual slaves listed on the 1759 census.

CHAPTER 8

1. *Slave and Citizen*, 45.
2. *Ley de Siete Partidas* (1931), trans. by John Vance, *et al*, 90, 671, 891, 901–903, 979–86, 1305, 1342–45.
3. In the 1540's King Charles I prohibited castration as a form of punishment for runaway slaves, see Richard Konetzke, ed. and comp., *Colección de documentos para la historia de la formación social de Hispanoamerica*, 3 vols., I, 237–41.
4. King Philip II permitted castration for runaways in 1578 stating, "This is the punishment they fear the most." Cited in Arboleda, *Historia de Cali*, 3 vols., I, 91.
5. AHNC, Reales Cédulas 29, fols. 57–65 (1789).
6. Meiklejohn, "Negro Slave Legislation," 64.
7. AHNC, Visitas del Cauca 5, fols. 16–18 (1804); Governor Nicolás Díaz de Perea to the Pueblo de Murrí, Nóvita, August 13, 1764, Biblioteca Nacional de Colombia, Bogotá, Libros Raros, Manuscrito 179 #4.
8. AHNC, Visitas del Cauca 5, fols. 5–15, 29–41, 77–82 (1804).
9. Klein noted exceptions to this, but his overall thesis supports the idea that slave laws were upheld in most instances—especially in the cities (*Slavery in the Americas*). Norman Meiklejohn, in his study of slave legislation in New Granada, contends that in many regions of Colombia slaves had access to the Spanish courts and officials even went beyond the letter of the law to defend slaves. However, he does admit that local magistrates were prone to favoritism to protect wealthy local inhabitants in rural areas. See "Negro Slave Legislation," 113.
10. Konetzke, "Charles III to Bishop of Popayán," *Colección de documentos*, III, 382–83.
11. AHNC, Negros y Esclavos del Cauca 1, fols. 671–74 (1795).
12. AHNC, Censos de Varios Departamentos 6, fol. 377 (1782).
13. AHNC, Miscelánea 85, fols. 601–603 (1720).
14. Klein, *Slavery in the Americas*, 97–98.
15. AHNC, Censos de Varios Departamentos 6, fols. 375–76.
16. AHNC, Historia Eclesiástica 1, fols. 615–16 (1800); AHNC, Visitas del Cauca 5, fols. 288–89 (1809).

17. AHNC, Reales Cédulas 7, fols. 745–48 (1722); AHNC, Miscelánea 123, fols. 176–78 (1727); AHNC, Caciques e Indios 59, fols. 266–68 (1727).

18. AHNC, Negros y Esclavos del Cauca 2, fols. 961–62 (1755); AHNC, Negros y Esclavos del Cauca 4, fols. 568, 574–75, 585 (1759).

19. AHNC, Empleados Públicos del Cauca 22, fol. 312 (1688); AHNC, Historia Eclesiástica 18, fols. 395–96 (1780); the stipend collected in 1739 amounted to two pesos per working slave (*esclavo útil*) each year, see AHNC, Minas del Cauca 5, fols. 835–36 (1739).

20. AHNC, Historia Eclesiástica 18, fols. 395–96 (1780).

21. AHNC, Minas del Cauca 2, fols. 997–99 (1757); AHNC, Minas del Cauca 3, fols. 433–34 (1794); AHNC, Minas del Cauca 5, fols. 282, 290 (1804).

22. AHNC, Minas del Cauca 5, fols. 273–77 (1805).

23. AHNC, Visitas del Cauca 5, fols. 11–27 (1779–83).

24. AHNC, Visitas del Cauca 5, fols. 9–10, 55–61, 77–82 (1804); AHNC, Minas del Cauca 5, fols. 76–80, 89–91 (1793), 200 (1799).

25. For a good explanation of slave rations see David Chandler, "Health and Slavery," 160.

26. AHNC, Visitas del Cauca 5, fols. 65, 76–80 (1804), 89–91 (1783), 288–302 (1720–1730).

27. AHNC, Milicias y Marinas 126, fols. 71–72 (1765); see also AHNC, Miscelánea 63, fols. 194–97 (1769); AHNC, Reales Cédulas 19, fols. 699–700 (1769).

28. Meiklejohn, "Negro Slave Legislation," 87.

29. AHNC, Visitas del Cauca 5, fols. 77–82 (1804).

30. AHNC, Minas del Cauca 5, fols. 288–89 (1724–1730).

31. AHNC, Visitas del Cauca 5, fols. 377 (1784), 5–15, 29–41 (1804).

32. Robert W. Fogel and Stanley L. Engerman stated that: "The slave diet [in the United States] was not only adequate, it actually exceeded modern (1964) recommended daily levels of the chief nutrients." *Time on the Cross*, I, 115.

33. AHNC, Visitas del Cauca 5, fols. 29–82 (1804).

34. *Time on the Cross*, I, 109–17.

35. In 1747, Lieutenant Governor José Pastrana advised against changing the course of a potentially rich stream because the work would be difficult and dangerous for slaves. Testimony supported Pastrana, and

Notes

the project was not undertaken. See AHNC, Minas del Cauca 5, fols. 848–49 (1747).

36. AHNC, Negros y Esclavos del Cauca 1, fols. 511–61 (1788–89).

37. King, "Negro Slavery in the Viceroyalty of New Granada," 226–29; See also John Potter Hamilton, *Travels through the Interior Provinces of Colombia*, I, 147–48. Of course, as Gilberto Freyre noted in *The Masters and the Slaves*, domestic servants, because of their close proximity to the masters and mistresses, were sometimes badly mistreated as owners used them to vent personal frustrations.

38. AHNC, Minas del Cauca 5, fols. 824–25 (1741); AHNC, Miscelánea 132, fols. 181–82 (1746).

39. AHNC, Juicios Criminales 135, fols. 542–45, 547–48 (1794).

40. *Ibid.*, fols. 247–52 (1748).

41. *Ibid.*, fols. 542–45, 547–48, (1794).

42. AHNC, Negros y Esclavos del Cauca 1, fols. 671–72, 787 (1795–96); AHNC, Empleados Públicos del Cauca 2, fols. 918–25 (1796).

43. AHNC, Miscelánea 1, fol. 831 (1803).

44. Alexander Von Humboldt, the famous German scientist who traveled in the Spanish colonies late in the colonial period, explained several inequities in the Spanish legal system: "But such is the state of the negroes, dispersed in places scarcely began to be cultivated, that justice, far from efficaciously protecting them during their lives, cannot even punish acts of barbarity that have caused their deaths. If an inquiry be attempted, the death of the slave is attributed to the bad state of his health, to the influence of a warm and humid climate, to the wounds which he has received, but which, it is asserted, were neither deep nor dangerous." (*Personal Narrative of Travels . . . 1799–1804*, 6 vols., III, 179–80).

45. AHNC, Minas del Cauca 1, fols. 948–50 (1783).

46. AHNC, Minas del Cauca 5, fols. 284–85 (1804).

47. AHNC, Miscelánea 130, fols. 631–47 (1741–43).

48. AHNC, Minas del Cauca 5, fols. 828–30 (1741).

49. *Ibid.*, fols. 284–85 (1804).

50. AHNC, Reales Cédulas 9, fols. 221–22 (1733).

51. Eugene Genovese presented a valuable critique of economic determinism and slavery; see "Materialism and Idealism in the History of Negro Slavery in the Americas," in *Slavery in the New World . . .*, 238–55.

Slavery on the Spanish Frontier

52. AHNC, Censos de Varios Departamentos 6, fol. 381 (1778).

53. By the 1780's and 1790's in most areas of Spanish America (including New Granada) free blacks outnumbered slaves, sometimes by as much as five or ten to one. For a good summation of these figures see Bowser, "Colonial Spanish America," 36–38.

54. The free black population increase for specific years was as follows: 3,160 in 1778; 3,348 in 1779; 3,612 in 1781; 3,899 in 1782; and 15,184 in 1808 (table 8).

55. Bowser, "Colonial Spanish America," 33–36; Klein, *Slavery in the Americas,* 197–99; Tannenbaum, *Slave and Citizen,* 58–59; Gonzalo Aguirre Beltrán, "The Integration of the Negro into National Society in Mexico," in *Race and Class in Latin America,* 15–16.

56. Klein (*Slavery in the Americas*) includes considerable detail on this type of manumission; see also Hubert H. S. Aimes, "*Coartación*: a Spanish Institution for the Advancement of Slaves and Freedmen," *The Yale Review* Vol. XVII (1908–1909), 412–31; Alexander Von Humboldt, *The Island of Cuba,* 212–18; Arthur F. Corwin, *Spain and the Abolition of Slavery in Cuba, 1817–1886,* 52.

57. Fogel and Engerman noted that the standard of living combined with the incentive system of bonuses meant that ". . . the typical field hand received about 90 per cent of the income he had produced." *Time on the Cross,* I, 5–6.

58. See for example AHNC, Protocolos 17, Notaría del Chocó, fols. 154–57 (1786–88).

59. Robert Cooper West suggested that owners accepted this because most of the freedmen continued to labor in the mines following manumission (*Colonial Placer Mining in Colombia,* 88–89). There is little evidence to sustain this contention for the Chocó. However, it may well be true for other regions of Colombia. See James J. Parsons, *Antioqueño Colonization in Western Colombia,* 52–53.

60. Meiklejohn recounted that slaves had direct recourse to the *audiencia real* in cases pertaining to manumission, and only in such cases ("The Observance of Slave Legislation," 89 n.1). This may well have been a contributing factor to the effectiveness of the manumission laws.

61. AHNC, Protocolos 17, Notaría del Chocó, fols. 154–57 (1786–88). Slaves in Cuba also purchased freedom in installments. See Klein, *Slavery in the Americas,* 78 and *passim.*

62. AHNC, Protocolos 17, Notaría del Chocó, fols. 154–57 (1786–88).

Although the archives and notarías in Quibdó and Nóvita pertaining to the colonial period were destroyed by fire, notary records extant in Quibdó for the years 1814–19 list dozens of examples of this type of manumission. See Notaría Pública de Quibdó, Quibdó, Años de 1814, 1815, 1817, 1818, 1819.

63. These slaves doubtless remained near the Spanish mines or population centers and may have been the freedmen to whom West referred (n. 59). Whether they hired out as free laborers or worked on their own accounts, however, is unknown.

64. Meiklejohn, "Negro Slave Legislation," 192–93. Meiklejohn included an excellent section on the various types of manumission possible in New Granada; see 153–84.

65. AHNC, Negros y Esclavos del Cauca 1, fols. 409–26, 508–10 (1738).

66. AHNC, Negros y Esclavos del Cauca 3, fol. 822 (1780); AHNC, Negros y Esclavos del Cauca 2, fols. 969–72 (1804).

67. AHNC, Negros y Esclavos del Cauca 2, fols. 617–18 (1732); AHNC, Negros y Esclavos del Cauca 3, fols. 822–26 (1780); AHNC, Miscelánea 2, fols. 390–91 (1791). Several of these cases involved freeing the deceased owners' mulatto children.

68. AHNC, Negros y Esclavos del Cauca 2, fols. 1–40 (1728); AHNC, Negros y Esclavos del Cauca 3, fol. 913 (1790).

69. AHNC, Negros y Esclavos de Cundinamarca 9, fols. 897–902 (1796).

70. AHNC, Negros y Esclavos del Cauca 2, fols. 1–40 (1728).

71. AHNC, Real Hacienda 40, fols. 276–78 (1797).

CHAPTER 9

1. *Slave and Citizen,* 100.

2. One of the best studies concerning the Spanish attitudes on race is Magnus Mörner, *Race Relations in the History of Latin America.*

3. Klein, *Slavery in the Americas,* 194–95.

4. Degler, *Neither Black Nor White,* 224–25. This view is also well presented by Harry Hoetink, specifically for the Caribbean and generally for the Americas. See *The Two Variants in Caribbean Race Relations . . .,* 167–90.

5. "Colonial Spanish America," in *Neither Slave Nor Free . . .,* 53.

6. Magnus Mörner, "El mestizaje en la historia de ibero-america," *Revista de Historia de America*, No. 53–54 (1962), 131.

7. J. H. Elliott, *Imperial Spain, 1469–1716*, 215.

8. Juan and Ulloa wrote that in Cartagena the social elite were the whites, the lowest class the blacks, and in between all the other castes structured according to their degree of whiteness. Through favorable unions the child of a black could be elevated into the ranks of the whites. The process took five generations, however. The children of a *quinteron* (one-sixteenth black) and a white were recognized as white. See *A Voyage to South America . . .*, I, 29–32.

9. See for example AHNC, Miscelánea 47, fols. 657–58 (1767), 633–34 (1792).

10. AHNC, Milicias y Marinas 134, fols. 253–65 (1766–72); AHNC, Impuestos Varios 10, fols. 117–18 (1779); AHNC, Poblaciones del Cauca 2, fol. 120 (1803).

11. AHNC, Contrabandos 20, fols. 541–42 (1799).

12. For a good summary of the advantages afforded to urban slaves see Bowser, "The African in Colonial Spanish America . . .," *Latin American Research Review*, Vol. VII (Spring, 1972), 81–82.

13. On February 22, 1587, the crown defined the job of *boga* on the Magdalena River as too difficult and intolerable for Indians and prohibited them from continuing this work. Recognizing, however, the importance of the trade along the Magdalena to the commerce of New Granada, the crown permitted—indeed demanded—freedmen to assume the vocation of *boga*. See Konetzke, *Colección de documentos* I, 573–79.

14. AHNC, Minas del Cauca 2, fols. 467–504 (1757).

15. AHNC, Visitas del Cauca 5, fols. 857–61 (1788).

16. AHNC, Negros y Esclavos del Cauca 2, fols. 961–64 (1755); AHNC, Negros y Esclavos del Cauca 4, fols. 558–90 (1759).

17. AHNC, Minas 3 (parte I), fols. 38–39 (1780–81); AHNC, Censos de Varios Departamentos 6, fol. 377 (1782).

18. ACC, Signatura 10362, fols. 50–90 (1752–68).

19. AHNC, Visitas del Cauca 5, fols. 277–78 (1808).

20. Konetzke, *Colección de documentos*, III, 622–23; See also Juan B. Quiros, "El contenido laboral en los códigos negros Americanos," *Revista Mexicana de Sociología*, Vol. V, No. 4, (1943), 475.

21. Konetzke, *Colección de documentos*, III, 331–32. The inequity between freedmen and whites and the desire of some of the freedmen to

be treated as equals led the Spanish to devise a special system toward the end of the colonial period known as a *cédula de gracias al sacar* whereby both crown revenues and egos were inflated. Upon payment of a fee to the crown, selected persons of mixed ancestry were able to secure the legal rights and privileges of whites. The fee was usually in proportion to the applicant's degree of whiteness and his ability to pay. Among other things, the holder of this *cédula*, or his family, could attend the university. See James Ferguson King, "The Case of José Ponciano de Ayarza: A Document of Gracias al Sacar," *Hispanic American Historical Review*, Vol. XXXI (1951), 641–42.

22. Klein, *Slavery in the Americas*, 223–24; Bowser, "Colonial Spanish America," 44; Alan Kuethe, "The Status of the Free Pardo in the Disciplined Militia of New Granada," *The Journal of Negro History*, Vol. LVI, No. 2 (April, 1971), 105–18.

23. AHNC, Virreyes 16, fols. 169–71 (1761).

24. AHNC, Milicias y Marinas 30, fols. 633–34 (1777).

25. AHNC, Virreyes 9, fol. 40 (1779); AHNC, Milicias y Marinas 52, fols. 478–79 (1782).

26. AHNC, Virreyes 9, fols. 4–6 (1782).

27. AHNC, Caciques e Indios 67, fol. 766 (1761).

28. There is a significant distinction between the settlement patterns of the freedmen of the Chocó and the "poor whites" of the American South. In the American South, ". . . the plantation system had driven these people to the less desirable lands . . . it had, to a very great extent, walled them up and locked them there. . . ." (W. J. Cash, *The Mind of the South*, 22).

29. AHNC, Negros y Esclavos del Cauca 2, fols. 414–15 (1785); AHNC, Poblaciones del Cauca 2, fols. 116–18 (1803).

30. For a discussion of this revolt see pp. 160, 169.

31. Aguirre, the last Spanish governor in the Chocó, demanded of others a rigid loyalty (as the king's chosen representative), and became an extremely unpopular figure with the white residents of the Chocó. Caycedo had many friends and relatives in the region who backed his position against the governor. See, AHNC, Miscelánea 22, fols. 667–71 (1809). White hatred against Aguirre increased and was one of the reasons the Chocó miners joined the 1810 independence movement against Spain. See Rogerio Velásquez, *El Chocó en la independencia de Colombia*, 93–94.

32. The literature concerning *palenques* (or *quilombos* in Brazil) has increased rapidly in recent years. Although no study treats the Chocó, works of interest include: Roger Bastide, *Las Americas negras* . . .; Edison Carneiro, *Guerras de los Palmares*; G. Porras Tronconis, *Cartagena Hispanica 1533 a 1810*; Norman E. Whitten, *Black Frontiersmen: A South American Case.*

33. Population figures including male and female statistics for Spanish America are surprisingly difficult to locate and there is a need for future investigation along these lines. Most authors simply state that male slaves outnumbered female slaves. In one recent book, for example, the author stressed the predominantly male nature of black immigration to the Americas as extremely important for the development of the black community, but no statistics were given. See Franklin Knight, *The African Dimension in Latin American Societies.*

34. The Chocó presents striking differences with regard to the percentage of *libre* women in a region where self-purchase was common. In Cuba the majority of blacks who were able to purchase freedom were male, and Frederick P. Bowser noted: "If this example is at all typical for the rest of Spanish America, one would expect to find more adult males entering the ranks of the free colored population. . . ." ("Colonial Spanish America," 32).

35. AHNC, Impuestos Varios 8, fols. 377–81 (1805), 457–59 (1806).

36. For example "Cantos de mi Tierra y de mi Raza," sung by Leonor Gonzáles Mina (Medellín, Sonolux).

37. Thomas J. Price Jr., "Estado y necesidades actuales de las investigaciones Afro-Colombianas," *Revista Colombiana de Antropología* No. 2 (1954), II, 24.

38. Velásquez says these folktales relate "the secret rebellion of the abandoned against the powers that control." See "Cuentas de la raza negra," *Revista Colombiana de Folclor* No. 2 (1959), 2,5.

39. For one of the best recent studies on aspects of magic, organization, and survival of the black in Western Colombia see David Paul Pavy, "The Negro in Western Colombia" (Ph.D. dissertation, Tulane University, 1967); see also Whitten, *Black Frontiersmen.*

40. Antonio Cuervo, ed. and comp., *Informe de los Padres misioneros de Putumayo y Caqueta*, September 17, 1773, *Colección de documentos inéditos sobre la geografía y la historia de Colombia*, IV, 256–57.

41. *Neither Black Nor White*, 51–52.

42. It should be noted, however, that since no statistics were compiled for *cimarrones* in the Chocó, the inventories listing women as runaways may be the exception. There were incidents of male *cimarrones* raiding mining camps to capture women. See AHNC, Miscelánea 100, fols. 365–66 (1767).

43. AHNC, Negros y Esclavos del Cauca 2, fols. 413–16 (1788).

44. AHNC, Minas 3 (parte II), fols. 315–18 (1815), 439–41 (1819).

45. AHNC, Miscelánea 100, fols. 365–66 (1767); AHNC, Negros y Esclavos del Cauca 3, fols. 963–64 (1802–1803); AHNC, Juicios Criminales 134, fols. 195–223 (1802).

46. AHNC, Minas del Cauca 6, fol. 895 (1728); AHNC, Real Hacienda 28, fols. 1033–1034 (1730).

47. AHNC, Esclavos 1, fol. 500 (1789).

48. AHNC, Negros y Esclavos del Cauca 1, fols. 511–61 (1788–89); AHNC, Juicios Criminales 133, fols. 223–24 (1802); AHNC, Juicios Criminales 134, fols. 195–223 (1802).

49. AHNC, Caciques e Indios 23, fols. 849–53 (1686); AHNC, Minas del Cauca 6, fol. 649 (1702).

50. AHNC, Reales Cédulas 9, fols. 225–28 (1733).

51. Meiklejohn, "Negro Slave Legislation," 87.

52. AHNC, Negros y Esclavos del Cauca 2, fols. 196–97 (1781–1808).

53. AHNC, Milicias y Marinas 126, fol. 160 (1803).

54. AHNC, Milicias y Marinas 124, fols. 1119–21 (1806).

55. AHNC, Milicias y Marinas 134, fol. 254 (1767).

56. At that time Quibdó contained only twenty whites and, according to Lieutenant Governor Juan Jiménez, "ten other citizens of some recommendation." *ibid.*, fol. 253 (1767).

57. AHNC, Milicias y Marinas 126, fols. 185–86 (1766).

58. AHNC, Milicias y Marinas 134, fols. 254–55 (1767). It is interesting to note that shortly following this altercation a militia unit was formed in Quibdó.

59. AHNC, Miscelánea 100, fols. 365–66 (1767).

60. AHNC, Milicias y Marinas 134, fols. 258, 264 (1767).

CHAPTER 10

1. *The Economics of Slavery and other Studies in Econometric History*, 43–44, 82.

2. *Time on the Cross*, I, 68–70.

3. *Ibid.*, 4.

4. AHNC, Minas del Cauca 5, fols. 848–49 (1747).

5. See table 5. Same was also true for the freedmen who were counted by the census takers.

6. AHNC, Minas del Cauca 6, fols. 954–55 (1723).

7. AHNC, Negros y Esclavos del Cauca 4, fols. 558–90 (1759).

8. AHNC, Minas del Cauca 5, fol. 64 (1790); ACC, Signatura 10362, fols. 55–57 (1768).

9. AHNC, Minas del Cauca 5, fol. 636 (1800).

10. AHNC, Empleados Públicos del Cauca 5, fols. 262–64 (1747).

11. AHNC, Contrabandos 19, fols. 83–84 (1786); AHNC, Minas del Cauca 5, fols. 546–48 (1802).

12. AHNC, Empleados Públicos del Cauca 5, fols. 262–64 (1747); AHNC, Minas del Cauca 5, fols. 636–37 (1800).

13. AHNC, Minas del Cauca 5, fol. 834 (1739).

14. *Ibid.*, fols. 848–49 (1747).

15. *Ibid.*, fols. 571 (1726), 288–302 (1730).

16. ACC, Signatura 10362, fols. 37–42, 86–90 (1768).

17. See AHNC, Visitas del Cauca 2, fol. 961 (1755); AHNC, Minas del Cauca 2, fols. 882–83 (1757).

18. See for example AHNC, Minas del Cauca 5, fols. 180–85 (1800), 293, 297 (1730), 830–36 (1737); AHNC, Minas del Cauca 3, fols. 424–26 (1792); ACC, Signatura 10362, fols. 50–90 (1752–68).

19. See for example AHNC, Minas del Cauca 2, fols. 882–83 (1756); AHNC, Minas del Cauca 5, fols. 274–77 (1805), 288–302 (1720–30), 830–35 (1737).

20. In 1759, 3,578 out of 3,918 slaves existed on *cuadrillas* numbering more than 30. Eighteen slaveholders out of a total of 58 owned more than 100 slaves and another 24 owned more than 30. See AHNC, Negros y Esclavos del Cauca 4, fols. 558–90.

21. Where documentation permitted, the 23-peso average was cross-checked and found to be very close to the actual costs on the large *cuadrillas*.

22. This decision is based upon data from individual *cuadrillas* and the comprehensive slave census of 1759. In the 1759 census, for example, 1,569 out of 3,918 slaves were registered as *chusma* (40.05 per cent). See AHNC, Negros y Esclavos del Cauca 4, fols. 558–90.

23. See for example property belonging to Francisco de Saavedra (slaves—27,952 pesos, other property—8,777 pesos), AHNC, Minas del Cauca 4, fols. 167–75 (1725); property belonging to Francisco Gonzáles (slaves—30,860 pesos, other property—11,424 pesos), AHNC, Minas del Cauca 5, fols. 21–27 (1779).

24. ACC, Signatura 10362, fol. 42 (1768).

25. An owner had invested approximately 350 pesos in a slave by the time he reached working age (20 pesos a year for maintenance, and another 50 pesos in time off for the mother, extra food, and so forth). The average return from a prime slave (figured from table 15) was 265 pesos a year. Thus a prime slave paid off the owner's total investment with slightly less than two years' work.

26. Slaves who purchased their own freedom are not a capital loss for the owner since they paid the top price permitted for their liberty. Thus the owner lost potential earning power but retained his capital investment on a slave who purchased freedom.

27. AHNC, Minas del Cauca 5, fols. 358–65 (1690).

28. AHNC, Minas del Cauca 4, fols. 288–94 (1734); AHNC, Minas del Cauca 5, fols. 288–302 (1720–30), 571 (1726), 298 (1730).

29. AHNC, Minas del Cauca 5, fols. 824–36 (1729–41); AHNC, Miscelánea 121, fols. 564–65 (1739–41).

30. AHNC, Minas del Cauca 5, fols. 848–49 (1747).

31. AHNC, Negros y Esclavos del Cauca 2, fol. 963 (1755); Restrepo, *Estudio sobre las minas*, 87.

32. AHNC, Negros y Esclavos del Cauca 4, 558–64 (1759).

33. AHNC, Minas del Cauca 2, fols. 882–83, 891 (1755–58).

34. AHNC, Minas 1 (parte II), fols. 91–107 (1766–71); AHNC, Negros y Esclavos del Cauca 4, fol. 574 (1759).

35. ACC, Signatura 10362, fols. 37–42 (1752).

36. *Ibid.*, fols. 37–105 (1752–68).

37. AHNC, Minas del Cauca 6, fols. 794–95 (1790).

38. On the world market today 80,000 pesos worth of gold (6,400 ounces at $180 dollars an ounce) would be equal to $1,152,000.

39. AHNC, Minas del Cauca 5, fols. 64–66 (1784–89).

40. *Ibid.*, fols. 101–102 (1790).

41. AHNC, Minas 3 (parte II), fols. 140, 142–44, 174, 191 (1803); AHNC, Visitas del Cauca 5, fols. 135 (1804), 270 (1806).

42. "Commerce and Enterprise in Central Colombia, 1821–1870"

(Ph.D. dissertation, Columbia University, 1965), 366, 372.

43. *Ibid.*, 380–81.

44. Luis Ospina Vásquez, *Industría y protección en Colombia, 1810–1930*, 35. The usual lending rate was 5 per cent.

45. See for example ACC, Signatura 10362, fols. 55–58 (1753–54).

46. D. A. Brading, *Miners and Merchants in Bourbon Mexico, 1763–1810*, 295.

47. *Ibid.*, 121–24.

48. *Ibid.*, 216–17.

49. The Bourbon reforms had varying effects on the economy of New Granada. William McGreevey stated that exports were up as a result of the greater freedom of trade but that "at the end of the eighteenth century Colombia was still very much a traditional society with all that implies for the working of the economy." See *An Economic History of Colombia, 1845–1930*, 21–23.

50. The Arboledas (Manuel María) and Mosqueras (José María) retained an agent in Cádiz, Luis Jiménez, who purchased goods for them in Spain and then remitted these goods to Cartagena. See ACC, "Cuentos de gastos de recivo y embarque . . ." (1802), José María de Mosquera Collection.

Bibliography

I. *Unpublished Documents*

A. Archival Sources

Archivo Central del Cauca, Popayán, Colombia.

Signatura: 1831, 1933, 2561, 2761, 3124, 3144, 3372, 6233, 8174, 9757, 9983, 10362.

Archivo del Congreso de Colombia, Bogotá, Colombia.

Archivo de la Compañía Minería Chocó Pacifico, Andagoya, Chocó, Colombia. Land titles and documents related to mining in the Chocó, 1776–1974.

Archivo General de Indias, Seville, Spain.

Audiencia de Santa Fe, *legajos*: 362, 381, 411, 835, 837, 881, 882, 883, 901, 902.

Contaduría, *legajos*: 1590, 1603, 1604.

Archivo Histórico Nacional de Colombia, Bogotá, Colombia.

Aduanas, vol. 5; Aguardientes del Cauca, vols. 4, 5; Alcabalas, vol. 17; Archivos, vol. 4; Caciques e Indios, vols. 10, 14, 16, 17, 23, 26, 32, 38, 59, 67; Censos de Varios Departamentos, vols. 6, 8; Contrabandos, vols. 3, 5, 10, 17, 18, 19, 20, 22, 23, 24, 27; Esclavos, vol. 1; Empleados Públicos del Cauca, vols. 2, 5, 22; Estadística, vol. 11 (parte I); Gobernación del Chocó (Cajas Misceláneas); Gobernación del Chocó (República), vols. 15, 16; Gobernaciones (República), vols. 166, 195; Historia Eclesiástica, vols. 1, 9, 11, 18; Impuestos Varios, vols. 1, 8, 10, 18, 24; Juicios Criminales, vols. 133, 134, 135, 136, 151; Mejores Materiales, vols. 2, 17; Milicias y Marinas, vols. 30, 40, 52, 60, 111, 116, 124, 126, 134, 142; Minas, vols. 1 (parte II), 3 (parte I), 3 (parte II); Minas del Cauca, vols. 1, 2, 3, 5, 6; Miscelánea, vols. 1, 2, 18, 19, 22,

38, 42, 47, 59, 63, 72, 79, 85, 95, 100, 119, 121, 123, 129, 130, 132, 135, 141; Negros y Esclavos del Cauca, vols. 1, 2, 3, 4; Negros y Esclavos de Cundinamarca, vol. 9; Poblaciones del Cauca, vol. 2; Protocolos (Notaría del Chocó), vols. 16, 17; Reales Cédulas, vols. 4, 7, 8, 9, 10, 17, 19, 29, 35; Reales Cédulas (anexo), vols. 657, 664; Real Hacienda, vols. 10, 25, 27, 28, 29, 30, 34, 36, 40, 42, 43, 45, 48; Real Hacienda (anexo), vols. 7, 8; Viverryes, vols. 9, 16; Visitas del Cauca, vols. 2, 5.

National Archives of the United States of America, Washington, D.C. Post Records of the Department of State, Quibdó, Republic of Colombia, 1913–1915 (Record Group # 84).

Notaría Pública de Quibdó, Quibdó, Chocó, Colombia. Años de 1814, 1815, 1817, 1818, 1819.

B. Manuscript Collections

José María Mosquera Papers, 1735–1830. Unsorted collection with an unknown number of items. Letters and papers are tied together sometimes by the year, and sometimes by the name of either the recipient or the sender of the letter. Archivo Central del Cauca, Popayán, Colombia.

Tomás Cipriano de Mosquera Papers, 1815–1868. Unknown number of items arranged chronologically in folders. Archivo Central del Cauca, Popayán, Colombia.

Popayán Papers, 33 Boxes. Papers of several prominent families in the Popayán region of Colombia, 1650–1898. Southern Historical Collection, University of North Carolina, Chapel Hill.

C. Public or Official Documents

Censos Generales de población de la República de la Nueva Granada (1835). Unpublished volume in Archivo Histórico Nacional de Colombia, Bogotá, Colombia.

Censos Generales de población de la República de la Nueva Granada (1843). Unpublished volume in Archivo Histórico Nacional de Colombia. Bogotá, Colombia.

Censos Generales de población de la República de la Nueva Granada (1851). Unpublished volume in Archivo Histórico Nacional de Colombia, Bogotá, Colombia.

Bibliography

Governor Nicolás Díaz de Perea to Pueblo de Murrí, Nóvita, August 13, 1764. Biblioteca Nacional de Colombia, Bogotá. Libros Raros.

II. Printed Primary Sources

A. Newspapers

El Atratense, 1880, Quibdó, Chocó, Colombia.
El Chocoano, 1889. Quibdó, Chocó, Colombia.
El Ensayo, 1908. Quibdó, Chocó, Colombia.

B. Collections and Documents

Cuervo, Antonio B., ed. *Colección de documentos inéditos sobre la geografía y la historia de Colombia*, 4 vols. Bogotá, 1891–94.

Donnan, Elizabeth, ed. and comp. *Documents Illustrative of the History of the Slave Trade to America*, 4 vols. Washington, D.C., 1930–35.

El Cabildo de Quibdó a la nación y al Congreso, Quibdó, July 17, 1851. Printed in Cartagena, Colombia, 1851.

Friede, Juan, ed. and comp. *Documentos inéditos para la historia de Colombia*, 10 vols. Bogotá, 1955–60.

Konetzke, Richard, ed. and comp. *Colección de documentos para la historia de la formación social de Hispanoamerica*, 3 vols. Madrid, 1953.

Ortega, Ricaurte, Enrique, ed. *Historia documental del Chocó*. Bogotá, 1954.

Ortíz, Sergio Elias, ed. and comp. *Escritos de los economistas coloniales, Don Antonio Narváez y la Torre y Don José Ignacio de Pombo*. Bogotá, 1965.

Posada, Enrique and Ibáñez, P.M., comps. *Relaciones de Mando: Memorias presentadas por los gobernantes del Nuevo Reino de Granada*. Biblioteca de Historia Nacional, VIII. Bogotá, 1910.

Scott, Samuel Parsons; Lobingier, Charles Sumner; and Vance, John, comps. *Las Siete Partidas*. New York, 1931.

C. Chronicles, Diaries, Memoirs and Travel Accounts

Castellanos, Juan de. *Elegías de varones ilustres de Indias*, 3 vols. Bogotá, 1955.

Cieza de León, Pedro de, *The Travels of Pedro Cieza de León, A.D. 1532–1550, Contained in the First Part of His Chronicle of Peru.* Trans. and ed. by Clements R. Markham. London, 1864. (Hakluyt Society, Series I, Vol. XXXIII.)

Cochrane, Charles Stuart. *Journal of a Residence and Travels in Colombia During the Years 1823 and 1824,* 2 vols. London, 1825.

Codazzi, Agustín. *Jeografía física i política de las provincias de la Nueva Granada por la comisión corográfica bajo la dirección de* ———: *provincias de Cordoba, Cauca, Popayán, Pasto and Tuquerres,* IV. Bogotá, 1959.

De Pons, Francisco. *Travels in South America during the Years 1801, 1802, 1803, and 1804 . . .,* 2 vols. London, 1807.

Fermín de Vargas, Pedro. *Pensamientos políticos sobre la agricultura, comercio y minas del virreinato de Santafé de Bogotá . . . .* Bogotá, 1968.

Hamilton, John Potter, *Travels through the Interior Provinces of Colombia,* 2 vols. London, 1827.

Humboldt, Alexander de [Von], *Personal Narrative of Travels to the Equinoctial Regions of the New Continent, During the Years 1799–1804, by* ——— *and Aimé Bonpland; with Maps, Plans, etc.,* Trans. by Helen María Williams. 6 vols. London, 1818.

———. *Political Essay on the Kingdom of New Spain,* Translated by John Black. 4 vols. London, 1811. (Reprint, New York, 1966).

———. *The Island of Cuba.* Trans. by J. S. Thrasher. New York, 1856.

Juan, Jorge, and Ulloa, Antonio de. *A Voyage to South America . . .,* Trans. by John Adams. 2 vols. London, 1807.

Silvestre, Francisco. *Descripción del reyno de Santa Fe de Bogotá: Escrita en 1789 por* ———, *secretario que fue del virreinato y antiguo gobernador de la provincia de Antioquia.* Bogotá, 1968.

Trautwine, John C., "Rough Notes of an Exploration for an Inter-Oceanic Canal Route by Way of the Rivers Atrato and San Juan, in New Granada, South America," *Journal of the Franklin Institute,* vol. LVII (1854), 145–54, 217–31, 289–99, 361–73; vol. LVIII (1854), 1–11, 73–84, 145–55, 217–26, 289–99.

Ulloa, Antonio de, see Juan, Jorge.

[Walker, Alexander.] *Colombia: Being a Geographical, Statistical, Agricultural, Commercial, and Political Account of that Country. Adapted*

Bibliography

for the General Reader, the Merchant, and the Colonist, 2 vols. London, 1822.

Walton, William. Present State of the Spanish Colonies . . ., 2 vols. London, 1810.

III. Secondary Sources

A. Books

Acosta, Joaquín. Historia de la Nueva Granada. Bogotá, 1942.

Aguirre Beltrán, Gonzalo. La población negra de Mexico 1519–1810, estudio etnohistórico. Mexico, 1946.

Alvarez Lleras, Jorge. El Chocó. Bogotá, 1923.

Arboleda, Gustavo. Historia de Cali desde los orígenes de la ciudad hasta la expiración del periodo colonial, 3 vols. Cali, Colombia, 1956.

Arcila Robledo, Fray Gregorio. Apuntes históricos de la provincia Franciscana de Colombia. Bogotá, 1953.

Bastide, Roger. Las Americas negras: Las civilazaciones Africanas en el nueva mundo. Madrid, 1969.

Boxer, C. R. The Golden Age of Brazil, 1695–1750. Berkeley and Los Angeles, 1962.

Carneiro, Edison. Guerras de los Palmares. Mexico, 1946.

Cash, W. J. The Mind of the South. New York, 1941.

Conrad, Alfred H., and Meyer, John. The Economics of Slavery and other Studies in Econometric History. Chicago, 1964.

Cordoba, Francisco. Nociones de geografía e historia del Chocó. Quibdó, Chocó, Colombia, 1933.

Corwin, Arthur F. Spain and the Abolition of Slavery in Cuba, 1817–1886. Austin, 1967.

Curtin, Philip. The Atlantic Slave Trade: A Census. Madison, 1969.

Davis, David Brion. The Problem of Slavery in Western Culture. Ithaca, 1966.

Degler, Carl. Neither Black Nor White: Slavery and Race Relations in Brazil and the United States. New York, 1971.

Díaz Soler, Luis M. Historia de la esclavitud negra en Puerto Rico. Barcelona, 1970.

Elkins, Stanley. Slavery, A Problem in American Institutional and Intellectual Life. Chicago and London, 1958.

239

Elliott, J. H. *Imperial Spain: 1469–1716*. New York, 1964.

Fogel, Robert W. and Engerman, Stanley. *Time on the Cross: The Economics of American Negro Slavery*. 2 vols. Boston and Toronto, 1974.

Freyre, Gilberto. *The Masters and the Slaves: A Study in the Development of Brazilian Civilization*. Trans. by Samuel Putnam. 2d ed. New York, 1956.

Genovese, Eugene, *The World the Slaveholders Made*. New York, 1969.

Geografía económica de Colombia, VI, Chocó. Contraloría general de la República. Bogotá, 1942.

Haring, Clarence. *The Spanish Empire in America*. New York, 1963.

Harris, Harvin. *Patterns of Race in the Americas*. New York, 1964.

Hart, Francis Russell. *The Disaster of Darién: The Story of the Scots Settlement and the Causes of its Failure, 1699–1701*. New York, 1929.

Henao, Jesús María and Arrubla, Gerardo. *History of Colombia*. Trans. and ed. by J. Fred Rippy. Chapel Hill, 1938.

Hoetink, Harry. *The Two Variants in Caribbean Race Relations. . . .* Trans. by Eva Hooykaas. New York and London, 1967.

Klein, Herbert. *Slavery in the Americas: A Comparative Study of Virginia and Cuba*. Chicago, 1967.

Knight, Franklin. *African Dimensions in Latin American Societies*. New York, 1974.

McGreevey, William Paul. *An Economic History of Colombia, 1845–1930*. Cambridge, 1971.

Mendoza Nieto, Jorge, *Geografía ilustrada del Chocó*. Bogotá, 1942.

Mörner, Magnus, *Race Relations in the History of Latin America*. Boston, 1968.

Olano, Antonio, *Popayán en la Colonia*. Popayán, Colombia, 1910.

Ospina Vásquez, Luis, *Industría y protección en Colombia, 1810–1930*. Medellín, Colombia, 1955.

Parsons, James J., *Antioqueño Colonization in Western Colombia. Ibero-Americana: 32*. Berkeley, 1949.

Pierson, Donald. *Negroes in Brazil: A Study of Race Contact at Bahia*. Chicago, 1942.

Porras Tronconis, G. *Cartagena Hispanica 1533 a 1810*. Bogotá, 1954.

Prebble, John. *The Darién Disaster: A Scots Colony in the New World, 1698–1700*. New York, 1968.

Restrepo, José Manuel. *Historia de la revolución de Colombia en la America Meridional*, 4 vols. Besanzon, France, 1858.

Bibliography

Restrepo, Vicente. *Estudio sobre las minas de oro y plata de Colombia*, 2d ed. Bogotá, 1888.

——. *Estudio sobre las minas de oro y plata de Colombia*. Bogotá, 1952.

Roca Castellanos, Manuel. *10 luces sobre el futuro*. Bogotá, 1935.

Romoli, Kathleen. *Balboa of Darién: Discoverer of the Pacific*. Garden City, 1953.

Stein, Stanley. *Vassouras: A Brazilian Coffee County*. Cambridge, 1957.

Tannenbaum, Frank. *Slave and Citizen, the Negro in the Americas*. New York, 1947.

Technical Paper for the Atrato-Truandó Geophysical Survey: Research Triangle Institute Report GL 6. Durham, N.C., 1965.

Velásquez, Rogerio. *El Chocó en la independencia de Colombia*. Bogotá, 1965.

Wassen, Henry. *Estudios Chocoes*. Goteborg, 1963.

West, Robert Cooper, *Colonial Placer Mining in Colombia*. Baton Rouge, 1952.

——. *The Pacific Lowlands of Colombia: A Negroid Area of the American Tropics*. Baton Rouge, 1957.

Whitten, Norman. *Black Frontiersmen: A South American Case*. New York and London, 1974.

Williams, Eric. *Capitalism and Slavery*. Chapel Hill, 1944.

B. Unpublished Doctoral Dissertations

Chandler, David Lee. "Health and Slavery: A Study of Health Conditions among Negro Slaves in the Viceroyalty of New Granada and its Associated Slave Trade, 1600–1810." Tulane University.

King, James Ferguson. "Negro Slavery in the Viceroyalty of New Granada." The University of California, 1939.

Meiklejohn, Norman. "The Observance of Negro Slave Legislation in Colonial Nueva Granada." Columbia University, 1969.

Pavy, David Paul. "The Negro in Western Colombia." Tulane University, 1967.

Safford, Frank. "Commerce and Enterprise in Central Colombia, 1821–1870." Columbia University, 1965.

Whitten, Norman E. "An Analysis of Social Structure and Change: Profile of a Northwest Ecuadorian Town." The University of North Carolina, 1964.

C. Articles and Miscellaneous

Aguirre Beltrán, Gonzalo. "The Integration of the Negro into National Society in Mexico." In *Race and Class in Latin America*. Ed. by Magnus Mörner. London, 1969.

Aimes, Herbert H. S. "*Coartación*: A Spanish Institution for the Advancement of Slaves and Freedmen." *The Yale Review*, Vol. XVII (1908–1909), 412–31.

Arboleda, José Rafael, S. J. "La historia y la antropología del negro en Colombia," *Universidad de Antioquia*, No. 157 (April–June, 1964), 233–48.

Bowser, Frederick P. "Colonial Spanish America." In *Neither Slave Nor Free: The Freedman of African Descent in the Slave Societies of the New World*. Ed. by David W. Cohen and Jack P. Greene. Baltimore and London, 1972.

———, "The African in Colonial Spanish America: Reflections on Research Achievements and Priorities." *Latin American Research Review*, Vol. VII (Spring, 1972), 77–94.

Cantos de mi Tierra y de mi Raza. Vocal by Leonor Gonzáles Mina. Medellín, Colombia, Sonolux, 1968.

Genovese, Eugene. "Materialism and Idealism in the History of Negro Slavery in the Americas." In *Slavery in the New World: A Reader in Comparative History*. Ed. by Laura Foner and Eugene Genovese. Englewood Cliffs, 1969.

Hoz, Enrique de la. "Música contemporánea de Colombia." *Cuadernos Hispanoamericanos*, Vol. XXXII, No. 93 (1957), 338–54.

Jaramillo Uribe, Jaime. "Esclavos y señores en la sociedad Colombiana del siglo XVIII." *Anuario Colombiano de Historia Social y Cultura*, Vol. I, No. 1 (1963), 3–62.

Kuethe, Alan. "The Status of the Free Pardo in the Disciplined Militia of New Granada." *The Journal of Negro History*, Vol. LVI, No. 2 (1971), 105–18.

King, James Ferguson. "The Case of José Ponciano de Ayarza: A Document on Gracias al Sacar." *Hispanic American Historical Review*, Vol. XXXI (1951), 640–48.

Meiklejohn, Norman. "The Implementation of Slave Legislation in Eighteenth Century New Granada." In *Slavery and Race Relations in Latin America*. Ed. by Robert Brent Toplin. Westport, Conn., 1974.

Mörner, Magnus. "El mestizaje en la historia de Ibero-America." *Revista*

Bibliography

de Historia de America, Nos. 53–54 (June–December, 1962), 127–69.
Murphy, Robert Cushman. "The Earliest Spanish Advances Southward from Panama along the West Coast of South America." *Hispanic American Historical Review*, Vol. XXI (1941), 3–29.
———. "Racial Succession in the Colombian Chocó." *Geographical Review*, Vol. XXIX (1939), 461–71.
Price, Thomas J. "Estado y necesidades actuales de las investigaciones Afro-Colombianas." *Revista Colombiana de Antropología*, No. 2 (1954), II, 11–36.
Quiros, Juan B. de. "El contenido laboral en los códigos negros Americanos." *Revista Mexicana de Sociología*, Vol. V, No. 4 (1943), 473–510.
Russell-Wood, A.J.R. "Colonial Brazil." In *Neither Slave Nor Free: The Freedman of African Descent in the Slave Societies of the New World.* Ed. by David W. Cohen and Jack P. Greene. Baltimore and London, 1972.
Sharp, William F. "El negro en Colombia: manumisión y posición social." *Razón y Fábula: Revista de la Universidad de los Andes*, No. 8 (July–August, 1968), 91–107.
———. "Una imagen del negro." *Revista de la Dirección de Divulgación Cultural: Universidad Nacional de Colombia*, No. 2 (January–March, 1969), 171–85.
Velásquez, Rogerio. "Cuentas de la raza negra." *Revista Colombiana de Folclor*, No. 2 (1959), Series 2, 1–61.

Index

Slavery on the Spanish Frontier

stallment purchase, 143–44; objections to, 144–45; as escape valve, 146–47, 157; of women, 154; *see also coartación*
Martínez, Gov. Francisco: 52
Martínez de Escobar, Gov. Manuel: 67&n., 68
Martínez Malo, Joseph Joachín: 75, 77
Maturana, Francisco: 70–71, 180–81
Mazamorreros: 46, 49, 59, 70, 116, 125, 131, 151
Meiklejohn, Norman: 138n.
Mellet, Julian: 15
Messía de la Zerda, Viceroy Pedro: 52n.
Mestizos: 31, 51, 104
Mexico: 185–86
Meyer, John: 171
Michaeli, Gov. Joseph: 56–57, 59, 106, 108
Middle passage: 112
Militia: 152–53
Mines: location of, 13–14; and mine owners, 56, 77–78, 116–17; *see also* gold, gold production, mining
Mining: development of, 38, 77; taxes on, 42, 44, 54–57, 62–65, 67–69; code, 46; regulations concerning, 46–47, 51, 53–57, 59, 63, 65, 67, 77; use of water in, 47–49; description of, 48–49; folk techniques in, 49n., 51–52, 59; profits of, 115, 190; *see also* gold, gold production, *quinto*, *mazamorreros*, platinum

Miscegenation: 18, 148–49
Mita: 104
Montes, Gov. Bartolomé: 70
Moreno, Miguel: 180
Mosquera, Ignacio: 49
Mosquera, Jaciento de: 113–14
Mosquera, José Marcelino de: 55
Mosquera, José María: 188
Mosquera, Pedro de: 174–75, 180
Mulattos: 21n., 31, 51, 55, 104, 150, 152–53, 160; *see also* blacks, freedmen, slaves
Murrí: 10

Negroes: 21n.; *see also* blacks, freedmen, mulattos, slaves, *zambos*
Noanamá: 10, 17, 21, 23, 31, 35–36, 38, 75, 101, 103, 107
Noanamaes: 19, 26, 30, 36
Nóvita (town): 10, 14, 23, 29, 31, 35ff., 71ff., 101, 103, 107, 118, 181–83; importance of, 14; location of, 14–15; description of, 15; 55; demise of, 16; *see also* province of Nóvita
Nóvita (province): *see* province of Nóvita

Ordóñez, Antonio de: 40
Oro blanco: *see* platinum
Orta, Francisco de: 26
Overseers: 50, 102, 104, 131, 146, 176

Palacios, Matías: 184&n.
Palenques (runaway slave settlements): 154–56

250

Safford, Frank: 185
Salviejo, Pedro: 181
San Clemente, Manuel: 58
San Juan River: 38–39; location of, 9–10; regulations concerning, 10&n., 40–42, 61, 75, 77, 112; headwaters of, 12; travel on, 13, 26, 41, 55–56; *vigía* (fort) of, 39–40, 65, 76
San Juan de la Rivera, Marqués de: 43
San Pablo (Istmina): 10, 38
San Pablo Isthmus: 47
Santa Fe de Bogotá: 18, 28, 32ff., 56–59, 62–63, 66, 72, 103, 107, 111, 169
Santo Domingo (Haiti): 159
Serranía de Baudó: 9, 12
Silvestre, Francisco: 71–73
Sipí: 17, 23, 103
Slave gangs: *see cuadrillas*, slaves
Slaveholders: 115–16, 151, 177
Slave codes: 127–28, 139–41, 143n., 147
Slaves: in mining, 18, 48–49, 53, 111ff., 191; early use of, 20–21; number of, 21–23, 38, 117–18, 123–25; diseases of, 22, 112–13; location of, 22–23, 115–16; insurrections of, 29, 141, 156–60; in farming, 47, 144, 174; holidays for, 49, 130, 134–36, 142, 144–45, 145n.; hiring-out system, 49–50, 57, 136, 173; in transportation, 57, 175; crimes by, 57–58, 133, 138, 140, 144–45, 145n., 146, 156–57; punishment of, 59, 127–28, 138–40, 156–57, 169; fear of, 108, 118,

141, 147, 157–59; and Spanish law, 111, 127–29, 137–41, 143–46; mortality rate of, 112–13, 124–25, 178–79; value of, 113–14, 118–22, 145&n., 178; special skills of, 120, 137, 173; marriages of, 124, 127, 139–41; birth rates of, 124–25; opportunities for, 124, 133, 142, 146–47, 156, 192; free time for, 129, 134–36, 142; education of, 129, 139–40, 170, 193; mistreatment of, 130, 136–41, 144, 174; rations for, 131–35, 139–41, 174; diet of, 133–35, 139; arming of, 134, 158–59, 159n., 170; in domestic service, 137–38; and *coartación*, 142–43; assimilation, 148–49, 190; *see also* African influence, blacks, capitanejos, church, manumission, *zambos*
Slave trade: 22, 80, 112–13, 117–20, 125–26, 171–72; reasons for decline of, 187–88
Smith, Gov. Carlos: 53
Soliman, Miguel: 151
Sonora, Marqués de: 52–53
Sotomayor, Gov. Carlos de: 35
South Sea Company: 114
Spain: 10, 42, 47, 52, 54, 73, 75, 101, 117
Spanish Main: 10
Suárez, Juan: 56–59
Supplies in Chocó: 37–38, 40–41, 61, 75

Tadó: 10, 12ff., 31, 49, 55–56, 100–102, 107, 141, 158